D0773221

PARADISE LOST AND THE COSMOLOGICAL REVOLUTION

This volume brings John Milton's *Paradise Lost* into dialogue with the challenges of cosmology and the world of Galileo, whom Milton met and admired: a Universe encompassing space travel, an Earth that participates vibrantly in the cosmic dance, and stars that might be "world[s] / Of destined habitation." Milton's bold depiction of our Universe as merely a small part of a larger Multiverse allows the removal of Hell from Earth's center to a location far off in the abyss of Chaos. In this wide-ranging work, Dennis Danielson lucidly unfolds early modern cosmological debates, engaging not only Galileo but also Copernicus, Tycho Brahe, Kepler, and the English Copernicans, thus placing Milton at a rich crossroads of epic poetry and the history of science.

DENNIS DANIELSON is Professor of English at the University of British Columbia. He is also a member of the Milton Society of America and an associate member of the American Astronomical Society. Danielson's previous books include *Milton's Good God: A Study in Literary Theodicy* and *The Cambridge Companion to Milton*.

PARADISE LOST
AND THE COSMOLOGICAL
REVOLUTION

DENNIS DANIELSON

University of British Columbia

CAMBRIDGE
UNIVERSITY PRESS

CAMBRIDGE
UNIVERSITY PRESS

32 Avenue of the Americas, New York, NY 10013-2473, USA

Cambridge University Press is part of the University of Cambridge.

It furthers the University's mission by disseminating knowledge in the pursuit of
education, learning and research at the highest international levels of excellence.

www.cambridge.org
Information on this title: www.cambridge.org/9781107033603

© Dennis Danielson 2014

First published 2014

Printed in the United Kingdom by Clays, St Ives plc

A catalog record for this publication is available from the British Library.

Library of Congress Cataloging in Publication Data
Danielson, Dennis Richard, 1949–
Paradise lost and the cosmological revolution / Dennis Danielson.
pages cm
ISBN 978-1-107-03360-3 (Hardback)
1. Milton, John, 1608–1674–Knowledge–Science.   2. Milton, John, 1608–1674–Knowledge–
Science.   3. Milton, John, 1608–1674. Paradise lost.   4. Galilei, Galileo, 1564–1642–Influence.
5. Literature and science–England–History–17th century.   6. Cosmology in literature.   I. Title.
PR3592.S3D36 2014
821'.4–dc23   2014024211

ISBN 978-1-107-03360-3 Hardback

With gratitude to
Patrick Grant, John Carey, and Owen Gingerich
and
in affectionate memory of
Martin Evans

Contents

Illustrations

Permissions:

Figures

Foreword and acknowledgments

The chapters in this book appear in the order in which they were written. The book's themes *felt* as if they were unfolding in a logical order – one that I trust is also evident to readers. Chapter 1 offers astronomical and cosmological background, highlighting elements to which John Milton and many of his age responded. Chapter 2 seeks to address one of the boldest aspects of the imagined world of *Paradise Lost*; indeed, the vocabulary of "world" and "Universe" is inadequate to describe the larger Multiverse within which Milton situates Hell, Heaven, and our Cosmos. Zooming in on that Universe in Chapter 3, we not only examine Copernicus's cosmological challenge to the model described in Chapter 1 but also glimpse the range of proposals offered by cosmological bricoleurs through the middle of the seventeenth century. Chapter 4 addresses the first exhilarating telescopic discoveries of Galileo and the deep-seated resistance of a figure such as Francis Bacon to accepting Galileo's Copernican conclusions. However, Chapter 5 shows Galileo's influential binary of the "two chief world systems, Ptolemaic and Copernican," to be anachronistic and tendentious, offering a rhetorical and scientific backdrop against which Milton's apparent tentativeness about Copernican cosmology is seen to be more deft and responsible than many have thought. Chapter 6 examines the Sun's location, symbolism, and theology amid the cosmological debates and offers an appreciation of Milton's treatment of solar themes. Milton's exuberantly Galilean treatment of Earth – a wandering star whose affinity with the rest of the Universe poetically sexualizes and enlivens the heavens – is examined in Chapter 7. Chapter 8 extends the discussion of Earth's role in a living, perhaps extraterrestrially populated, navigable, and purposeful Cosmos. These chapters are liberally punctuated with close readings of Milton's own challenging and beautiful cosmological passages. The epilogue concludes by offering remarks on the position and achievement of *Paradise Lost* as a node of cosmological reflection in the seventeenth century and perhaps for the future.

I would like to think that almost any curious, intelligent person might find interesting a discussion of the greatest epic in the English language interwoven with aspects of a truly momentous set of developments in humankind's understanding of the Universe. In addressing a hoped-for wide audience with inevitably varied backgrounds, however, I might occasionally, in my pedantic way, tell students of Milton or aficionados of the history of science things they already know. Should this happen, I beg my readers' kind forbearance.

Already the recipient of much kindness, I wish to record thanks to the Social Sciences and Humanities Research Council of Canada for a grant supporting the research that went into this book. I am also grateful to the Alexander von Humboldt Foundation for awarding me the Konrad Adenauer Forschungspreis in 2011–12. This permitted me seasons of appropriately monklike concentration in Munich, during which much of the book was composed. In addition, I offer thanks to Janet Henshaw Danielson, Christopher Graney, Javier Ibáñez, and John Leonard for reading parts of my manuscript and suggesting improvements, likewise to Ray Ryan at Cambridge University Press for his interest and encouragement, and to the press's three anonymous readers for their generous, helpful critique. For wonderful teachers and mentors over the years – four of whom I seek to honor in the dedication – I am also deeply grateful. Nothing can convey sufficient thanks to my immediate family, especially Janet. I alone am to thank for whatever faults remain in this book, the writing of which has been for me an inexpressible privilege. *Soli Deo gloria.*

Note on text and usage

I follow the style of the International Astronomical Union in capitalizing Earth, Sun, Moon, Universe, Cosmos, etc., when these designate a single astronomical entity (parallel to the standard usage, whereby one capitalizes Mercury, Venus, and the proper names of other planets). When a word is generic or plural, however, it is not capitalized (e.g., "Galileo discovered Jupiter's four moons," "Humans are created from earth," etc.).

I use American punctuation and spelling except for the word *storey*. Part of my historical account concerns the traditional distinction between upper and lower storeys of the Universe and retaining that spelling helps keep architectural or cosmological structures from being confused with narratives or stories.

In transcriptions of Latin and English texts, I have retained original capitalization and spelling but have regularized i/j, u/v, and long "s" and have expanded abbreviations, such as those formed with superscripts, tildes, ampersands, and the like. I have not adhered to the seventeenth-century convention of italicizing proper names.

In citations of writings in which no published translation is indicated, the translation is my own. For some lesser-known works, I provide the original Latin in the footnotes. For better-known authors whose original works are readily available on the World Wide Web (e.g., Copernicus, Gilbert, Galileo, Bacon), I quote either my own or a standard published translation – with references to or strategic samples of the original only when these seem to be of particular interest. For biblical quotations, I have chosen to use the King James (or Authorized) version. One is always wise, of course, given enough time, to consult the original languages and other translations. All quotations from *Paradise Lost* (*PL*) are from the Modern Library Classics edition, edited by William Kerrigan, John Rumrich, and Stephen M. Fallon.

Preface: A cosmical epic

In poems, equally as in philosophic disquisitions, genius produces the strongest impressions of novelty, while it rescues the most admitted truths from the impotence caused by the very circumstance of their universal admission. Truths, of all others the most awful and mysterious, yet being, at the same time, of universal interest, are too often considered as *so* true, that they lose all the life and efficiency of truth, and lie bed-ridden in the dormitory of the soul, side by side with the most despised and exploded errors.

Samuel Taylor Coleridge, *Biographia Literaria*[1]

The decisive thing [about the 1969 Moon landing] is that it brought to an end the Copernican trauma of the Earth's having the status of a mere point – of the annihilation of its importance by the enormity [*Übergröße*] of the universe. . . . The successive increases in the disproportion between the Earth and the universe, between man and totality, have lost their significance. . . . One can also put it this way: Equivalence is established between the microscopic and the telescopic sides of reality – absence of difference, in a sense that no longer has any tinge of Pascal's abysses of the infinities.

Hans Blumenberg, *The Genesis of the Copernican World*[2]

One of the glories of Milton is that, like other great poets, he permits us to see significant things afresh – perhaps even to see things we have never quite seen before. The notion of recuperation, of renovation, and of "repair[ing] the ruines"[3] stands at the threshold of his early treatise *Of Education* and it can be seen as the essence of *Paradise Lost*. Famously, the prospect of a regained paradise, of a restoration of humankind, appears in the fifth line of that epic, even before the story of loss quite gets under way. One must not,

---

[1] S. T. Coleridge, *Biographia Literaria* (New York, 1834), p. 56.
[2] Hans Blumenberg, *The Genesis of the Copernican World*, trans. Robert M. Wallace (Cambridge, MA: MIT Press, 1987), pp. 678–9; cf. Blumenberg's original, *Die Genesis der kopernikanischen Welt* (Frankfurt: Suhrkamp, 1975), pp. 786–7.
[3] *Of Education* (London, 1644), the preface to Samuel Hartlib.

of course, minimize the depths of loss that Milton explicitly or implicitly explores: humankind's fall and exile from paradise; our loss of harmonious communion with God, with angels, with Earth, with each other; our forfeiture of cosmic mobility and of immortality; and Milton's own sorrows arising from losses physical, political, ecclesiastical, and domestic. However, in *Paradise Lost*, we are surprised not only by sin but also by joy, by bliss, by wonder. The "awful and mysterious" truths (in Coleridge's words) are not merely or always terrifying; they are often exhilarating. For Milton, those truths include the delicate sheen left behind by "Minims of nature" – by lowly worms – "Streaking the ground with sinuous trace" (7.482, 481) as well as awe-inspiring and poignant glimpses of our Earth viewed from the Sun or of our entire Cosmos caught sight of from outer Chaos. Milton's "argument" is as much about a rescue as it is about a loss. And for Milton, there is no unbridgeable gulf between the microscopic and the macroscopic or between small things of human interest and grand things of universal interest.

For more than a century now, critic Walter Raleigh's comment that *Paradise Lost* is "a monument to dead ideas,"[4] regardless of whether he intended it as hostile, has typified a sleepy neglect of the magnificence and vibrancy of the cosmic canvas that Milton unfurls in his epic. It is true that significant (although sometimes equivocal) contributions toward an understanding of Milton's engagement with astronomy and cosmography were offered in the first two-thirds of the twentieth century by such critics as Allan Gilbert, Grant McColley, Marjorie Nicolson, and Walter Clyde Curry. And there have been other similarly equivocal contributions in more recent decades.[5] But no one has yet mounted the full rescue mission required if we are to experience and to relish the astonishing engagement of the plot, persons, and poetry of *Paradise Lost* with the Cosmos – to recognize it, in David Masson's apt words, as "a cosmical epic which was without a precedent and remains without a parallel."[6]

It is not only critics who have contributed to the neglect of Milton's "universal interest." With some few exceptions, historians of science and popularizers have for centuries fallen into clichés and generalizations about

---

[4] Walter Raleigh, *Milton* (London, 1900), p. 88.
[5] As I shall acknowledge more fully later, John Leonard's *Faithful Labourers: A Reception History of Paradise Lost, 1667–1970* (New York: Oxford University Press, 2013) [henceforth cited as *FL*], especially Chapter 11 (pp. 705–819), has done an exceptional job of evaluating critical responses to astronomical issues in *Paradise Lost* and hence of clearing the ground for a study such as this one.
[6] David Masson, *The Life of John Milton: Narrated in Connexion With the Political, Ecclesiastical, and Literary History of His Time*, 7 vols. (London: Macmillan, 1859–1894), 6:535.

the shape and meaning of the cosmological revolution that stretched roughly from Copernicus to Newton. Most notably, the story of the rise of heliocentrism has been told with uncritical Whiggish assumptions about struggles between the forward looking and the backward looking, between the scientific and the religious, between enlightened and obscurantist. Against such a monochrome backdrop, it is little wonder that Milton is readily lumped together with traditional defenders of "the discarded image"[7] – of the model of the Universe usually associated with the name of Ptolemy. But such oversimplifications concerning the rise of Copernicanism – some of them already starting to take hold in the mid-seventeenth century – too easily desensitize us to the depth and complexity of debates still going on (and for good scientific reasons) when Milton wrote *Paradise Lost* and, thus, to the colorful richness of Milton's cosmic imagination.

Part of the somnolence I am describing is simply something that happens with the passage of time, with the changes that take place within a language, and, as Coleridge indicates, with the loss of "life and efficiency" that accompanies years of repetition and habituation. My ambition in this book is to help cast off that sleepiness through carefully attending to what Milton wrote and to how his cosmological context engaged him and was engaged by him. According to late nineteenth-century German philosopher Wilhelm Dilthey, the historian shares with the poet a capacity to apprehend and reenact a complex of thoughts, feelings, circumstances, and characters in such a way that readers may relive or experience (*nacherleben*) a world from which they would otherwise be quite cut off – a "world that stretches our horizon of lived human possibility otherwise inaccessible to us."[8] Milton is indeed that kind of poet and my aim is to serve as his accessory by facilitating the kind of historical understanding Dilthey adumbrates.

It is a commonplace of Milton criticism that to deepen one's understanding of the debates with which Milton was surrounded – for example, regarding politics, theology, or poetic theory – also potentially deepens one's appreciation of his works. In this respect, what the present study attempts is hardly different methodologically from much else that has contributed to the ongoing conversation about Milton amid his milieu.

---

[7] I borrow the phrase from C. S. Lewis, *The Discarded Image: An Introduction to Medieval and Renaissance Literature* (Cambridge: Cambridge University Press, 1964), one of the most eloquent and sympathetic expositions of that model.

[8] Wilhelm Dilthey, *Plan der Fortsetzung zum Aufbau der geschichtlichen Welt in den Geisteswissenschaften; Gesammelte Schriften 7* (Göttingen: Teubner, 1958): 215–16.

In the area of cosmology, however, the task may be even more daunting than it usually is, given historical changes in vocabulary. One can imagine, for example, placing a seventeenth-century and a twenty-first-century politician or theologian or poet together in a room and finding that they could, if perhaps with great effort, communicate with each other on some level about what it is that politicians, theologians, or poets actually do. Such a thought experiment is considerably harder to conduct in almost any area whose substance concerns what we now call *science*. The word *science* was indeed in use in Milton's day, although it did not mean then what it does today despite the persistence of some significant seventeenth-century roots. "Scientist," on the other hand, was a nineteenth-century coinage,[9] as was "Copernicanism." "Cosmology" itself does seem to have come into modest use in the mid-seventeenth century. But it is highly doubtful whether a present-day cosmologist would find much in common with anyone at all in the seventeenth century with regard to the methods, problems, and vocabulary of cosmology.[10] Too much has changed.

This is why I need to introduce in a relatively basic way the problems and lexicon of seventeenth-century cosmology – and to try, as much as one can, to peer behind more recent construals of science history, including popular binaries – most notably "Copernican vs. Ptolemaic" – with all the cultural and historical baggage it has come to entail. The discussion I pursue will not artificially eschew vocabulary developed after the seventeenth century, although I shall try to remain aware of terminological dangers, including that of anachronism. As the first two chapters implicitly argue, we need to revisit the cosmological background of Milton's age and, in a way that attends carefully to the canvas of creation he unfurls, crucially extend our lexicon so we might more adequately comprehend the structure and magnitude of the world Milton portrays.

The main piece of new vocabulary I will introduce to describe Milton's canvas of creation is "Multiverse." Although technically anachronistic, the term is highly useful for a discussion of Milton's cosmology, given that the synonyms "Universe" and "Cosmos" bespeak, respectively, unity and order and that, therefore, neither term can properly be employed to denote Milton's Chaos, which is boundless and disordered. "Multiverse" was first coined by William James in 1895 and is actively employed by cosmologists

---

[9] See Danielson, "Scientist's Birthright: How a New Name Embodied Ideals of Connection and Inclusiveness," *Nature* 410 (26 April 2001): 1030–31.

[10] I am speaking, of course, generally. It might be amusing to imagine possible exceptions, such as two holders of the Lucasian Chair in Mathematics at Cambridge – one from the late seventeenth century and a more recent holder from the early twenty-first century.

today.[11] Historically, it has occasionally been used pejoratively to substitute for "Universe" – to reflect a pessimistic view according to which the Universe, not living up to its name, shows signs of fragmentation. In relation to Milton, however, I shall use the term nonpejoratively to denote a maximal, comprehensive ensemble of potential cosmic components – some of which may be selected (or may have been selected) to make up the pieces of an actual universe or possibly more than one. This lexical maneuver protects "Universe" and "Cosmos" (whose main seventeenth-century synonym was simply "world") from being arbitrarily and incoherently employed to denote entities ordered and disordered.

This book, as will become evident, is more about Milton and his context than about Milton studies. My principal quarry is what Milton wrote and what he invites us to imagine – together with the strands of historical, scientific, and literary fabric that help make his achievement intelligible. I do not take as my principal task a developed critique of the history of the reception and interpretation of *Paradise Lost*. While valuing such reception history and particularly appreciating John Leonard's recent magisterial rooting out of persistent misreadings, I shall resist letting the long, intriguing course of the Miltonist conversation deflect attention from more primary and (in my view) even more interesting matters. Thus, for the most part, I shall foreground discussions and controversies that Milton was or might have been aware of – that he might reasonably be seen to be engaging in – and shall acknowledge a range of Milton critics' pertinent contributions on broadly cosmological issues chiefly, although still visibly, in the footnotes.

Before turning to those primary matters, however, I would like to comment on a handful of publications bearing on Milton's cosmology that have appeared since 1970 (the *terminus ad quem* of Leonard's *Faithful Labourers*) – my purpose being to illustrate tendencies I positively wish to avoid. The work most closely aligned to the present one in its scope and purpose is Harinder Singh Marjara's impressive *Contemplation of Created Things: Science in Paradise Lost*. Marjara sets out to situate Milton's ideas "in their scientific and metaphysical context, occasionally going back to their ancient and medieval roots."[12] Despite this laudable aim, however, Marjara's discussion is weakened by his tendency to assume, rather than

---

[11] One of the most comprehensive collections on this topic is *Universe or Multiverse?*, ed. Bernard Carr (Cambridge: Cambridge University Press, 2007).

[12] Harinder Singh Marjara, *Contemplation of Created Things: Science in Paradise Lost* (Toronto: University of Toronto Press, 1992), p. 13.

argue, that certain elements formed part of Milton's intellectual furniture. He states that "the framework [of Milton's ideas] was basically Aristotelian" and goes on to worry repeatedly about how the poet conforms to or diverges from a peripatetic position. While praising Milton's description of Chaos as a realm extending endlessly beyond the bounds of our finite Universe, Marjara accordingly frames this achievement by saying that Milton "sacrifices the compatibility of his universe with his Aristotelianism" (p. 107). Moreover, Marjara's assumptions about Milton's basic Aristotelianism naturally appear to lend credence to other assumptions about "his geocentrism" and its supposed affinity to anthropocentrism (p. 135) – mistaken attributions, as I shall argue, in spite of how frequently they have been applied to Milton over the centuries. To its credit, Marjara's learned book aims to resist any simplistic construal of Milton as "old-fashioned" (p. 14). But by unnecessarily shackling Milton with tenets of a science either already or about to be discredited, Marjara in effect "retreats to a defense of Milton based on poetic license" and ends up "damn[ing] with faint ambiguities."[13]

Indeed, very few critics succeed in transcending the persistent progressivist binary that portrays individual characters on the stage of history as playing roles that are either backward looking or forward looking (the former, in keeping with the modernist paradigm, of course being bad and the latter being good). The true picture is seldom that simple and often much more interesting than the binary suggests. To acknowledge and celebrate the genuine progress and achievements of science since the time of Copernicus need not entail what Antonio Pérez-Ramos has called an "ideology of success" nor justify the habit of treating "allegiance to Copernicanism ... as *the* mark of modernity and progressiveness."[14] Much more will be said in Chapters 6 and 7 about modernity's paradoxically self-congratulatory tendencies as they relate to the historiography of science and in particular of Copernicanism. But while probing and praising Milton's achievement, I explicitly eschew attempts to make him a hero of the rise of science or to engage in "Whiggish ancestor-chasing" (Pérez-Ramos, p. 198), as if identifying his sources or influences could adequately perform the task of authentic assessment and interpretation.

[13] Stephen Fallon, his review of Marjara, *The Journal of English and Germanic Philology*, 93.3 (July 1994): 428–31; and Diane Kelsey McColley, "Milton and Nature: Greener Readings" (Review Article), *Huntington Library Quarterly*, 62.3/4 (1999): 423–44 (p. 432).
[14] Antonio Pérez-Ramos, "Francis Bacon and Astronomical Inquiry," *British Journal for the History of Science* 23.2 (June 1990): 197–205 (pp. 197, 199).

Perhaps the most compact illustration of how complex the imagined march of science can actually be is the case of Francis Bacon (1561–1626), to which I shall return in Chapter 4. In 1667, the year *Paradise Lost* was first published, Bacon was already being hailed by Abraham Cowley in the verse preface to Thomas Sprat's *History of the Royal Society* as a pioneer of the new science:

> *Bacon*, like *Moses*, led us forth at last,
> The barren Wilderness he past,
> Did on the very Border stand
> Of the blest promis'd Land,
> And from the Mountains Top of his Exalted Wit,
> Saw it himself, and shew'd us it.[15]

As we shall see, however, despite this near apotheosis of Bacon as Mosaic deliverer of natural philosophy, he had in fact openly dismissed Copernicanism as "the speculations of one who cares not what fictions he introduces into nature, provided his calculations answer."[16]

But some Miltonists continue to practice "ancestor chasing" – one of the most notable recent contributions in the area of Milton's cosmology fingering Bacon as just such an ancestor. Catherine Gimelli Martin has called Milton "perhaps the most Baconian poet of the seventeenth century," and throughout her long and often helpful article, she repeats her thesis concerning that affinity.[17] While this may be a slightly more fruitful approach than labeling Milton "basically Aristotelian," there is scarcely any firm evidence supporting it; it seems something more asserted than properly argued. Milton and Bacon may indeed share a vocal dislike for things monkish and scholastic; moreover, both vigorously seek to interpret experience independent of preconceived orthodoxies or idolatries. But their sharing certain antipathies does not confirm Martin's contention, and one worries that linking Milton to Bacon may be unduly motivated by a desire to have some of Bacon's

---

[15] Abraham Cowley, "To the Royal Society," lines 93–8; in Thomas Sprat, *The History of the Royal-Society of London, For the Improving of Natural Knowledge* (London, 1667), sig. B2ᵛ.

[16] *The Works of Francis Bacon*, ed. James Spedding et al., 15 vols. (London: Longman, 1857), 10:427–8; 7:304: *ejus sunt viri qui quidvis in natura fingere, modo calculi bene cedant, nihil putet.* The work cited is Bacon's *Descriptio Globi Intellectualis*, composed probably in 1612 but published only posthumously, in Amsterdam, in 1653.

[17] Catherine Gimelli Martin, "'What If the Sun Be Centre to the World?': Milton's Epistemology, Cosmology, and Paradise of Fools Reconsidered," *Modern Philology* 99.2 (Nov. 2001): 231–65 (p. 231).

prestige as "the hero of the revolution in scientific method"[18] rub off on the often scientifically undervalued epic poet.

Against such an attempted renovation of Milton's scientific credentials, William Poole has responded with his "Milton and Science: A Caveat."[19] Poole's stimulating short essay casts doubt on Martin's cheerfully arranged affiliation between Milton and Bacon. Poole's is a generally wise, heavily documented admonition against exaggerating the depth of Milton's contact with the new science or the new scientists. However, although he claims not to be consigning Milton "back to the dustbin of the old science," Poole declares "it must be conceded that the epic nonetheless upholds the Ptolemaic model as dominant" (p. 28). This claim constitutes quite precisely a consignment to a dustbin, although it is a consignment decreed rather than argued. In spite of his largely astute critique of those who press the case for a "forward looking" Milton, Poole thus, in spite of his efforts to encourage a more rigorously contextualized reading of Milton, ends his discussion by offering something much like the backward-looking poet portrayed by so many earlier critics.

A further example of ancestor-chasing is worth mentioning here because it still often afflicts not only Milton studies but also the historiography of cosmology more generally. One of the most colorful characters in sixteenth-century intellectual history is undoubtedly Giordano Bruno, whose caché was cemented by the fact that on February 17, 1600, the Roman Inquisition burnt him at the stake. In his place of execution, Rome's Campo de' Fiori, there still stands a statue of Bruno, erected in 1889, whose inscription includes the words "A Bruno Il Secolo da lui Divinato" ("To Bruno, from the generation he foresaw [or divined]") – itself a concise instance of ancestor appropriation. Few scholars any longer give credence to the notion that Bruno was burnt for his cosmology or his Copernicanism. Indeed, Ernan McMullin has shown how poorly Bruno understood Copernicus, commenting that "to call Bruno a 'Copernican' requires one to empty the label of all content save the assertion that the earth and planets move around the sun."[20] Frances Yates, the twentieth century's most influential interpreter of Bruno, referring to Bruno's *La Cena de le Ceneri* (*The Ash Wednesday Supper*, written in England and

[18] The phrase, quoted by Martin (p. 234), is William Whewell's, from *Philosophy of the Inductive Sciences Founded Upon Their History*, 2d ed., 2 vols. (London, 1857), 2:230.

[19] William Poole, "Milton and Science: A Caveat," *Milton Quarterly* 38.1 (March 2004): 18–34. With "the newer school of criticism," Poole associates Kester Svendsen, Stephen Fallon, Harinder Singh Marjara, John Rogers, Karen Edwards, and Martin.

[20] Ernan McMullin, "Bruno and Copernicus," *Isis* 78.1 (Mar., 1987): 55–74.

published in 1584), commented that "Copernicus might have well bought
up and destroyed all copies of the *Cena* had he been alive."[21]
The dominant current in Bruno's thought was in fact Hermeticism, a
mystical, ultimately pantheistic amalgam of ideas based on the supposedly
Mosaic-era writings of Hermes Trismegistus. Bruno used pantheism's
identification of God and Cosmos to undermine Aristotle's doctrine of
the finitude of the Universe, for "it is fitting that an inaccessible divine
countenance should have an infinite likeness with infinite parts – such as
those countless worlds I have postulated. . . . There must be innumerable
individuals such as those great creatures are (of which our earth is one – the
divine mother who gave birth to us, nourishes us, and will finally receive
us again into herself). [And] to encompass these innumerable creatures
requires an infinite space."[22] Bruno's pantheistic presumption that life is
present everywhere in the universe, combined with his affection for
atomism, led him to postulate a homogeneous Cosmos with stars and
earths distributed throughout empty space. Such an account may superficially appear to anticipate (for example) Newtonian absolute space, but
philosophically it more anticipates New Age than new science.[23]

Yet Bruno still keeps getting dragged into otherwise worthwhile discussions of Milton and science. Setting aside the raw incompossibility of
the claims and methods, for example, of Galileo and Bruno (even the
most recent space telescopes cannot penetrate to nor justify conclusions
about infinity), we should recognize that the spirit and aims of Bruno's
mystically tinged cosmology evince very little affinity indeed with
modern science.

A footnote by Catherine Gimelli Martin affords an instructive cau-
tionary instance of how Bruno's supposed influence may worm its way
into discussions of Milton. Having claimed that Milton's science is
"heavily permeated with Neoplatonic forms of thought" descending
ultimately from Nicholas of Cusa – "probably . . . via the voluminous
propagandizing of Giordano Bruno" – Martin offers the following note:
"Both Harris Fletcher . . . and Frances Yates . . . have found connections

---

[21] Frances A. Yates, *Giordano Bruno and the Hermetic Tradition* (Chicago: University of Chicago Press,
1964), p. ix.
[22] *The Book of the Cosmos: Imagining the Universe From Heraclitus to Hawking*, ed. Dennis Danielson
(hereafter *BOTC*), p. 142; my translation (with kind advice from Arielle Saiber) from *De l'infinito
universo et Mondi*, 1584; original text reprinted in *Le opere italiane di Giordano Bruno*
(Göttingen, 1888).
[23] It would be wrong, of course, to deny *any* connection between Hermeticism and a figure such as
Newton.

between Milton and Bruno" (Martin, p. 263). Martin's note offers no
specific citation of Yates – only the title of her book. But if one searches
that volume, one indeed finds a reference to Milton and Bruno. Yates
quotes *Il Penseroso*:

> Or let my Lamp at midnight hour,
> Be seen in som high lonely Towr,
> Where I may oft out-watch the Bear,
> With thrice great Hermes, or unsphear
> The spirit of Plato to unfold
> What Worlds, or what vast Regions hold
> The immortal mind that hath forsook
> Her mansion in this fleshly nook. . . .
>
> (ll. 85–92)

Yates comments: "These lines (which to my mind have a Brunian ring
through the mention of the Bear, where the reform of the heavens begins
in *Spaccio*) brilliantly suggest the atmosphere of the Hermetic trance"
(Yates, p. 280). Who could object to Yates's hearing a "Brunian ring" in
these early lines of Milton? But this scarcely justifies the assertion that she
actually "finds a connection" between Milton and Bruno.

Moving on to Fletcher, one in fact finds him offering the following
tenuous line of reasoning. He points out that Milton's father (John
Milton Sr.), Alexander Gill the Elder (who became headmaster of
St. Paul's School), John Florio (eventual translator of Montaigne), and
Bruno were in 1583 "perhaps all at Oxford at the same time." As he
openly concedes, "it is a fascinating but vain speculation to suggest that
the elder Milton knew the other three." Nevertheless, in the next breath,
Fletcher avers that "such a suggestion is revealing in connection with the
father's urging of the boy Milton to learn the Continental
vernaculars. . . . Through Bruno and Florio, the elder Milton, if he was
at Oxford, would have been impressed by the linguistic interests
centering in these two Italians."[24] Thus does a "vain speculation"
instantly become a "suggestion" – one that is "revealing" – and then
in turn, decades later, becomes in the hands of Martin a "connection"
between a visiting Italian writer and Milton, whose father might
have breathed the same Oxford air with Bruno in 1583 – a quarter-
century before the future epic poet was born.

---

[24] Harris Francis Fletcher, *The Intellectual Development of John Milton*, 2 vols. (Urbana: University of
Illinois Press, 1956), 1:302.

Enough about ancestor-chasing – except only this: Often, in thought as well as in life, we simply do not know our own ancestors, even though we do have them, as did Milton. However, it is not to belittle the influence of ancestors to suggest that the story of influence is seldom the most interesting one to tell or to hear. In this book, I shall try to situate Milton and *Paradise Lost* nonreductively in a wider culture of thought, replete with influences, that stretches backward and forward in time – indeed, to the present day – and to examine and illuminate his poem's rich engagement with astronomy and cosmology.

CHAPTER I

The discarded image

In Book 8 of *Paradise Lost*, Raphael opens his response to Adam's questions about astronomy with these words:

> "To ask or search I blame thee not; for heav'n
> Is as the book of God before thee set,
> Wherein to read his wondrous works, and learn
> His seasons, hours, or days, or months, or years:
> This to attain, whether heav'n move or Earth,
> Imports not, if thou reckon right; the rest
> From man or angel the great Architect
> Did wisely to conceal, and not divulge
> His secrets to be scanned by them who ought
> Rather admire; or if they list to try
> Conjecture, he his fabric of the heav'ns
> Hath left to their disputes, perhaps to move
> His laughter at their quaint opinions wide
> Hereafter, when they come to model heav'n
> And calculate the stars, how they will wield
> The mighty frame, how build, unbuild, contrive
> To save appearances, how gird the sphere
> With centric and eccentric scribbled o'er,
> Cycle and epicycle, orb in orb."
>
> (8.66–84)

Raphael begins this speech with an important biblical and Christian commonplace that underpinned the serious study of the world for centuries (and in some quarters still does): that the world is a kind of book – not only a thing in itself but, in a manner analogous to speech or writing, a vehicle for communicating the power and divinity of its Creator. "The heavens declare the glory of God," exclaimed the Psalmist (Ps. 19:1); "the invisible things of [God] from the creation of the world are clearly seen, being understood by the things that are made, even his eternal power and Godhead," wrote St. Paul (Rom. 1:20); "the whole

I

world is a shadow, a way, a trace; a book with writing front and back," reechoed St. Bonaventure in the thirteenth century.[1] Milton himself, in the invocation to Book 3 of the epic, has already lamented his own loss of visual access to that book:

> . . . for the book of knowledge fair
> Presented with a universal blank
> Of Nature's works to me expunged and razed,
> And wisdom at one entrance quite shut out.
>
> (3.47–50)

This fundamental analogy justified astronomical study and, Milton would assume, transcended virtually all controversy as far as his poem's fit audience was concerned. For, as John Calvin wrote in his *Commentary on Genesis*, astronomy "is not onely pleasant to be knowen but also verie profitable. It cannot be denied but that the same Arte doth set forth the wonderfull wisedome of God" – even if, regrettably, "certeine phrentike persons . . . boldly reject whatsoever is to them unknowen."[2]

A second relatively noncontroversial claim Raphael makes in this part of his response concerns one of the main practical uses of astronomy – the formation and regulation of the calendar: "seasons, hours, or days, or months, or years." Reform of the calendar had been a pressing ecclesiastical theme in the sixteenth century because of the urgency of reestablishing a proper date for Easter. Pope Gregory XIII had established a calendar reform commission, which eventuated in the papal bull of 1582, *Inter Gravissimas*, and in the calendar known to this day as the Gregorian.[3] Moreover, although astronomers were essential contributors to calendar reform, Raphael is perfectly correct to state that the regulation of the calendar ("This to attain . . .") is unaffected by claims for or against Earth's movement. Raphael does *not* declare astronomy is general unimportant. Rather, it merely "imports not" when it comes to our "learn[ing] . . . seasons, hours, or days, or months, or years." What is critical in this regard is "reckon[ing] right." For fathoming the practical, calendrical dimensions of time is more a task for mathematics than for physics or cosmology.

[1] *Collationes in Hexameron* 12.14; in *The Works of Bonaventure*, trans. José de Vinck (Paterson, NJ: St. Anthony Guild Press, 1970). For more on the "two books" theme, see the excellent contribution by Kenneth Howell, *God's Two Books: Copernican Cosmology and Biblical Interpretation in Early Modern Science* (South Bend, IN: University of Notre Dame Press, 2002).

[2] John Calvin, *A Commentarie of John Calvine, Upon the First Booke of Moses Called Genesis*, trans. Thomas Tymme (London, 1578), sig. C.iii.ʳ.

[3] See, among numerous other accounts, James M. Lattis, *Between Copernicus and Galileo: Christoph Clavius and the Collapse of Ptolemaic Cosmology* (Chicago: University of Chicago Press, 1994), pp. 20–1.

Raphael's next point, about the great Architect's policy of concealment, presents a greater challenge to interpretation. Perhaps Milton (via Raphael) is merely echoing (and Christianizing) the Presocratic philosopher Heraclitus: "Nature loves to hide" (φύσις κρύπτεσθαι φιλεῖ). As for the reference to God as "Architect," Copernicus had similarly spoken of the Creator of the Universe as *Opifex* (maker, framer, artist, or artisan). Behind these lines may lurk the double meaning of "mystery" familiar to students of the late medieval mystery cycles, in which artisans, protectors of trade secrets, nonetheless play a role in bringing to light the secrets of divine revelation. In any case, the Architect's policy of concealment is nondiscriminatory: The workings of the Universe are divulged to neither humans nor angels. What follows in this speech as well as in subsequent ones, however, implies that the concealment is no permanent or complete ban on astronomical understanding. Instead, Raphael's language indicates the need for effort and reverence in the process of acquiring knowledge. God does not "divulge" his secrets – etymologically "make them public" (literally, "vulgarize" them) – to be "scanned by them who ought / Rather admire." The latter word reemphasizes the normative wonder evoked earlier (line 68), while "scanned" carries a strong sense, contrary to the piety one ought to exercise in beholding the heavens, of standing in criticism or judgment of a particular work of art (OED, 2.a.&b.). The now-familiar meaning of "scan" as involving mere visual, neutral, and possibly hurried examination does not appear in the English language until more than a century after Milton. Thus, Raphael is emphatically *not* saying "Don't look," and Milton is not merely engaging in the "scientific obscurantism" that Grant McColley identifies as the last refuge of literalists who (he thinks) oppose enlightened enquirers' reading "the open book of the world."[4]

Indeed, the "or" of line 75 implies a large measure of permission: "or if they list to try / Conjecture, he his fabric of the heav'ns / Hath left to their disputes, perhaps to move / His laughter." Given Raphael's opening metaphor of "the book of God," one naturally expects readers to attempt conjecture or interpretation. Such hermeneutical activity is practicable and permissible within the prescribed bounds of reverence. And although within this text it is hard to tell whether God's imagined laughter is derisive or merely amused, what is clear is that the practice of cosmological interpretation will result in disputes, will prove controversial, and will include

[4] Grant McColley, "The Ross-Wilkins Controversy," *Annals of Science* 8.2 (April 15, 1938): 153–89 (p. 187).

the danger of creaturely pride – in particular, forgetfulness regarding who actually made and governs the "fabric" or edifice of the world.

Scientifically, the key (and still useful) term in these lines is "model," which Milton concisely employs as a verb. What astronomers do is to make models of the heavens in order to "save appearances." More will be said about the latter phrase farther on in this chapter and elsewhere. But it is perhaps wise here to belabor the point that as long as one is consciously making a model, one is aware that one's proposals are subservient to a larger reality.[5] If one forgets that subservience, however, then impiety or scientific category mistakes can arise. For example, in 1541, Reformer Philipp Melanchthon complained in a letter about various "absurdities" plaguing churches and schools – a complaint he illustrated by reference to "that Polish astronomer who moves the Earth and immobilizes the Sun."[6] Having heard only distant reports of the new cosmology of Copernicus, whose work had not yet been published, Melanchthon suspected the new teaching of a *lack* of the kind of subservience to reality just referred to, hence the word *absurdity* and his clearly ironic description about the astronomer moving Earth. Such irony, however – along with an awareness of the distinction between models and reality – is often in rather short supply, even today. Journalistic and Internet summaries of science history still repeatedly talk about how Copernicus "removed Earth" from the center of the Universe. Actually, he did not: It was never there in the first place. What he did, quite piously and consciously, was to propose an alternative model that he considered superior to – more faithful to reality than – the one taught by his predecessors and contemporaries.

Thus, to return to Raphael's words, astronomers should piously recognize that what they "wield" (or "govern," OED, 1.a.) is their models rather than the "mighty frame" itself. That right balance will require them to acknowledge who truly holds the pen when it comes to authoring the "book of God." But again, as with "scan[ning]" earlier in the excerpt, the temptation will be to play the role of the self-important literary critic and to "scribble" over the substance of that text. Apparently, Milton and Raphael – and, as we shall see, Copernicus and others – found many of the scribblings of astronomers themselves to be inelegant and potentially risible.

---

[5] A helpful introduction to models can be found in Ian G. Barbour, *Myths, Models, and Paradigms: A Comparative Study in Science and Religion* (New York: Harper & Row, 1974); see for example p. 69.

[6] Melanchthon to Mithobius, 16 Oct. 1541; in *Corpus Reformatorum, Philippi Melanchthonis Opera*, eds. C. G. Bretschneider and H. E. Bindsell, 28 vols. (Halle: Schwetschke, 1834–60), vol. 4, col. 679, letter #2391: *ille Sarmaticus Astronomus, qui movet terram et figit Solem.*

The technical astronomical terms that Raphael mentions in his first response to Adam – "centric and eccentric . . . Cycle and epicycle" – apply mainly, although not exclusively, to what is sometimes collectively called *Aristotelian/Ptolemaic astronomy*. In Whiggish narratives of science history, this set of beliefs and explanations is often passed over dismissively. For any student of the history of thought, however, that system and its cultural, philosophical, and religious fabric are fascinating and essential for an understanding of Renaissance and early modern literature. Perhaps the most sympathetic account is that offered by C. S. Lewis's study *The Discarded Image*, a title I here borrow as a convenient name for the broadly Aristotelian/Ptolemaic model. As with any disused artifact seen only (if at all) in a book or a museum, its power and usefulness may initially be hard for present-day observers to grasp. But the magnitude of the scientific achievement of Copernicus and his heirs in the sixteenth and seventeenth centuries is most fully appreciated by those who glimpse the greatness as well as the flaws of the cosmology that was eventually and by circuitous paths superseded. For that "image" was a thing of considerable beauty and aspects of it had been delighting human beings for almost 2,000 years.

Although the phrase "Aristotelian/Ptolemaic" suggests an equal yoking of Aristotle (384–322 BC) with Ptolemy (ca. 90–168 AD), it is best to emphasize (with some oversimplification) that the former was a physicist and philosopher and the latter an astronomer and mathematician. In fact, in the sixteenth century and earlier, "mathematician" and "astronomer" were virtually interchangeable terms, while physicists studied a quite distinct subject matter.

Most of us have much more practical experience with physics than with astronomy. Although we notice when it is winter and when it is summer, when the Sun rises and sets, and perhaps whether the Moon is waxing or waning, we generally leave the actual details and meaning of those things to specialists – professional astronomers, calendar-makers, meteorologists. In contrast, everyone is continuously at work doing physics: estimating the weight of objects, determining which ones we had better not drop on our toes, judging the speed of vehicles so as to avoid getting knocked down in the street, measuring the temperature of the air outside our doors or of the heating elements under our frying pans. Most sports that people watch or play are complex, skillful explorations of practical physics, although almost none are connected in any direct way to astronomy. In short, there are very few real astronomers. But in myriad practical ways, everyone is a physicist.

Such elementary observations offer some insight into why Aristotle, the first thinker to formulate a systematic physics, was so influential for so long. From his teacher Plato, Aristotle learned an abiding respect for order, for precision of ideas, and for mathematical truths – especially those of geometry – even if these could never be fully embodied in this world in physical "reality." Plato had tried, by means of the exercise of philosophical reason, to see beyond this imperfect physical world: to discern Justice with a capital "J" and to comprehend the perfections of geometry that Euclid would later systematize. For Plato, it was these unchanging and incorruptible "forms" and mathematical verities that properly constituted reality. This is why quotation marks appear in the phrase physical "reality" – because real reality, for Plato, is not physical at all.

Aristotle by no means rejected all his master's teachings, but he is striking for his this-worldly, hard-nosed, commonsense application of the love of order, perfection, and unity he inherited from Plato. The poet Goethe said that whereas Plato is like a pointed flame striving heavenward, Aristotle assembles materials from far and wide and step by step upon an earthly foundation erects his edifice, also rising heavenward, but like a pyramid.[7] This picture conveys Plato's hard-to-systematize upward striving as well as its contrast with Aristotle's clear, well-proportioned solidity firmly rooted to this Earth.

What kind of world did Aristotle "construct"? One commentator has called it a "two storey" Universe.[8] Before the time of Plato and Aristotle, there were opposite tendencies in Greek thought, typified by Heraclitus and Parmenides.[9] Parmenides declared that all things are one and unchanging and that change itself is merely illusory. Heraclitus, by contrast, asserted that "everything flows and nothing abides; everything gives way and nothing stays fixed."[10] Strife is the very nature of reality. However, Aristotle established a peaceful coexistence between these two contrary philosophical temperaments by assigning them "separate territories" in his

[7] Paraphrase of Johann Wolfgang Goethe, *Geschichte der Farbenlehre*, in *Goethes Werke*, vol. 14 (Hamburg: Christian Wegner Verlag, 1960), p. 54: "[Aristoteles] umzieht einen ungeheuren Grundkreis für sein Gebäude, schafft Materialien von allen Seiten her, ordnet sie, schichtet sie auf und steigt so in regelmäßiger Form pyramidenartig in die Höhe, wenn Plato, einem Obelisken, ja einer spitzen Flamme gleich, den Himmel sucht."

[8] Arthur Koestler, *The Sleepwalkers: A History of Man's Changing View of the Universe* (1959; Harmondsworth, UK: Penguin, 1982), pp. 61–5.

[9] For more on the history of the contrary Heraclitean and Parmenidean tendencies, see Hélène Tuzet, "Cosmic Images," *Dictionary of the History of Ideas*, ed. Philip P. Wiener (New York: Scribner's, 1968), 1:513–23.

[10] *The Presocratics*, ed. Philip Wheelwright (New York: Odyssey Press, 1966), p. 70. The next quotation is from p. 71.

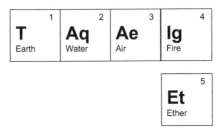

Figure 1.1   Aristotelian Periodic Table of the Elements

two-storey Universe. The upper storey – the world beyond the Moon – is where no change takes place. There, the spheres of the stars move in perfect regularity and harmony and nothing comes into being or passes away. But below the Moon, within the "sublunary" sphere, is the domain of time and mutability. Here, everything changes and, as Heraclitus said, "you cannot step twice into the same river."

For Aristotle, these two domains are made of qualitatively different kinds of stuff. He accepted the teaching of Empedocles that there are four "elements": earth, water, air, and fire (from heaviest to lightest). But, Aristotle added, beyond the Moon, everything is ethereal – literally made of ether, also known as the fifth element ("quintessence"). This system is illustrated by the rather lighthearted "periodic table of the elements" that appears in Figure 1.1.

The primitive appearance of this "periodic table" should not, however, hide the practical, commonsense basis of Aristotle's system. By "earth," Aristotle referred not merely to soil but more generally to that which is solid, including, of course, virtually everything other than water that constitutes Earth. Based on observation, one knows that whatever is made of earth – a rock, for example – will when released from one's hand drop straight down through the air and through any water it meets until it rests upon Earth's solid surface. Water will also fall down through the air but will stop at or in some body of water, such as a sea or a lake, that rests in turn upon solid earth. In the same way, air that is trapped beneath the surface of a lake will bubble up when released and rejoin the air that rests upon the surface of the water. Similarly, fire, as everyone can observe, strives upward through the air just as air rises through water.

Aristotle's theory of the four elements thus harmonizes with what he calls "natural place." In modern physics, to express it in rough Newtonian terms, stones or raindrops fall toward Earth because Earth, as a massive body, gravitationally attracts other things that have mass – including stones, raindrops, and also air. However, air is less dense than water – it has less mass per unit of volume – just as water is in turn less dense than rocks. This is why water displaces air and rocks displace air and water. But for Aristotle, it is *place*, not body or mass, that exerts the attractive influence. When a rock falls, it is seeking or being drawn to its proper place. Likewise, when a bubble rises, it is not so much that the water is *dis*placing the air as that the air is seeking what was its natural place to start with. Such are Aristotle's influential ideas about what he calls "the potency of place."[11]

That concept of place is intimately related to Aristotle's concept of motion. *Natural* motion, he asserts, is of two different kinds, in accordance with which "storey" of the Universe it occurs in. In the upper storey – in the heavens – what is natural is uniform circular motion about a center. But down here, where humans live, in the lower storey, natural motion is straight-line motion toward or away from the center. In the earlier examples of the stone and the bubbles, the stone naturally falls straight downward toward the center of the Universe (where Earth's center, on account of Earth's heaviness, also happens to be). And the bubble rises heavenward, following a vertical, rectilinear trajectory away from the center of the Universe.

As one observes daily, however, not all objects follow this straight-down or straight-up trajectory. Tennis balls, for example, do not spend most of their travel time going straight up or straight down, for there is also such a thing as unnatural or "violent" motion. When a player tosses a ball straight up in the air, that is violent motion. But nature gradually takes over and reverses the ball's course so it falls back to Earth. Even when a player hits the ball over the net with a rising stroke, one can see how nature starts to take over – to mitigate the violence done to the tennis ball – and to pull its trajectory toward one that is vertical and centripetal.

Finally, the distinction between natural and violent motion is one that applies only in the lower storey of the Universe. In the heavens, not only is all motion circular, but all motion is natural. One might object that meteors and comets do not appear to display circular motion about a center. This, however, is one of the reasons why Aristotle and most other astronomers for almost 2,000 years presumed that meteors and comets pursued their courses within the sublunary sphere – high up, to be sure, but still within the lower storey of the Universe.

[11] Aristotle, *Physics*, in *The Works of Aristotle*, ed. W. D. Ross (Oxford: Clarendon Press, 1930), vol. 2, 208b–209a.

As one moves from the lower storey of the Universe to the upper storey, one moves from physics to astronomy and also to what Aristotle dubbed *metaphysics* – "that which is beyond physics." It is worth repeating that the upper storey of the Universe, according to this model, is, properly speaking, not physical but ethereal – made of different stuff and characterized by different laws of motion. This motion, as already observed, is for Aristotle uniform and circular. In fact, the assumption concerning the incorruptibility of the heavens and the uniform circularity of the spheres persisted, astonishingly, even beyond the time of Copernicus, who did not challenge it. In Chapters 3 to 5 and elsewhere, we shall see how Milton engaged controversies concerning this powerful and persistent binary: perfection up there; imperfection down here.

In its most schematic form, Aristotle's astronomy is nicely illustrated by a picture (Figure 1.2) published in 1539 and again many times through the sixteenth century in Peter Apian's *Cosmographia*. The picture is, of course, a Christianized view of Aristotle's Universe, although much Islamic and Jewish thought of the Middle Ages was also deeply Aristotelian.

Examining the picture from inside out, one sees the four sublunary domains corresponding to the four elements – earth and water together in the inmost sphere, with air and then fire above them – followed by the first planetary sphere: that of the Moon. Then come the rest of the planetary spheres: of Mercury, Venus, the Sun, Mars, Jupiter (or Jove), and Saturn. Other items today included in the category of planets – Uranus, Neptune, and (some people still think) Pluto, none of which had yet been discovered – are no part of Aristotle's Universe, whereas for him and his followers, the Moon and the Sun are indeed two of the seven planets.

One observes, furthermore, that the planets are pictured *between* the circles inscribed in this graphic. This might be surprising, for the modern concept of an orbit – depicted as a circle (or ellipse) marking a planet's trajectory – tends to be read anachronistically back into such schematic models. Modern depictions naturally show planets *on* the lines rather than between them. However, this is not how Aristotle or the Middle Ages understood planetary locomotion. Each planet was thought to be carried by an ethereal sphere. The thickness of the shell of each sphere, as in this picture, is at least as great as the planet's diameter. Moreover, also perhaps surprisingly, there is absolutely no space between the spheres, for that would imply a vacuum, which Nature abhors. The "orbs" are all tightly nested one within the other, like the firm, perfectly spherical, and translucent layers of a cosmic onion. Of course, they all turn at different speeds, but the "friction" thus created produces not dissonance but

Figure 1.2   Aristotle's universe as illustrated in Apian's *Cosmographia* (1539)

(some thought) music: the harmony of the spheres – although this idea
originated not with Aristotle but with the Pythagoreans.

Beyond the final planetary sphere (of Saturn) comes that which is
labeled *Firmamentum* – the term for the heavens that appears in the
Vulgate version of the biblical creation account of Genesis 1 – and more
commonly known as the sphere of the fixed stars. The next or ninth
sphere is apparently empty but not in the sense of forming a vacuum;
rather, it is also crystalline (*Cristallinum*) – here marked out with the
signs of the Zodiac. Finally, at the extremity of the world is the *Primum
Mobile*, the prime mover, the sphere that encompasses and governs the
movement of all the other spheres. Thus far, the Universe. But, of course,
literally above and beyond it, in this Christianized version – indicated
although not depicted – is the "empyreal" Heaven, the dwelling place
of God and all the elect (saints and angels): *coelum empireum, habitaculum
dei et ominium electorum.*

Aristotle's Universe, especially its upper, superlunary storey, offers a satisfying and orderly picture, even if it leaves us earthly humans, down here in the lower storey, feeling a certain claustrophobia. The claustrophobia is an issue especially if one excludes the religious prospect of moving beyond the visible heavens to an ultimate, divine Heaven. For Aristotle himself, in any case, there was no such "beyond." Even if one focuses exclusively on astronomy, however – on the movements of the stars and the planets – there are problems with the Aristotelian system. To be sure, pictures such as Apian's are schematic. It would be wrong to insist that it somehow offers a "literal" picture of the world as the Middle Ages or sixteenth century imagined it. Set alongside what Ptolemaic astronomers in fact described, its relative scale, its flatness, its up-down orientation, and its presentation of a minimal number of crystalline spheres are all obviously graphical devices to make it accessible to the human observer. It is, in a word, symbolic.

But even given that concession, the Aristotelian system displays real weaknesses when it comes to actually describing what happens in the heavens. In fact, part of its legacy was almost two millennia worth of headaches for astronomers.

When Milton put into Raphael's mouth the claim that astronomers would contrive "[t]o save appearances," he employed an expression (σώζειν τα φαινόμενα) that had been in use since possibly the time of Plato.[12] It refers to any attempt to harmonize astronomical theory and observation. The attempt is necessary precisely because reconciling physics and astronomy – the way things ought to be and the way things appear to be – is so difficult. It should be emphasized that the concept of saving the appearances (or the phenomena) spans various cosmologies; it is by no means tied to a geocentric system. As early as the first century, Plutarch (ca. 46–120 AD) has a character use the phrase in relation to Aristarchus of Samos – sometimes now thought of as an ancient Copernicus: "that great man attempted 'to save phenomena' with his hypothesis that the heavens are stationary, while our Earth moves round in an oblique orbit, at the same time whirling about her own axis."[13]

---

[12] This according to Simplicius in his commentary on Aristotle's *De caelo*, ed I. L. Heiberg (Berlin, 1894), p. 489.
[13] Plutarch, *The Face Which Appears on the Orb of the Moon*, trans. A. O. Prickard (Winchester, UK: Warren and Son, 1911), p. 20.

Nonetheless, understanding the main problems that Aristotle's geocentrism posed for astronomy – and vice versa – demands a small amount of patience and a few fundamental pieces of vocabulary (which will appear in boldface). To begin, imagine that you are standing in the Northern Hemisphere under open skies, facing north, on a clear starlit night. You locate the North Star, Polaris. If you are near the equator, Polaris will be just above the northern horizon, although the farther north you are, the higher in the sky Polaris will appear. Because you are facing north, your right hand will be toward the east; your left, toward the west. And if you watch the stars for some time, you will notice that while Polaris apparently stands still, the other stars on the near side of it are moving in counterclockwise circles across the sky from right to left or from east to west. If you are somewhat north of the equator, you will also see stars on the far side of Polaris and they will appear to be moving in arcs from left to right but still counterclockwise.

This scene creates no particular problem for Aristotle's cosmology. For, assuming a central and immobile Earth and also uniform circular motion in the heavens, you see just what you would expect: a sphere of "fixed" stars (i.e., in fixed positions relative to each other) turning uniformly about an axis that runs from Polaris through the center of the Universe (also coincidentally through Earth's center), ending at the south polar star, assuming there is one. And it matters not whether it be summer or winter: The pole star invariably stands true north (almost) and the other stars move in regular circles about it.

If you repeat your nighttime observations, however, you will notice that the stars do not attain the meridian – achieve their highest point in the sky – at the same time each night. To explain this fact, one must remember that for Earth dwellers, "time of day" is governed by the Sun and that the Sun's sphere (in the system here imagined) is distinct from that of the fixed stars in two main respects. First, even though both spheres turn from east to west, the Sun's rising and setting do not synchronize with the revolutions of the stars. In fact, the Sun's position slowly "slips backward" relative to the stars, with this slippage adding up to 360 degrees – one full cycle – in the course of a year. And during this time, of course, the Sun itself goes through one annual cycle of adjusting its north-south elevation, appearing farthest north in June (on the summer solstice) and farthest south in December (on the winter solstice).

However, neither is this solar behavior much of a problem for Aristotelian cosmology. True, the heavenly spheres must be concentric, but no one said they had to be coaxial. As long as their different axes

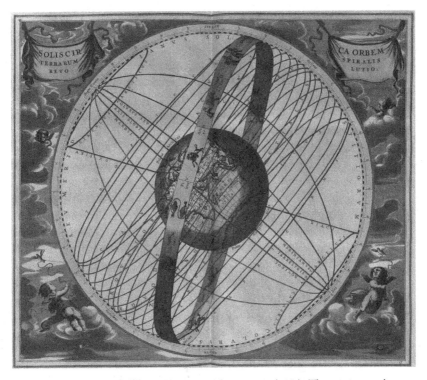

Figure 1.3   From Cellarius, *Harmonia Macrocosmica* (1660). The caption reads:
"The spiral revolution of the Sun about the Earth"

intersect at the center of the Universe, the spheres *are* concentric.
Accordingly, a standard depiction of the geocentric Sun shows its orb at
the familiar 23½-degree incline from that of the stellar sphere, ringed with
signs of the Zodiac, through which the Sun travels on its annual movement relative to the stars . In Figure 1.3, one can see the zodiacal band
delineating the Sun's pathway, known as the **ecliptic**. Of course, a solar
eclipse can occur only when (with other necessary conditions) the
Moon's pathway intersects the ecliptic. Andreas Cellarius's picture shows
the northward "rising" of the Sun in the first half of the year and places the
vernal equinox in the foreground – just to the right of Pisces and partway
into Aries, the Ram. The picture also helpfully includes straight lines
marking the stellar and solar axes.

For the sake of simplicity, one can ignore some relatively small difficulties caused by the fact that the Sun's rate of travel along the ecliptic
measurably accelerates and decelerates over the course of the year

(because in actuality, Earth's orbit is elliptical, not circular). One can also, at this level of discussion, ignore the Moon,[14] although Aristotelians were able to come pretty close to saving the solar and lunar phenomena – to account for a deceleration here or a wobble there – by including in their model some extra concentric but noncoaxial crystalline spheres.[15] Such systems of so-called **homocentric** ("same-centered") spheres remained the great hope of Aristotelian astronomers right up to the time of Copernicus. Only five years before the appearance of *De Revolutionibus*, Girolamo Fracastoro, Copernicus's former fellow student at Padua, was still trying to save the appearances by this means in his book *Homocentricity* (1538).

However, the most baffling problem of all was the planets. Although we now sharply distinguish stars and planets, the ancients called them all stars and merely divided them into two kinds based on their motions: the fixed stars and the wandering stars. It is the latter designation from which the word *planet* is derived; in Greek, the word means "wanderer" (πλανήτης αστήρ; cf. Latin *stella errans*). For planets are wanderers indeed, with Mars being a typical and particularly disturbing example.

As Figure 1.4 illustrates, not only does Mars speed up, slow down, and wander from the path of the ecliptic, but also, every 780 days, it appears to loop back across its own track. This phenomenon is known as **retrograde motion** and it does not do much to support Aristotle's belief in celestial uniform circular motion about a center. It is this problem more than any other that inspired the most heroic efforts of late antiquity and the Middle Ages to save the appearances. And to a degree, it is the sheer strenuousness of those efforts that ultimately drove Copernicus to champion a different cosmology.

The astronomer most persistently associated with attempts to save the appearances is Claudius Ptolemy (ca. 100–ca. 175). He was not the originator of all the ideas associated with his name, but he deserves credit as a great astronomical synthesizer. He is best known as the author of the single most influential astronomy textbook ever written. Originally titled

---

[14] An excellent discussion of the Moon's "behavior" can be found in Duncan Steel, *Eclipse: The Celestial Phenomenon That Changed the Course of History* (Washington, DC: Joseph Henry, 2001).

[15] Eudoxus of Cnidus (ca. 400–ca. 347 BC), who initiated this system of extra spheres, attributed three spheres each to the Sun and Moon. Aristotle attributed five each to the Sun and Moon and a total of fifty-six when all the spheres of the stars and of the planets and the extra "counterturners" are included. See Michael J. Crowe, *Theories of the World From Antiquity to the Copernican Revolution* (New York: Dover, 1990), pp. 23–6.

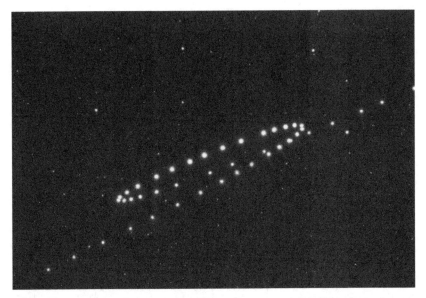

Figure 1.4   The retrograde motion of Mars as revealed by photos taken at intervals of five to seven days between October 2011 and July 2012.

Mathematical Syntaxis, the book came to be known as *Almagest* – which means "the greatest." This advanced technical work encompassed enormous numbers of diagrams, charts, and mathematical equations. It first appeared in Greek, in Alexandria, probably shortly after year 150 and it also survived many centuries in Arabic. In the entire Mediterranean area and in Europe east and west, supplemented by Ptolemy's *Planetary Hypotheses*, *Almagest* became the standard authority on astronomy for more than 1,000 years.[16]

Ptolemy and his followers tackled the vexing problem of the planets – of the wandering stars – by means of three main devices he employed in his model. Although these are employed in combination with each other, they may for the sake of clarity be considered one at a time. Precisely because they are parts of a discarded system, it is worth pointing out the brilliance of each one as well as its awkwardness. As already suggested, ancient and medieval cosmology can be viewed as one grand series of negotiations

---

[16] See *Ptolemy's Almagest*, trans. G. J. Toomer (New York: Springer, 1984). See also Bernard R. Goldstein, "The Arabic Version of Ptolemy's Planetary Hypotheses," *Transactions of the American Philosophical Society*, New Series 57.4 (1967): 3–55.

between the physics of Aristotle on the one hand and observational astronomy on the other – the goal of the negotiations being a state of concord in which the appearances are saved. But as in many negotiations, so in this one there were a number of items "on the table." It is interesting to notice which "demands" the natural philosophers were willing to compromise or give up in their efforts to "reach an agreement" with the appearances.

The original Aristotelian demands in this grand negotiation were five aspects of the following descriptive phrase: (1) uniform (2) circular motion (3) upon crystalline spheres (4) turning about a universal center point, which, for reasons of heaviness, is occupied by (5) an immobile Earth. However, Ptolemy as a practical negotiator and mediator did his best, as he must, to make concessions to the appearances without relinquishing – or admitting he was relinquishing – any of the original demands. The three devices already mentioned constitute in effect Ptolemy's concessions.

The first device is known as the **epicycle**, as mentioned by Raphael in his first astronomical response to Adam. Mars is typical of the problem. One can save the appearance of its retrograde motion by postulating that the planet moves uniformly and circularly on a small sphere that in turn is centered on a point moving uniformly and circularly on a larger sphere. The combined "spirograph" effect is that the planet's motion displays a series of loops (Figure 1.5), which, if viewed more or less from the center of the larger sphere, will periodically make the planet appear to move backward (hence retrograde motion).

This device works pretty well within limits. Epicycles do offer a possible way of harmonizing theory and observation. But at what cost? What has been negotiated away? Initially, one might be tempted to answer "simplicity" or "elegance." There is no doubt that the introduction of epicycles adds a multiplicity of new entities into the cosmic model. But more specifically, what has been bargained away in this part of the negotiation is the uniqueness of the center of the Universe as the geometrical center of all the celestial spheres. It is true that Aristotle had distinguished between different meanings of "center": the figurative sense of "core" or "heart" on the one hand and literal, geometrical centrality on the other.[17] With the advent of the epicycle, however, the literal meaning itself is fragmented. The device serves uniform circular motion about a center, *but now it is*

[17] Aristotle, *On the Heavens I and II*, ed. and trans. Stuart Leggatt (Warminster, UK: Aris & Phillips, 1995), pp. 149–51 (*De Caelo* 293a-b). See also Leggatt's notes, pp. 251–5.

DE MOTIB. STELLÆ MARTIS

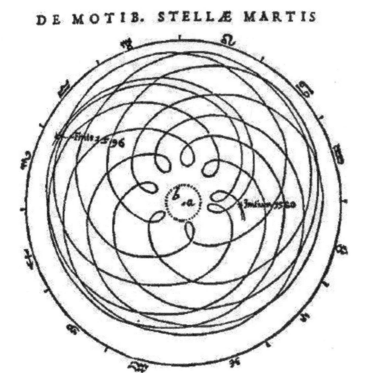

Figure 1.5   The path of Mars, as described by Kepler (*Astronomia Nova*, 1609), with its distinctive "pretzel shaped" orbit around a static, central Earth.

simply any center. The once-unique geometrical role of the universal midpoint has been divided, distributed, devolved.

This dispersion is carried one stage further by the second Ptolemaic device, known as **eccentrics** (see Figure 1.6), which are also mentioned by Raphael. Astronomers postulated these perfect circles as a way of explaining why a planet appears to speed up during half of its circuit about Earth and to slow down during the other half. Everyone today has had the experience of watching an airplane flying high overhead – and it seems to be moving slowly – while if one observes the same plane from close range, its motion seems fast. The technical reason for this difference is that, visually, one judges velocity by **angular motion** – by how much one has to turn one's head or move one's eyes to follow a moving object.

In the same way, if a planet is carried in a sphere that turns uniformly about a point that is eccentric – off center from where Earth

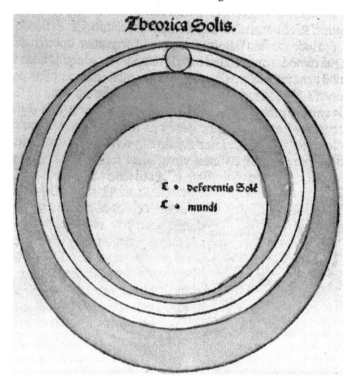

Figure 1.6   From Georg Peurbach, *Theoricae Novae Planetarum*, 1482.

is located – then, from Earth, the planet will appear to move more slowly when it is farther away and more rapidly when it is closer. Because this variation in velocity is really observed in the case of the planets, such eccentric circles help to save the appearances while supporting continued belief in the circularity and uniformity of celestial motion.

Again, though, something has been bargained away. Not only do eccentrics indicate a further erosion of the geometrical uniqueness of the universal center point, but they also introduce a definite asymmetry into the supposed perfection of the picture of the heavens. Eccentrics are literally off center – a feature that might well be construed as a celestial "imperfection." Finally, for anyone who sets a high value on the overall harmony of the world, eccentrics must also appear an imperfect device in the absence of any physical explanation for *why* the planetary spheres should turn about "centers" that have no fundamental relation to the whole – with no logical reason for being situated where they are.

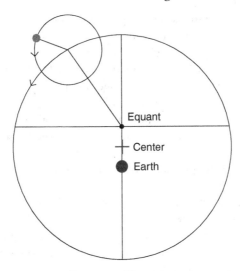

Figure 1.7   The equant

The third Ptolemaic device is a supplement to eccentrics and operates in conjunction with them. It accounts for the lack of uniform circular motion that remains when eccentrics have done all they can do. This notorious device is known as the **equant** and was the one most decisively rejected by Copernicus.[18] Given a line that includes the center of the Universe (where Earth is supposed to be located) as well as the center point of a planet's (eccentric) sphere, the equant is a point on that line located at the same distance from the sphere's center as Earth is but in the opposite direction. This complicated description is rendered quite simple by a diagram, as in Figure 1.7.

To grasp the function of the equant, one may recall the concept of angular motion and conduct a brief thought experiment. Imagine yourself standing at the very center of a circular racetrack watching a horse trotting around the course at a uniform speed. In order to keep the horse in the center of your vision, you will need to pivot yourself around and this *angular motion* on your part will happen uniformly (a) because the horse's *proper motion* is uniform and (b) because you are observing from the center. However, now imagine that you are watching the same horse on

[18] See Georg Joachim Rheticus (Copernicus's sole student and "apostle"), *Narratio Prima*; in *Three Copernican Treatises*, trans. Edward Rosen, 3rd edition (New York: Octagon Books, 1971, p. 135: "[M]y teacher dispenses with equants."

the same circular racetrack but from a viewpoint some distance away from the center. If the horse keeps up its uniform pace, your pivoting about will have to speed up when the horse is on the nearer part of the track and slow down when it is on the part farther from you. But now imagine that from this off-center vantage point you find you can observe the horse by pivoting yourself around at a uniform rate. If this were the case, then you could conclude that the horse's proper motion was *not* uniform. In this last scenario, if you replace the horse with a planet, then what you are standing on is the equant point. The equant is an equalizer. From it, the planet's motion *appears* uniform, even though, in fact, it is not.

This thought experiment helps to show not only how the equant works but also how it constitutes in effect a mathematical game of bait and switch. It saves the appearances by trading away the original definition of uniform circular motion. For was not uniform motion supposed to be "proper" motion – motion actually belonging to the moving object? But in the theory of the equant, this is abandoned in favor of angular motion. And the awkward thing about uniform angular motion is that it renders actual uniformity of motion a mirage – an optical illusion. As is evident in the thought experiment, if an object moving about a circle displays uniform angular motion as measured from an eccentric point, then it cannot possibly possess uniform proper motion. Therefore, to assert a planet's uniform *angular* motion as hypothetically observed from the equant is to sabotage any assertion of the planet's uniform *proper* motion. One can almost imagine Aristotle turning over (perhaps nonuniformly) in his grave – or, with Milton, hear God laughing.

What, then, from an Aristotelian viewpoint, was bargained away in Ptolemy's negotiations with the astronomical appearances? Again, the original theoretical demands were (1) uniform (2) circular motion (3) upon crystalline spheres (4) turning about a universal center point, which, for reasons of heaviness, is occupied by (5) an immobile Earth. The first of these (1), in its original definition of uniform proper motion, is quietly relinquished (in the theory of the equant) in exchange for angular motion. The idea of crystalline spheres (3) is not openly relinquished but severely compromised by the equant and by epicycles. The equant implies that the supposed crystalline sphere itself has nonuniform proper motion and this in turn raises the unanswerable question of *why* it does. Epicycles similarly diminish the credibility of the spheres by entailing the question of how – by what mechanism – small spheres can perform their rotations within larger ones. The concept of a universal center (4), although not openly relinquished, is in effect given less work to do: Most of its former tasks are delegated to eccentrics and to the centers of epicycles.

In short, the Ptolemaic negotiation leaves only (2) and (5) intact: the celestial circles and Earth's immobility. Heavenly uniformity of motion is gone – at least in its original sense. The crystalline spheres are rendered more imaginary than real in the absence of any physics that might describe how or why they function as they do or why they are situated where they are. Moreover, the idea of a universal center point, although not abandoned, suffers a devolution and contraction of its geometrical and mechanical role.[19]

By the time of Copernicus in the sixteenth century, the saving of astronomical appearances had thus already de facto spelled a severe loss of physical harmony and coherence in what was then the standard model of the Universe. And by Milton's lifetime, various aspects of Ptolemaic cosmology became objects of ridicule. Already by 1621, Robert Burton in his "digression of the Aire" in the *Anatomy of Melancholy* was calling "reall orbs, excentricke, concentricke, circles aequant &c. . . . absurd and ridiculous. For who is so mad to thinke that there should be so many circles, like subordinate wheeles in a clock, al impenetrable and hard, as they faine, adde and substract at their pleasures"?[20]

Among Ptolemy's successors, however, supporters as well as opponents expressed embarrassment at the awkward implications of his model. One early critic of Ptolemy was Proclus (412–85), an admirer of those he called the "professional astronomers" – "people like Aristarchus, Hipparchus, [and] Ptolemy." But he advocated applying a "critical mind" to their doctrines and made no effort to hide his discomfort with some of the devices used to save appearances. His comments go to the heart of the problem:

> What shall we say of the eccentrics and the epicycles of which [the astronomers] speak so much? Are they only conceptual notions or do they have a substantial existence in the spheres with which they are connected? If they exist only as concepts, then the astronomers have passed, without noticing it, from bodies really existing in nature to mathematical notions and, again without noticing it, have derived the causes of natural movements from something that does not exist in nature.[21]

[19] For a more fine-grained account than is possible here, see Lattis, *Between Copernicus and Galileo: Christoph Clavius and the Collapse of Ptolemaic Cosmology*, Chapter 6.

[20] Robert Burton, *The Anatomy of Melancholy*, ed. Holbrook Jackson (New York: Random House, 1977), Part 2, p. 50.

[21] Proclus, *Hypotyposis astronomicarum positionum*, trans. Abraham Wasserstein, in *Physical Thought From the Presocratics to the Quantum Physicists*, ed. Shmuel Sambursky (London: Hutchinson, 1974), p. 114.

By engaging the issue of causes derived "from something that does not exist in nature," Proclus also points to a distinction sometimes employed by modern historians of science: that between "realism" and "instrumentalism." In short, do Ptolemaic astronomers believe that epicycles and other devices describe entities that actually exist in nature (in which case they are realists) or do they claim only that the devices save the appearances but are not or might not be actual features of physical or celestial reality (in which case they are instrumentalists)?

Another admirer/critic of the Ptolemaic system was the medieval Jewish philosopher Moses Maimonides (1135–1204), who also raised the specter of the absurdity born from the union of Aristotle's physics and Ptolemy's astronomy. Maimonides' brilliant summary is worth quoting at some length:

> The theory that [the spheres] move regularly, and that the courses of the stars are in harmony with observation, depends ... on two hypotheses: we must assume either epicycles, or eccentric spheres, or a combination of both. Now I will show that each of these hypotheses is irregular, and totally contrary to the results of Natural Science. Let us first consider an epicycle ... rotating on a sphere, but not round the centre of the sphere that carries it. This arrangement would necessarily produce a revolving motion; the epicycle would then revolve, and entirely change its place. But that anything in the spheres should change its place is exactly what Aristotle considers impossible. ... (1) It is absurd to assume that the revolution of a cycle has not the centre of the universe for its centre; for it is a fundamental principle in the order of the universe that there are only three kinds of motion – from the centre, towards the centre, and round the centre. But an epicycle does not move away from the centre, nor towards it, nor round it. (2) Again, according to what Aristotle explains ... there must be something fixed, round which the motion takes place. This is the reason why the earth remains stationary. ...
>
> Consider, therefore, how many difficulties arise if we accept the theory which Aristotle expounds in Physics. For, according to that theory, there are no epicycles, and no eccentric spheres, but all spheres rotate round the centre of the earth! How then can the different courses of the stars be explained? How is it possible to assume a uniform perfect rotation with the phenomena which we perceive, except by admitting one of the two hypotheses or both of them? The difficulty is still more apparent when we find ... that the calculations according to these hypotheses are perfectly correct, within one minute; and that their correctness is confirmed by the most accurate calculation of the time, duration, and extent of the eclipses, which is always based on these hypotheses.[22]

---

[22] Moses Maimonides, *The Guide of the Perplexed*, trans. M. Friedländer (London, 1881–1885); excerpted in *BOTC*, ed. Danielson, pp. 84–5.

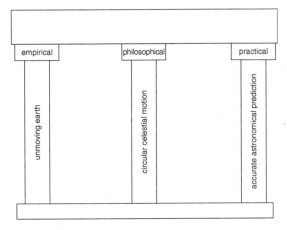

Figure 1.8   The three pillars of pre-Copernican (geocentric) cosmology

Maimonides masterfully grasps both horns of the Ptolemaic dilemma. The first, negative one has already been mentioned: The Ptolemaic model has much about it that is awkward and contrived. But the second horn is this: The model, broadly speaking, *works.* As Maimonides implies, any system that could successfully undergird the business of calculating "seasons, hours, or days, or months, or years" – even accurately predicting such astronomical phenomena as eclipses – was immensely impressive. Thus, while it is important to see how cumbersome many aspects of the Ptolemaic system were – for these were indeed the seeds of its destruction – it is equally important to glimpse the sources of its strength. It lasted for more than a millennium not because people's minds were weak but because its own powers were strong.

Those underpinnings can be seen as comprising three main pillars: one practical, one philosophical, and one empirical. (See Figure 1.8.) The practical pillar, just mentioned, is that the Ptolemaic system produced workable, relatively accurate results. The other two pillars – one philosophical and one empirical – are the two "Aristotelian demands" that remain after demands (1), (2), and (4) – uniformity of motion, the crystalline spheres, and the unique geometrical center – have been weakened or negotiated away. One of the survivors, then, is the perfect circularity of the heavenly spheres. The Ptolemaic negotiation leaves unshaken that deep-rooted philosophical belief in a realm that embodies the very symbol of perfection – the circle – never attainable here in the lower

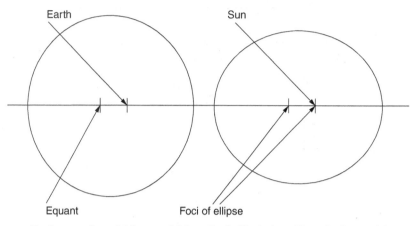

Basic equant model (geocentric)   Basic Keplerian ellipse (heliocentric)

Figure 1.9   Kepler's replacement of an eccentric point with one focus of an ellipse.

storey of the Universe. The third pillar, the empirical, is that other deep-rooted conviction founded on the assumption that our senses do not deceive us. And what we see, what we feel, is an Earth that does not move.

Of course, our senses are wrong – and so was Ptolemy. But such brilliant errors! Moreover, something that often goes unrecognized is how Ptolemy's devices themselves became, with some adjusting, components of the main cosmology that supplanted his. With Milton's God, we may laugh at eccentrics and epicycles, but what Galileo actually saw in those cold nights of telescopic observation in the early months of 1610 were the Jovian moons in their *epicycles* about Jupiter – proof that, in the words of Copernicus, there could be "numerous centers."[23] Moreover, with Kepler, all the orbits of the solar system came to be seen as elliptical and therefore *eccentric*. The Sun is eccentric relative to Earth's orbit, as Earth is eccentric relative to the Moon's.

Finally, the notorious equant was also rediscovered by Kepler to stunning effect. It would be pointless to claim that Ptolemy "anticipated" Kepler in any simplistic sense. However, as Figure 1.9 shows, it was but a short step from an eccentric circle with the equant and Earth symmetrically located on opposite sides of the center point to Kepler's proposal that planetary orbits are ellipses, with the Sun at one of the two focal points. Similarly, equant theory's replacement of uniform proper motion with angular motion – the latter being a composite of an object's motion and an observing subject's location – cracks open a door that Kepler eventually flung wide. For in

[23] Copernicus, *De Revolutionibus*, 1.9: *Pluribus ergo existentibus centris.*

keeping with his recognition that all things are "interconnected, involved, and intertwined,"[24] Kepler's second law unveiled a harmonious uniformity after all, in which time, radial distance, planetary distance traveled, and the observer's location all become part of the equation.

We shall return to various issues concerning the moving Earth in Chapter 7 and elsewhere, but it is worth noting here that alternatives to geostatic theory were formulated and acknowledged long before the sixteenth century and even long before Ptolemy. Even during the Middle Ages, a period popularly associated with monolithic geocentric cosmology, natural philosophers in fact routinely acknowledged the moving-Earth hypothesis – if only to reject it. Thomas Aquinas (ca. 1225–74), commenting on Aristotle's *On the Heavens*, asserts:

> Appearance of motion is caused either by the motion of the thing seen or by the motion of the one who sees it. For this reason some people, assuming that the stars and the whole sky rest, have posited that the earth on which we dwell is moved once daily from west to east around the equinoctial poles. Thus by our motion, it seems to us that the stars are moved in a contrary direction, which is what Heraclides of Pontus and Aristarchus are said to have posited.[25]

Aquinas, like Ptolemy before him, showed his true Aristotelian colors by rejecting the moving-Earth hypothesis. But less than a century later, John Buridan (ca. 1295–1358), rector at the University of Paris, offered a series of arguments illuminating late medieval cosmology from various angles.

Buridan's arguments raise a series of "significant" or "difficult" doubts, including the following:

> Whether the earth is directly in the middle of the Universe so that its centre coincides with the centre of the Universe. . . .

> Whether the . . . conclusion of Aristotle is sound, namely, if the heaven is by necessity to be moved circularly forever, then it is necessary that the earth be at rest forever in the middle. . . .

> Whether, in positing that the earth is moved circularly around its own center and about its own poles, all the phenomena that are apparent to us can be saved.

[24] Johannes Kepler, *New Astronomy*, trans. William H. Donahue (Cambridge: Cambridge University Press, 1992), p. 48.
[25] Aquinas, "Commentary on Aristotle's *On the Heavens*" [II.8.289b.5–7], trans. Edward Grant, in *A Source Book in Medieval Science*, ed. Edward Grant (Cambridge, MA: Harvard University Press, 1974), p. 67.

Given that the theory of eccentrics had so muddied the location and function of the center (or possibly *centers*), Buridan's first doubt is hardly surprising. The second doubt, even in its parallel structure ("moved circularly forever ... at rest forever"), shows a tendency to view the heavens' mobility and Earth's stability as correlative propositions and therefore potentially exchangeable. As for the third doubt, Buridan goes on to cite the "persuasion" that "just as it is better to save the appearances through fewer causes than through many, ... so it is better to save [them] by an easier way than by one more difficult. Now it is easier to move a small thing than a large one. Hence it is better to say that the Earth, which is very small, is moved most swiftly and the highest sphere is at rest than to say the opposite."[26] Here again is the argument from economy – the very argument with which Adam opens the dialogue on astronomy in Book 8 of *Paradise Lost*.

Although Buridan spoke from a position of respect for Aristotle, his freedom to entertain propositions inimical to Aristotle stands as a reminder that pre-Copernican European or Christian natural philosophy was no mere Aristotelian monolith.[27] In 1277, some 200 years before the birth of Copernicus, the bishop of Paris, Étienne Tempier, issued a condemnation of 219 articles, many of them Aristotelian. Among these was one stating "that the First Cause cannot make many worlds" – a claim worthy of rejection because it implied a limitation of God's omnipotence. Thus, the condemnation of 1277 operated like a piece of antimonopoly legislation, encouraging competition in the marketplace of ideas. It opened the door to philosophical speculation about a range of issues, including Earth's mobility and the possibility of a plurality of worlds[28] – speculation in which Buridan, along with many others after him, including Milton, took part.

There was long and rich precedent, therefore, for the engagement of such "conjecture" and "disputes" as those mentioned by Raphael in the discussion of astronomy in Book 8 of *Paradise Lost*. But before turning to them, let us ponder the breathtakingly larger backdrop against which, Milton recognized, controversies about the "cosmologically local" structure of our Universe should be placed.

---

[26] John Buridan, Questions on the Four Books on the Heavens and the World of Aristotle, trans. Marshall Clagett, in Clagett, *The Science of Mechanics in the Middle Ages* (Madison: University of Wisconsin Press, 1959), pp. 594–5.

[27] See Edward Grant, *The Foundations of Modern Science in the Middle Ages: Their Religious, Institutional and Intellectual Contexts* (Cambridge: Cambridge University Press, 1996), pp. 144–8.

[28] See Steven J. Dick, *Plurality of Worlds* (New York: Cambridge University Press, 1982), pp. 28–9.

CHAPTER 2

Multiverse, Chaos, Cosmos

In the beginning God created the heaven and the earth. And the earth was without form, and void; and darkness was upon the face of the deep. And the Spirit of God moved upon the face of the waters.

The Bible, Genesis (also known as the First Book of Moses), 1:1–2

It was a most ancient and in a manner Universally received Tradition amongst the Pagans ... that the *Cosmogonia* or Generation of the World took its first Beginning from a *Chaos* (the *Divine Cosmogonists* agreeing herein with the *Atheistick* ones;) ... Neither can it reasonably be doubted, but that [this tradition] was *Originally Mosaical*, and indeed at first a *Divine Revelation*. ... Wherefore those *Pagan Cosmogonists* who were *Theists*, being *Polytheists* and *Theogonists* also, and asserting besides the One *Supreme Unmade Deity*, other *Inferiour Mundane Gods*, *Generated* together with the World (the Chief whereof were the *Animated Stars*) they must needs according to the Tenor of that Tradition, suppose them as to their Corporeal Parts at least, to have been Juniors to *Night* and *Chaos*, and the Off-spring of them, because they were all made out of an Antecedent *Dark Chaos*.

Ralph Cudworth, *The True Intellectual System of the Universe*[1]

One of the most conspicuous and wide-spread characteristics of many Renaissance thinkers through into the seventeenth century was their desire to conflate or at least harmonize ancient philosophies with each other and with more recent developments of thought. Milton's fusion of classical epic and biblical narrative is symbolic in this regard, as is, perhaps, counterbalancing that tendency, his repeated subordination of Greek and Roman myth to Christian purposes. Harmony, of course, was not always possible – certainly not with regard to the large philosophical and religious matter of cosmogony (theories about the origin of the Universe) nor with regard to astronomical issues, such as Earth's movement. In the second

---

[1] Ralph Cudworth, *The True Intellectual System of the Universe* (completed 1671) (London, 1678), p. 248.

epigraph, however, Milton's contemporary Ralph Cudworth is typical in his efforts to distinguish among ancient schools as to whether they are theistic and where possible to trace their shared debt to a common biblical source.

For Milton, in *Paradise Lost*, as maker of a "world" as well as poet of a theodicy – a justification of "the ways of God" (1.26) – there was a great deal at stake regarding cosmogony beyond its obvious interest as an account of the origins of the visible Universe. For part of that theodicy involved the assertion that God is omnipotent, a proposition implying in turn that nothing beyond his power, will, or goodness constrains his creative acts. Ancient pagan cosmogonies did generally posit some such constraint or else denied divine origins altogether, thus *a fortiori* denying (in Cudworth's precise phrase) "One *Supreme Unmade Deity*."

The constraint that many ancient thinkers posited as limiting divine creative activity and against which theologians reacted from the beginnings of Christianity is typified by the dualistic characterization of creation presented in Plato's *Timaeus*, which offers a "likely account" of how the world began. "God," says Timaeus in the dialogue, "wishing that all things should be good, and so far as possible nothing be imperfect, and finding the visible universe in a state not of rest but of inharmonious and disorderly motion, reduced it to order from disorder."[2] In this way, God is conceived to have done the best he could with preexisting and disharmonious materials. Thus, as Timaeus says later in his account, "this world came into being from a mixture and combination of necessity and intelligence."[3] Such a view is contrary to the biblical teaching that "there is but one God ... of whom are all things" (1 Cor. 8:6), for it supposes that something other than God alone is primordial – that something apart from him existed in the beginning, limiting his creativity.[4] Even if Plato's God achieves a high degree of success in imposing his will on Chaos, the very assumption that the latter is primordial entails for the Christian an inadmissible limitation of divine power.

Nevertheless, the hint in Genesis of an early if not primordial state of disorder was enough to encourage centuries-long Christian efforts to syncretize pagan and biblical accounts. What one might call the passive

[2] Plato, *Timaeus*, trans. Desmond Lee (Harmondsworth: Penguin, 1965), 30 (p. 42).
[3] *Timaeus* 48 (p. 65). See also John Hick's discussion of the *Timaeus* and dualism, in which he suggests that Plato's "necessity" signifies not rigid determination ... but something more like chaos and randomness"; *Evil and the God of Love* (London: Macmillan, 1966), p. 33.
[4] On the contrast between biblical and dualistic views, see Langdon Gilkey, *Maker of Heaven and Earth* (New York: Doubleday, 1959), pp. 48–51.

aspect of the biblical analogue is represented by darkness and water: "The earth was without form, and void; and darkness was upon the face of the deep." Not unlike the account that appears in the *Timaeus*, this text suggests that creation was accomplished over against something contrary: in opposition to an uncreated state or even an anticreational force. As Bruce K. Waltke has shown, "At least in a dozen texts of the Old Testament, reference is made to the LORD's conflict with the dragon or sea monster variously named as Rahab, 'The Proud One,' or Leviathan, 'The Twisting One' or Yam, 'The Sea.' Moreover, at least five of these texts are in a context pertaining to the creation of the world."[5] Others have shown the affinities between these figures and the personified destructive forces that appear in ancient Near Eastern literature, such as the Enuma Elish.[6]

How, then, were such images of Chaos and even hostility harmonized with a Christian cosmogony declaring the primordiality and omnipotence of God the Creator? Again, the main teachings were forged in a context of controversy. In early Christianity, Gnosticism, and, somewhat later, Manichaeism were the forms of radical dualism that presented the greatest threat to the doctrine of creation – the latter being succinctly asserted against the Gnostics by Irenaeus near the end of the second century:

> It is proper ... that I should begin with the first and most important head, that is, God the Creator, who made the heaven and the earth, and all things that are therein ... and to demonstrate that there is nothing above Him or after Him; nor that, influenced by any one, but of His own free will, He created all things, since He is the only God, the only Lord, the only Creator, the only Father, alone containing all things, and Himself commanding all things into existence.[7]

Contrasted with this view is that of Manichaeism, a close kin of Gnosticism, which arose in the third century and posited a primordial opposition of Good and Evil, Light and Darkness, God and Matter. It was this "heresy" (in fact, a separate religion) that St. Augustine spent the first stage of his career as a Christian theologian attacking. Like Irenaeus, Augustine reasserted that there is but one God and that "of him, and through him, and to him, are all things" (Rom. 11:36). To bolster

---

[5] Bruce K. Waltke, *Creation and Chaos: An Exegetical and Theological Study of Biblical Cosmogony* (Portland, OR: Western Conservative Baptist Seminary, 1974), p. 5.

[6] See J. Martin Evans, *Paradise Lost and the Genesis Tradition* (Oxford: Clarendon Press, 1968), p. 12.

[7] Irenaeus, *Against Heresies* 2.1.1; in *The Ante-Nicene Fathers*, ed. Alexander Roberts and James Donaldson (rpt. Grand Rapids, MI: Eerdmans, 1975), vol. 1.

his anti-Manichaean defense, Augustine adopted certain aspects of Neoplatonic thought and developed the concept of evil as privation. Because evil by its very nature is thus parasitic, it need not be viewed as being in any way primordial or original.

Against the Manichaeans, Augustine argues that natures (created things) are corruptible not because of a mixture of good and evil principles but because they are created *ex nihilo*: "All corruptible natures ... are natures at all only so far as they are from God, nor would they be corruptible if they were of Him; because they would be what He himself is. Therefore of whatever measure, of whatever form, of whatever order, they are, they are so because it is God by whom they were made; but they are not immutable, because it is nothing of which they were made."[8] Furthermore, lest the Manichaeans should resort to the familiar conception of a primal, formless matter and identify that with their evil principle, Augustine asserts that matter is also from God the Creator:

> Neither is that material, which the ancients called *Hylē*, to be called an evil. ... By *Hylē* I mean a certain material absolutely formless and without quality, whence those qualities that we perceive are formed. ... Nor is that *Hylē* ... to be called an evil which cannot be perceived through any appearance, but can scarcely be thought of through any sort of privation of appearance. ... If form is some good, ... even the capacity of form is undoubtedly something good. ... And because every good is from God, no one ought to doubt that even matter, if there is any, has its existence from God alone.[9]

Thus, in the most orthodox of writers, we find at least a hint of how the formless matter of the ancient pagan cosmogony might be syncretized with a Christian, nondualistic view of creation by a wholly good God.

The seventeenth century offers many further examples of apologists and polemicists who articulated the connections among creation, Chaos, evil, and omnipotence. In a work titled *The Originall Cause of Temporall Evils* (1645), Meric Casaubon, son of the more famous Isaac Casaubon, sets out to oppose two theories concerning the origin of evil that, he says, the devil, before the time of "Epicurisme," introduced into men's opinions (1) "that God was of an envious nature: ... which was ... the very argument

---

[8] Augustine, *De Natura Boni Contra Manichaeos*, Chapter 10; in *A Select Library of the Nicene and Post-Nicene Fathers of the Christian Church*, ed. Phillip Schaff (rpt. Grand Rapids, MI: Eerdmans, 1974), vol. 4.

[9] Augustine, *De Natura Boni*, Chapter 18; in *Patristic Studies* vol. 88 (Washington, DC: Catholic University of America Press, 1955).

[the devil] used to our first father and mother . . . to make them transgress" and (2) an error they fell into later, "not altogether so impious, but more absurd, that God is not omnipotent, and wanted not will, but power to amend what they conceived to be amiss in the world: or, that there were two Authors and Creators of all things, the one good, and the other evill."[10] As Casaubon recognized, there is an apparent dilemma concerning God's power and goodness, with the result that "among [the ancients] that were agreed concerning the goodnesse of God, there was no small controversie concerning his power. For, said they, were God as omnipotent, as he is good, why hath he not made all things as goodnesse would have prompted?" This sort, among whom Casaubon lists Seneca and Epictetus, "did put all the fault of all that was done amisse in the world upon the ὕλην [*hylēn*], or, *materiam*, that God was to work upon, and was not able (so they) to rectify." Casaubon adds: "I cannot excuse *Plato*, though some have taken great pains to doe it; . . . his words are plain, that ανάγκη [*anankē*, "necessity"], or, *materia prima*, as eternall as God himselfe, did concurre with him, to the making of all things."[11]

Some of the most intriguing ancient atheistical cosmogonists were the atomists, of whom the most prominent were Democritus and Epicurus among the Greek Presocratics and first-century-BC Roman poet and popularizer Lucretius, whose long poem *De Rerum Natura* was rediscovered in Florence in 1417 and received multiple translations into English in late seventeenth-century England.[12] Despite the original atomists' apparently thoroughgoing materialism and desire to account for the workings and origins of the world without recourse to divine explanation, significant numbers of Renaissance writers sought to harmonize a theistic cosmogony with atomist principles.

In France, for example, Pierre Gassendi spent his career developing a Christian Epicureanism – an atomism intended to offer an alternative to the kind of Aristotelian physics sketched in Chapter 1. In England, Walter Charleton, "Gassendi's English popularizer" and friend of Thomas Hobbes,[13] championed atomism while carefully distancing himself from the atomists' radical materialism. Charleton rejects what he calls that "execrable delusion" that the Universe was not created by God but resulted

---

[10] Meric Casaubon, *The Originall Cause of Temporall Evils* (London, 1645), the preface (n.p.).

[11] Casaubon, *The Originall Cause*, pp. 28–9.

[12] See *BOTC*, ed. Danielson, Chapter 4, "Atoms and Empty Space," and Stephen Greenblatt, *The Swerve: How the World Became Modern* (New York: Norton, 2011).

[13] Stephen Fallon, *Milton Among the Philosophers: Poetry and Materialism in Seventeenth-Century England* (Ithaca: Cornell University Press, 1991), p. 46.

fortuitously from "an infinite *Chaos* of *Atoms*."[14] The epitome of this view Charleton translates from Lucretius:

> The Worlds *Materials* having first been tost,
> An infinite *Time*, within an infinite *Roome*,
> From this to that uncircumscribed coast,
> And made by their own *Tendency* to roame
> In various *Motions*; did at last quiesce
> In these *Positions*, which they now possess.
>   (p. 42; *De Rerum Natura*, 1024–8)

Charleton rejects "this old Romance of the spontaneous result of the World from ... that Abysse of Atoms ... rowled up and down, to and fro, by an impetuous and continual inquietude ... or civil war" and he carefully identifies those elements of the Epicurean view that make it unacceptable to the Christian. Expressly to be denied are the claims "(1.) *that the Chaos of Atoms was nonprincipiate*, or as antient as Eternity: (2.) that they were not created *ex nihilo* ... by God: (3.) that they were not becalmed, separated, ranged, and disposed into their proper stations ... by the artifice of any other *Cause*, but the blind Ordination ... of *Fortune*" (p. 43). "And yet notwithstanding," Charleton goes on to say, "I have never yet found out any justifiable ground, why *Atoms* may not be reputed *Mundi materies*, the Material Principle of the Universe, provided that we allow, that God created that first *Matter* out of *Nothing*" (p. 44).

> Suppose we, in short, that God in the first act of his Wisdome and Power, out of the *Tohu*, or nothing, creates such a ... mass of Atoms, as was necessary to the constitution of the Universe: ... and then will all the subsequent operations of nature remain so clear and easie, that a meer *Ethnick* by guidance of ... *Sense* and *Ratiocination*, may progress to a physical theory of them, and thereby salve all the Phaenomena's with less apostasie from first Principles proposed, then by any other hypothesis yet excogitated. (p. 47)

Thus, Charleton, like Augustine and countless other Christian thinkers, seeks to render pagan philosophy for its "Egyptian gold" and, by using that refined substance for the saving of appearances, to further the attack against paganism's dualistic or antitheistic tenets.

That Milton similarly adapts pagan cosmological and cosmogonic sources is not in dispute. At one level, the pagan sources of his Chaos

---

[14] Walter Charleton, *The Darknes of Atheism Dispelled by the Light of Nature: A Physico-Theologicall Treatise* (London, 1652), p. 40.

have been adequately noted by his editors and commentators.[15] However, the simple citing of a pagan source in connection with a work like *Paradise Lost* may too easily call to mind possible similarities with paganism – without regard for their accompanying contrasts. Charleton's discussion, at least, makes explicit the attempt to separate out the dross. At the same time, the use of pagan terminology in connection with the biblical account of creation was in the seventeenth century such a commonplace that its appearance should not generally be read as implying anything scandalous for Christian cosmogony. Milton's contemporary Thomas Goodwin, for example, unflinchingly reads the first verse of Genesis thus: When "it is said, that on the *first day God created the heaven and the Earth*, . . . by Earth is meant the confused *Chaos*, the matter of Sun, and Moon, and Stars, and Men, and Beasts, and Fire, and Water, and Earth, and all."[16] Milton's treatment of Chaos, however, I shall argue, transcends in fresh ways its pagan roots and the commonplace, occasionally bland syncretizing of those roots with Christian theology. It may also be seen, in its literary and theological boldness, to stand apart from even his contemporaries' critical efforts at saving appearances of creation and Chaos.

As already mentioned, ancient atomism entailed a thoroughgoing materialism that militated against any theistic cosmogony. How, then, can Milton, whose materialism is well established – and who rejects the traditional doctrine of *creatio ex nihilo* in favor of *creatio ex deo* – avoid being cast in the same mould with Democritus, Epicurus, Lucretius, and the rest? To answer this question, let us consider Milton's motivations for adopting two of his best attested "heresies." I would suggest that in

---

[15] See for example Merritt Hughes, *John Milton: Complete Poems and Major Prose* (New York: Bobbs-Merrill, 1957), pp. 179–180, in addition to textual notes on *Paradise Lost*; A. S. P. Woodhouse, "Notes on Milton's Views on the Creation: The Initial Phases," *Philological Quarterly* 28 (1949): 211–36; A. B. Chambers Jr., "Chaos in *Paradise Lost*," *Journal of the History of Ideas* 24 (1963): 55–84. Anyone interested in this general topic should also consult John Rumrich's landmark essay "Milton's God and the Matter of Chaos," *PMLA* 10.5 (1995): 1035–46 – whose position I generally endorse even if I might stop short of calling Chaos "God's womb" (p. 1043). Three other critics' discussions are pertinent here and certainly worth reading. Denis Saurat's *Milton: Man and Thinker* (London: J. M. Dent, 1944) goes far beyond my account of Milton's docrine of *creatio ex deo* and ascribes to Milton an essentially pantheistic "retraction theory" in his chapter "Ontology" (pp. 93–123). Regina Schwartz's *Remembering and Repeating: Biblical Creation in Paradise Lost* (Cambridge: Cambridge University Press, 1988) considers "an evil chaos so difficult to escape that it is not worth trying" (p. 11). She would probably find my position contributory to "something like a critical conspiracy to detoxify [Milton's] chaos" (p. 31). And John Rogers, in "Chaos, Creation, and the Political Science of *Paradise Lost*," Chapter 4 of *The Matter of Revolution: Science, Poetry, and Politics in the Age of Milton* (Ithaca: Cornell University Press, 1996), pp. 103–43, offers an account of creation with an emphasis on Milton's alleged relationship with seventeenth-century vitalism.

[16] Thomas Goodwin, *Of the Creatures, and the Condition of Their State by Creation* (1682), p. 112; in T. Goodwin, *The Works*, vol. 2 (London, 1683).

Milton's view, the doctrine of *creatio ex nihilo* offered no solution at all to the question of evil's origin but was actually part of the problem. Augustine, as we have seen, propounded a doctrine of creation out of nothing in order to undercut the Manichaeans, who explained evil by adducing creation's mixture of radical good and evil principles. Among Milton's contemporaries, Charleton is typical in qualifying materialistic atomism with the premise "that God created [the] first *Matter* out of *Nothing*." The risk, however, was a full conflation of the ideas of matter and nothingness, even to a point verging on the Manichaean notion of creation as a mixture of light and darkness. Peter Sterry (d. 1672), Oliver Cromwell's chaplain, goes so far as to say that "Man is composed of the light of God, and his own proper darkness. These two, the Schools call the Act and the potentiality; the form, and the matter; being, and not being, which constitute every Creature. The darkness or nothingness, which is the Creatures own, is the proper ground of sin."[17] Similarly, Thomas Goodwin declares that God "in making this Visible World ... began with a rude Lump, ... which was actually *Nothing*, potentially *All things*; therefore call'd *Earth and Waters*; but in truth a Darkness and deep Confusion without form." Goodwin also dangerously links the "nihility" of man's origins with moral evil: "The Creature being made out of Nothing, tends to a Deficiency."[18] As Robert Harris puts it: "Man was made out of *Nothing*, and therefore apt ... to return into his first principles, and ... prone to privations." But the fault, of course, is not God's; "man is the cause of his own naughtinesse."[19]

The term *naughtinesse* neatly fuses the moral and metaphysical implications of the doctrine of *creatio ex nihilo*[20] – implications that Milton takes pains to reject. First, as far as metaphysics is concerned, Milton asserts that God could not have created the world *ex nihilo* – "'could not', not from any lack of power or omnipotence, but because there had to be something already in existence which by being acted upon might receive the almighty force of his efficacy." This reasoning is based partly on what Milton conceived to be the exact meaning of Scripture. He argues that in Hebrew,

---

[17] Peter Sterry, *A Discourse of the Freedom of the Will* (London, 1675), p. 177.

[18] Goodwin, *Of the Creatures*, pp. 32, 25.

[19] Robert Harris, *A Brief Discourse of Mans Estate in the First and Second Adam* (London, 1653), pp. 9, 14.

[20] See Sidney's 1587 translation of Phillip DuPlessis-Mornay's *The Trewnesse of the Christian Religion*: "S. *Austine* sayth, that the *Latins* terme an evill man *Nequam*, and an evillnesse *Nequitiam*, that is to say, *Naughtie* and *Naughtinesse*"; in *The Prose Works of Sir Philip Sidney*, ed. Albert Feuillerat (1912; rpt. Cambridge: Cambridge University Press, 1962), 3:231.

Greek, and Latin and throughout Scripture, the verb "to create" implies "to make something out of matter."[21] Milton concludes, accordingly:

> And so, since both Holy Scripture and reason itself suggest that all these things were not made from nothing but from matter, it necessarily follows that matter either always existed outside God or at some time originated from God. That matter should have always existed outside God . . . by itself is not intelligible; nor, if it did not exist from eternity, is it any easier to understand where it eventually came from: There remains therefore only this [idea], especially as scripture guides us to it, that all things came out of God: see Rom. 11:36: *out of him, and through him, and into him are all things*; and 1 Cor. 8:6: *one God, the Father out of whom are all things* – ['out of', *ex*], as the Greek reads in both cases. (*DDC*, pp. 288–91)

This doctrine of *creatio ex deo* does not, of course, mean that God is material in the way in which tables and chairs are material, for as Raphael says in *Paradise Lost* in his own enunciation of the doctrine:

> . . . one Almighty is, from whom
> All things proceed, and up to him return,
> If not depraved from good, created all
> Such to perfection, one first matter all,
> Endued with various forms, various degrees
> Of substance.
>
> (5.469–74)

Although this one substance includes what is usually distinguished as "body" and "spirit" (5.478), Milton's doctrine clearly separates him from the tradition that views these as radically different kinds of substances – just as it involves him in a rejection of the world's original "naughtinesse." His high view of the goodness and power of God lies at the heart of his materialism as well as at the heart of his doctrine of *creatio ex deo*. These doctrines are indeed twins, for it is the latter that rescues matter from the taint of primordial evil. With the doctrine of *creatio ex deo*, matter can unequivocally be seen as created essentially good and no longer is doubt cast on the divine wisdom for creating a universe in a metaphysically evil state from its very beginning. Rather, asserts Milton, the "original matter is not to be thought of as an evil or worthless thing, but as a good thing, as a

---

[21] *The Complete Works of John Milton*, vol. 8: *De Doctrina Christiana*, ed. and trans. John K. Hale and J. Donald Cullington (Oxford: Oxford University Press, 2012), pp. 286–9 (cited hereafter as *DDC*). See George Newton Conklin, *Biblical Criticism and Heresy in Milton* (New York: King's Crown Press, 1949), p. 67, and Maurice Kelley's introduction to Milton's doctrine of creation, *Christian Doctrine*, in *Complete Prose Works of John Milton*, ed. Don M. Wolfe et al., 8 vols. (New Haven, CT: Yale University Press, 1953–81), 6:87–90.

seed bank of every subsequent good. It was a substance, and derivable from no other source than from the fountain-head of all substance; at first unarranged and disorganized, but afterwards God arranged it and made it beautiful" (*DDC*, pp. 292–3). In short, then, God is good and so is the stuff he makes – or the stuff that comes from him.

Finally, Milton takes care not to let materialism undermine God's freedom. He strives to purge such terms as *nature* and *fate* of any absolute, dualistic, or deterministic connotations. The etymology of these words, he contends, reveals that each is relative: "nature [*natura*] declares that it was born [*nata*]. … And what can fate [*fatum*] be but the divine decree [*effatum*] of some almighty deity?" (*DDC*, pp. 24–5). In this way, Milton signals early in his treatise that even when he uses terms drawn from pagan philosophy, he does so undualistically and in a manner consistent with a high view of divine omnipotence.

Before moving to Milton's poetic presentation of creation in *Paradise Lost*, I would offer this review of some main similarities and differences between Milton's position, as stated in *De Doctrina Christiana*, and that of his more orthodox contemporaries. William Pemble's chapter "Of Creation," which opens his *Treatise of the Providence of God*,[22] may be taken as representative of the latter. Pemble says that "creation … is the action of God, whereby out of nothing he brought forth Nature, and all things in Nature" (p. 265). Although agreeing about the relative status of nature, Milton declares that "God did not produce all things out of nothing but out of himself" (*DDC*, pp. 294–5). With Pemble, Milton would agree that there can be no "eternal substance, which is not God" (p. 266), but he avoids the doctrine of *creatio ex nihilo* by assuming that God *is* the eternal substance from which all other substances derive. Pemble, incidentally, believes "the world was created … *in the beginning*, that is, in the beginning of time, or together *with time*, rather than *in* time" (p. 267), but Milton sees no reason why time and motion, "according to the ideas of 'earlier' and 'later'," could not "have existed before this world was established" (*DDC*, pp. 298–9).

Pemble distinguishes the creation of "spiritual … substances, as the Angels, … which are void of matter," from "all corporall and materiall substances" (p. 267). As we have just seen, Milton teaches – from the mouth of an angel – that all things derive from "*one* first matter" (*PL*, 5.472). Both would agree that God created, as Pemble says, "of his

---

[22] William Pemble, *Treatise of the Providence of God*; in Pemble, *Works* (Oxford, 1659). In-text references are to this edition.

good pleasure, no necessity urging him, no power of the matter he took helping him" (p. 268). But whereas Milton, as already indicated, describes the production of matter as "at first unarranged and disorganized," Pemble describes the same thing only to reject it: "The first Matter, that huge lump, a rude and indigested heape, darke and obscure, ... the *Chaos* ... seemes not fit to be admitted." For, among other reasons, God "is not the Author of Confusion" (p. 267). Milton might well see this objection as part of the problem of evil as a whole: "how can something corruptible proceed from something incorruptible?" But the answer, he points out, is no easier even if one accepts *creatio ex nihilo*. And indeed, the same problem presents itself on the moral level: "How could something liable to sin issue, if I may so speak, from God?" (*DDC*, pp. 292–3). Milton's bold presentation of creation and Chaos in *Paradise Lost* is an integral part of his answer to these questions.

In *Paradise Lost*, the themes discussed so far in this chapter are summed up by God himself just before the account in Book 7 of the days of creation from Genesis 1. Speaking to the Son, the Father declares:

> "... 'thou my Word, begotten Son, by thee
> This [creation] I perform, speak thou, and be it done:
> My overshadowing Spirit and might with thee
> I send along, ride forth, and bid the deep
> Within appointed bounds be heav'n and earth,
> Boundless the deep, because I am who fill
> Infinitude, nor vacuous the space.
> Though I uncircumscribed myself retire,
> And put not forth my goodness, which is free
> To act or not, necessity and chance
> Approach not me, and what I will is fate.'"
>
> (7.163–73)

Even by the standards of *Paradise Lost*, this passage is an intertextual feast, of which I will note only a few elements. The Father's address begins by referencing the beginning not of Genesis but of John's Gospel: "In the beginning was the Word, and the Word was with God, and the Word was God. The same was in the beginning with God. All things were made by him; and without him was not any thing made that was made." Milton then reverses the syntactical sequence of Genesis 1, so the deep, which he will identify with Chaos, exists and is mentioned first; only afterward are physical bounds laid down. Until then, the deep of Chaos is boundless, but with this critical qualification: because "I am" (the identifying name of

Yahweh in his first address to Moses, Ex. 3:14) fills the infinitude. And it is primordially he, not the deep, that is "uncircumscribed" – a crucial difference from Lucretius, for whom the world's materials are "tost . . . From this to that uncircumscribed coast." (See p. 32.) Finally, in this account, in contrast to fundamentally dualistic cosmogonies, God has absolute freedom. He is not approached by necessity (the ἀνάγκη mentioned by Casaubon) and fate is merely what he wills – fate being, as already noted, nothing "but the divine decree [*effatum*] of some almighty deity."

One of the most memorable images of the grand creation narrative offered by *Paradise Lost* is that of the Almighty Power, or his Word, wielding his compasses on the face of the deep.[23] Like the Creator, actual cosmologists of the sixteenth and seventeenth centuries were also avid employers of compasses and some of the most widely known among their drawings are simply differently arranged circles – each drafted with a pair of compasses.[24] One such set of circles (Figure 2.1), printed in 1614 by the Jesuit astronomer Christoph Scheiner – a natural philosopher who employed the newly invented telescope and corresponded with Galileo and Kepler – graphically illustrates what I shall claim is the threefold structure of the creation as Milton presents it in his epic. Scheiner's *Disquisitiones* of that year, while supporting a geocentric (or geoheliocentric) and geostatic universe, describes and schematically depicts a range of alternative universes, including contemporary Ptolemaic, Tychonic, and Copernican proposals but also including what is labeled "The Mathematical [or Astronomical] System of the Ancients." After first summing up the traditional two-storey universe, Scheiner then goes on to sketch a schematic of an infinite Cosmos or (more precisely) Multiverse:

> Everything therefore that is corporeal either is the heavens or is contained
> by the circuit of the heavens; and standing far off is the Earth, appointed
> center of the heavens, and thus functioning as the center so far as percep-
> tion is concerned. Above Earth comes water, and above water air, which is
> surrounded by the ether, and this in turn by the womb of the heavens.

---

[23] The image is now probably best known graphically in William Blake's etching "The Ancient of Days," although the tradition of the Creator as a geometer, complete with compasses, was well known in the Middle Ages, as for example in the frontispiece of the thirteenth-century illuminated *Bible Moralisée*.

[24] As Dava Sobel points out in *A More Perfect Heaven: How Copernicus Revolutionized the Cosmos* (New York: Walker, 2011), in the manuscript copy of Copernicus's *De Revolutionibus*, in the center of his famous diagram of the heliocentric planetary spheres, the astronomer "inadvertently drilled a small hole" in the process of inscribing the diagram's eight circles (p. 183).

MATHEMATICÆ.

SYSTEMA ANTIQVORVM.

Sed veritas & Chriſtiana philoſophia hæc figmenta iam pridem exploſit; pro cuius rei ſtabilimento.

Figure 2.1   Scheiner and Locher (1614): "The Mathematical
[or Astronomical] System of the Ancients": the caption flatly reads
(in a wild overgeneralization): "But truth and Christian philosophy
have long since rejected such fictions in favor of something that
has stability."

These things accordingly make up the mass of the universe, and from these
in turn all other things come to be [*equibus deinde omnia caetera coalescent*].

Most ancient philosophers are opposed to this partition and many more
recent ones are opposed to that placement of things. And indeed, those
ancients along with many mathematicians have declared that the universe is

infinite. Within this they have distinguished two parts, one of which they assert to be this world or rather worlds, separate and finite in mass yet infinite in number; the other dispersed beyond the world, an infinite great heap of atoms, from which both already-created worlds might be fed and new worlds might from time to time be made.

Moreover, concerning our own world, philosophers have variously disagreed among themselves concerning its measure and structure. And so we may call their system somewhat formless and defective, according to the present diagram, except for the firmament marked ABCD, which is the highest heavens, in whose embrace the planets and other elements are held in place, but beyond which might surge an infinite Chaos, full of unformed atoms – within which this our universe might seem to swim, from which it might come into being, and into which it might eventually dissolve.[25]

Of the three circles that appear in Scheiner's graphic, the outer one is, of course, merely a pictorial convenience fitted to a finite page. The "INFINITE CHAOS OF ATOMS" is by definition not bounded. The next circle (ABCD), bounding the "Starry Heavens," indicates the separation of a finite sidereal sphere from the surrounding (theoretically) uncircumscribed Chaos. (The band of fixed stars depicted here is noticeably wider than in other roughly contemporary graphics of finite universes Ptolemaic, Tychonic, or Copernican.) Finally, in this schematic, the innermost circle merely demarcates the starry realm from the "place of the planets and of Earth." The latter is here left completely blank or rather black. Perhaps this is what Scheiner means by "formless and defective." Potentially, any arrangement of the planets and Earth – geocentric, heliocentric, geoheliocentric, and so on – could simply be cut and pasted into this bounded but otherwise undefined realm.

This account and graphic are remarkable for a number of reasons. Writing early in the seventeenth century, Scheiner clearly does not grasp the extent to which Christian cosmologists of his age and beyond will find (and in some cases have already found) the atomist infinitude attractive and potentially reconcilable with high doctrines of creation and of the Creator's omnipotence. Scheiner does grasp, however, the permeability of the circles and (at least at some point) the interrelations between outer Chaos and the inner realms of fixed stars, planets, and Earth. For the infinite atoms, according to the ancient school he mentions, constitute the

---

[25] Christoph Scheiner and (his student) Johan Georg Locher, *Disquisitiones Mathematicae, de Controversiis et Novitatibus Astronomicis* (Ingolstadt, 1614), pp. 16–17.

"heap" – the immense supply – of raw materials "from which both already-created worlds might be fed and new worlds might from time to time be made." Although that process of creation or coming-to-be of our Cosmos might have happened deep in the past, the ongoing existence of the surrounding Chaos entails a radical instability with regard to the location, status, and general security of the visible universe, which seems to "swim" and which might dissolve back into Chaos just as it coalesced from it. Little wonder, then, that the caption hastily declares a preference instead for "something that has stability."

The three-circle scheme thus offered but rejected by Scheiner affords a visual template that might assist an understanding of Milton's account of creation. As already mentioned, various thinkers from different epochs sought to combine elements of pagan cosmogony with the biblical account of Genesis 1. From early in the history of Christianity, in order to accommodate cosmogonies such as Plato's without incurring the charge of dualism, apologists, including Irenaeus and Tertullian, "proposed that God had created ... formless matter in advance of the six days' work"; other, later writers went even further and "postulated *two* creations: a first creation that resulted in the *ex nihilo* production of Chaos ('from Absolute Notbeing to Being'), and a secondary creation during which order was imposed upon the 'first matter' ('from Potentiality to Actuality')."[26] However, I would suggest that if *Paradise Lost* is permitted to speak for itself, the account it offers is one not of a twofold but of a threefold creation.

In *De Doctrina Christiana*, Milton does not distinguish various stages of creation as such. As we have seen, in describing the "original matter" that came from God, Milton simply says that it was "at first unarranged and disorganized, but afterwards God arranged it and made it beautiful." But in *Paradise Lost*, we can discern a first stage – not yet creation proper – in which prime matter is in some way "alienated" from God – rendered external to him; a second stage in which some (although not all) of that matter is chosen to be the stuff of this visible Universe; and a third stage in which that chosen stuff receives its actual forms. The result of the initial stage is Chaos and we first meet it in Book 2, where Satan, Sin, and Death look out from the gates of Hell[27] onto

---

[26] C. A. Patrides, *Milton and the Christian Tradition* (Oxford: Clarendon Press, 1966), pp. 30–1.
[27] Of course, Heaven and Hell have already been created; however, we can assume that *their* second and third stages of creation occurred before the second and third stages of the creation of our Universe.

> The secrets of the hoary deep, a dark
> Illimitable ocean without bound,
> Without dimension, where length, breadth, and highth,
> And time and place are lost; where eldest Night
> And Chaos, ancestors of Nature, hold
> Eternal anarchy, amidst the noise
> Of endless wars, and by confusion stand.
>
> (2.891–7)

We meet with Chaos again in Book 7, where this time, from Heaven's gates, the Father, Word, and Spirit view the same "immeasurable abyss / Outrageous as a sea, dark, wasteful, wild" (7.211–12). If we are concerned only with "traditional" notions, then the temptation will be to identify the domains viewed from the gates of Heaven and Hell with "the deep" or "the abyss" of Gen. 1:2[28] – which would be a mistake. For as far as Milton is concerned, these two terms are generic and the fact that they can describe Chaos does not mean that whenever Milton uses them it is Chaos proper to which he must be referring.

The distinction between Chaos and the deep of Gen. 1:2 first emerges in *Paradise Lost* at the beginning of Book 3. Here, the poet invokes that holy light, which "as with a mantle [did] invest / The rising world of waters dark and deep, / Won from the void and formless infinite" (3.10–2). Chaos is consistently acknowledged to be "infinite," "illimitable," "immeasurable," "without bound"; the world God creates in Gen. 1:1 is not so. According to the account of creation in Book 7 of *Paradise Lost*, God commands his Son to "ride forth, and bid the deep / Within appointed bounds be heav'n and earth, / Boundless the deep" (7.166–8). Heaven and Earth are thus bounded; Chaos – the "deep" referred to here – is bound*less*. What takes place in the second stage of creation broadly conceived (actually the beginning of this Universe per se, as in Gen. 1:1) is thus precisely the demarcating of limits – the drawing of circles. What is asserted in the first sentence of the Bible is what Milton depicts as the work of God's "golden compasses" in Chaos:

> "One foot he centered, and the other turned
> Round through the vast profundity obscure,
> And said, 'Thus far extend, thus far thy bounds,
> This be thy just circumference, O world.'"
>
> (7.228–31)

---

[28] In the Vulgate, Genesis 1:2 begins: *Terra autem erat inania et vacua, et tenebrae erant super faciem abyssi.*

God utters the great speech act whereby he names the territory demarcated within Chaos *world* – despite the fact that there is as yet nothing else qualitatively to distinguish this territory from the rest of Chaos. For, as Milton continues:

> "Thus God the heav'n created, thus the earth,
> Matter unformed and void: darkness profound
> Covered th' abyss."
>
> (7.232–4)

The circle God has traced with his compasses corresponds precisely with the second circle that appears in Scheiner's schematic drawing (ABCD), even though at this point in *Paradise Lost*, the inner realms of stars, planets, and Earth have not yet been formed.

The "matter unformed and void" mentioned here is accordingly not coextensive with Chaos as a whole. For although it may be the same sort of stuff as everything else in Chaos (and remains, temporarily, in a similarly disordered state), it has already been fenced off, demarcated, circumscribed – and so contrasts territorially, by virtue of those finite bounds, with "the void and formless *infinite*." In this sense, then, Chaos is "before the beginning"; it originated from God whenever God "retired" himself from it. The beginning of the universe itself, then, involves the circumscription just mentioned: the creation of a territory that is named by God and subsequently warmed and vitalized by the Spirit (7.234 ff.). And the third stage consists of the six days' work (or seven, if we include the Sabbath), of which we read in Genesis 1:3–2:3, recounted by Milton's Raphael in the rest of Book 7.

In connection with this three-stage process, Scheiner's "three circles" schema (no doubt unintentionally) offers a helpful diagrammatic insight into the relationship between Milton's Multiverse and his "world," or Universe, which encompasses what Raphael, echoing Genesis 1, calls "heaven and earth" – everything inside Scheiner's ABCD circle. Leaving aside for the moment the potentiality for plural worlds, one may therefore read Scheiner's second circle as a kind of Venn diagram indicating the set of cosmic components actualized and ordered in the creation of our Cosmos, which is accordingly a subset of all potential cosmic components.

The fact that Milton in *Paradise Lost* expands the process of creation from two stages to three – thus going beyond tradition and his own prose treatise – is of more than merely technical importance. The traditional two-stage theory has the limitation that all of Chaos gets used up in the second stage. But just as Milton needed the doctrine of *creatio ex deo* in order to establish that the "original matter" was "a good thing, . . . a seed bank of every subsequent good," so he also needed, in order to do justice to the fact of *evil*, to retain a robust Chaos even after the world was created[29] – not because the stuff of Chaos is inherently evil but because its status as a storm-tossed ocean and as an outdoor wilderness symbolizes the potentiality for loss of the order, beauty, cohesion, and culture that are embodied in our Cosmos. And yet, the potentiality for evil exists in dynamic balance with the potentiality for further good and for genuine creation. It may be worth noting here that the word *gas* was coined by J. B. Van Helmont (1579–1644) from the Greek χάος (*chaos*).[30] And the picture offered by Scheiner and Milton, I am suggesting, hints at the potentiality for ongoing interaction between that which lies outside Scheiner's circle ABCD and outside Milton's "opacous globe" and that which lies inside – just as gas, in the form of wind that may variously refresh or threaten, makes its unseen way beneath our doors, through cracks in our walls, and thence into our orderly (and perhaps too tightly sealed) homes.

Coexisting with this picture, in *Paradise Lost* as in *De Doctrina Christiana*, is a theology proclaiming that God is omnipotent, free, and wholly good while also fundamentally material. To allow the seeds of good to grow and bear fruit beyond himself, God first made a "beyond." Moreover, if all this is conceived spatially and if the "beyond" is not to be utterly surrounded by God, then it, like God, will be infinite. Because God is its origin, however, no dualism follows. Spoken by God himself, that point is emphatic: The deep exists and is unbounded because of God's infinitude and because of his inherent freedom to create – or not. Divine omnipotence is thus compromised by no pagan fate, no Platonic "necessity," not by any internal "pure actuality," not even by an infinity that he himself brings into being (7:168–70). Chaos is boundless only *because* God himself is boundless – and free, if he chooses, to place certain limits on himself for the sake of putting forth what amounts to a vast ocean of potentiality. Furthermore, although Milton undoubtedly believes that his account is "true," he also quickly reminds us that it is not literal but symbolic, accommodated to "process of speech," "told as earthly notion can receive" (7.178–9). In this way, he makes his presentation of

---

[29] Cf. Robert M. Adams's discussion "A Little Look Into Chaos," in *Illustrious Evidence: Approaches to English Literature in the Early Seventeenth Century*, ed. Earl Miner (Berkeley: University of California Press, 1975), pp. 75–6.

[30] See "gas," OED.

Chaos and creation consciously mythic, even while recognizing that symbol and myth have literal implications, thus presenting, from the very mouth of God, a remarkable case for the consistency of Chaos with divine omnipotence.

As already mentioned, in *Paradise Lost* we encounter Chaos principally in three substantial passages: in Book 2, as Satan exits the gates of Hell; in Book 3, as he alights on the outside of "this round world" (i.e., the Universe); and in Book 7, in the account of the "Noughth Day" of creation, when God, by his Word, applies his compasses to the face of the abyss. Because it is closest to our world and also closest to Scheiner's diagram, I would like to turn to the second of these passages before considering further the other two. The narrator segues from angels' hymns about redemption in Book 3 to the ongoing activity of Satan, who has weathered the storms of Chaos and reached our Cosmos, which from a great distance had appeared, at the end of Book 2, as a mere point of light but is now viewed up close:

> Meanwhile upon the firm opacous globe
> Of this round world, whose first convex divides
> The luminous inferior orbs, enclosed
> From Chaos, and th' inroad of darkness old,
> Satan alighted walks: a globe far off
> It seemed, now seems a boundless continent
> Dark, waste, and wild, under the frown of Night
> Starless exposed, and ever-threat'ning storms
> Of Chaos blust'ring round, inclement sky;
> Save on that side which from the wall of Heav'n
> Though distant far, some small reflection gains
> Of glimmering air less vexed with tempest loud:
> Here walked the fiend at large in spacious field.
> (3.418–30)

The "first convex" of line 419 coincides precisely with the circle inscribed in Book 7 by the Creator's compasses as well as with the second circle of Scheiner's graphic (ABCD), which demarcates the boundary between Chaos and our Cosmos. The technical difference, of course, is that Satan alights on a three-dimensional *sphere* – something that on a two-dimensional surface, such as a page, must be represented by a circle. We may note, moreover, that Milton accurately calls the surface "a boundless continent" – which it is not because it is boundless as Chaos is boundless (i.e., infinite) but in the strict geometrical sense in which the surface of any true sphere is boundless (although not infinite). For a line being etched or a creature making its way across the surface of a true sphere will never encounter a limit.[31]

However, the outer sphere, that "first convex," most certainly is a limit or boundary from the perspective of anyone or anything moving toward it in three dimensions from either above or below. That is precisely why Satan must here interrupt his earthward flight. And, of course, his night is starless because (for now) he remains beyond the cosmic bounds, outside the sphere, whereas the stars are inside, again as in Scheiner's diagram. And yet, Milton's narrative transcends any simple schematic, for in *Paradise Lost*, our Cosmos is not the only continent whose coasts face the ocean of Chaos. As we are reminded in this passage, Heaven itself is there, off in the distance, and its influences of calm and light are detectable even amid the "tempest loud."

The other remarkable feature that Milton builds into his depiction of the relationship among the continents of Hell, Heaven, and our Cosmos is that each, in keeping with the oceanic nature of Chaos, has a port. Heaven's inimitable "portal" appears at the top of the staircase that Satan "descries" (3.501). But at the foot of the same staircase appears the "passage" – the "opening" leading through into our Cosmos from Chaos. Because at this point in the narrative we are following Satan's trajectory, this port is most notable for the prospect it affords not of Chaos but of our own Universe – a prospect to which we shall return. Our two fullest visions of Chaos, however, are granted by views afforded from the other two gates: those of Hell and of Heaven.

Our first prospect coincides with that enjoyed by Satan, Sin, and Death. Sin has opened the gates of Hell and the infernal trinity peer outward. In keeping with Satan's own godless worldview, Milton offers in twenty-five lines a picture of which any atheist Epicurean might approve:

> Before their eyes in sudden view appear
> The secrets of the hoary deep, a dark
> Illimitable ocean without bound,
> Without dimension; where length, breadth, and heighth,

---

[31] Although etymology might suggest that "boundless" and "infinite" ought to mean the same thing, present-day cosmologists and mathematicians routinely distinguish between the two. See Robert Osserman's concise account, "Curved Space and Poetry of the Universe," in *BOTC*, ed. Danielson, pp. 350–5. Osserman quotes Max Born to the effect that "[The] suggestion of a finite, but unbounded space is one of the greatest ideas about the nature of the world which ever has been conceived." We can say with confidence that, as depicted in *Paradise Lost*, our Universe – like those proposed by Ptolemy, Copernicus, Tycho, and Kepler – is not infinite.

And time and place are lost; where eldest Night
And Chaos, ancestors of Nature, hold
Eternal anarchy, amidst the noise
Of endless wars, and by confusion stand.
For Hot, Cold, Moist, and Dry, four champions fierce
Strive here for mast'ry, and to battle bring
Their embryon atoms; they around the flag
Of each his faction, in their several clans,
Light-armed or heavy, sharp, smooth, swift, or slow,
Swarm populous, unnumbered as the sands
Of Barca or Cyrene's torrid soil,
Levied to side with warring winds, and poise
Their lighter wings. To whom these most adhere,
He rules a moment; Chaos umpire sits,
And by decision more embroils the fray
By which he reigns: next him, high arbiter
Chance governs all. Into this wild abyss,
The womb of Nature and perhaps her grave,
Of neither sea, nor shore, nor air, nor fire,
But all these in their pregnant causes mixed
Confus'dly, and which thus must ever fight. . . .

(2.890–914)

The boundlessness of Chaos extends to the scrambling or contesting of distinctions among commonsense categories, such as time and place, three-dimensionality, the four quadrants of the humoral system ("Hot, Cold, Moist, and Dry"), and the four Aristotelian elements of "sea . . . shore . . . air . . . fire." The components of Chaos are parodied in military terms – fittingly, given Satan's recent experience of war and his power-political views of government.

The irony of the passage is predominantly borne by the timing of the descriptions, with essential information held back until the end of a phrase, thus completing the bathos or paradox: "eldest Night / And Chaos . . . hold / Eternal anarchy . . . and by confusion stand"; these with their factions (described with lofty epic simile) fight their war, vying for supporters, and "To whom these most adhere / He rules *a moment*"; "Chaos umpire sits, / And by decision [. . .] more embroils the fray." Also fittingly, given the role of Chaos in offering raw materials from which a Cosmos may be created, the other main cluster of imagery relates to gestation, pregnancy, and birth. The phrase "womb of Nature and perhaps her grave" harmonizes not only with Satan's view of spontaneous "production" of worlds (cf. 1.650, 5.860–3) but also with Scheiner's account of the (in his view pagan) ancient cosmogony that envisages "an infinite Chaos, full of unformed atoms" – "within which this our Universe might seem to swim, from which it might come into being, and into which it might eventually dissolve." Moreover, the trumping of the confusion – one might say "the redemption of the pagan world picture" – is itself conveyed by a postponed phrase that the poet superadds to the content of Satan's atomist vision of Chaos and its elements:

> . . . which thus must ever fight,
> *Unless* th' Almighty Maker them ordain
> His dark materials to create more worlds.
> (2.914–16)

The potentiality signaled by the subjunctive "ordain" is actualized when the Almighty Maker does indeed perform creation out of the dark materials, as recounted in Raphael's narrative in Book 7. The beginning of this account forms the second panel of Milton's diptych on Chaos. In each panel, a trio of principal characters looks out – from the gates of Hell and the gates of Heaven, respectively – into what is recognizably the same abyss, whose chief features are those of a boundless and turbulent ocean, "immeasurable . . . Outrageous . . . dark, wasteful, wild." But in the second panel, Chaos and Chance emphatically do not form the government, and upon the "endless wars" depicted in the first panel, the Creator imposes a sudden ceasefire:

> "'Silence, ye troubled Waves, and thou deep, peace,'
> Said then the omnific Word, 'your discord end.'"
> (7.216–17)

This decree is followed by successive images of the cherubically borne chariot's entry into Chaos and the wielding of the divine compasses "to circumscribe / This universe, and all created things," which is the activity of creation earlier referred to as the Noughth Day – the framing narrative of Genesis 1:1–2, which precedes the first fiat of Day 1 ("Let there be light"). And in contrast to the warlike atmosphere of the first panel of the diptych, the verbs of this account bespeak divine activity that is nonviolent, deliberate, and almost domestic: outspread, infused, purged, founded, conglobed, disparted, spun, hung:

> ". . . darkness profound
> Covered th' abyss: but on the wat'ry calm
> His brooding wings the Spirit of God outspread,
> And vital virtue infused, and vital warmth
> Throughout the fluid mass, but downward purged
> The black tartareous cold infernal dregs

> Adverse to life: then founded, then conglobed
> Like things to like, the rest to several place
> Disparted, and between spun out the air,
> And Earth self-balanced on her center hung."
>
> (7.233–42)

Thus ends Raphael's account of the Noughth Day of creation – the biblical echoes of "darkness," "th' abyss," "wat'ry calm," "brooding wings," and "the Spirit of God" returning us to Milton's primary literary source as well as to the use of that same lexicon in his own exordium to the Spirit who was present from before creation's first fiat, "brooding on the vast abyss" (1.21). Like that invocation, Milton's entire multiportaled glimpse of Chaos draws upon, transcends, Christianizes, but does not merely discard, a rich array of pre-Christian materials. The robustly imagined origins and "cosmography" of his Multiverse undergird his justification of the ways of God by modeling the existence of a boundless ocean of potentiality – for good and evil – that entails neither ontological dualism nor any denial of divine omnipotence. But because that ocean, that surrounding wilderness, is still *there*, it also models the persistence of the potentiality for new goods, new evils, new creations, even new worlds. For us, of course, its inhabitants, the most interesting new world is the one that in Book 2 of *Paradise Lost* Satan sets off to explore: a Universe (a "heaven and earth") that was also in the seventeenth century and is still today being probed and imagined in new ways – and with great astonishment.

Milton's Multiverse

A. THE THREE STAGES OF ITS CREATION

Stage 1: God brings the Multiverse into being by "retiring" or withdrawing immediate control from a portion of his material substance (*PL*, 7.168–73). Thus, the matter of the Multiverse, which initially is coextensive with Chaos, is created *ex deo*, not *ex nihilo*. That matter, accordingly, although boundless and now in a "wild" and disordered state, is not inherently evil. The Book of Genesis is silent concerning this stage of creation.

Stage 2: The Son, the Word of God, employs his "golden compasses" to circumscribe and to demarcate territory within Chaos that will form the location and matter of our (large but finite) Cosmos, also known by the biblical collective noun phrase "the heaven and the earth" (cf. *PL*, 7.228–34). This "Noughth Day" of creation corresponds to the first two verses of Genesis 1. (See the epigraph at the beginning of this chapter.) Note that, initially, the demarcated territory of "the heaven and the earth" is qualitatively identical to the territory of Chaos outside the divinely circumscribed boundary. Moreover, Heaven (which Milton calls the empyreal Heaven to distinguish it from the heaven, or heavens, mentioned in Genesis 1:1) must also have originated from Chaos, as must Hell, although neither the Bible nor Milton offer any detailed account of the creation of Heaven and Hell. (The creation of Hell *is* mentioned by the personification of Chaos: *PL*, 2.1002–3.) At the end of the Noughth Day, within the now-bounded dark materials, cosmic organization begins to emerge with a purgation of things "Adverse to life" – with a conglobation of elements and with the hanging of Earth "self-balanced on her center" (7.234–42).

Stage 3:   This stage begins with the first divine fiat "Let there be light" and unfolds sequentially over the "days" of creation – one through seven (Gen. 1:3–2:3; *PL*, 7.243–634). Some traditions acknowledge only the first six days as constituting the creation (hence the term *hexameron*), but Milton's celebration of the Sabbath justifies its inclusion in the tapestry of creation.

B.   THE "COSMOGRAPHY" OF MILTON'S MULTIVERSE

1.   The Multiverse as a whole is everything that exists beyond God himself and includes (after the three stages of creation mentioned) (a) an infinite Chaos; (b) the empyreal Heaven; (c) Hell; (d) our "world," Universe, or Cosmos; and (e) any other worlds God might create from the stuff of Chaos. From the viewpoint of Hell, Heaven, and our Cosmos, therefore, Chaos remains literally "the great out-of-doors" – and Milton depicts it as such from the gates of Hell (Book 2), the gates of Heaven (Book 7), and the "cosmic hatch" that opens onto as well as out from our Universe (Book 3).

2.   Our Universe extends to and is enclosed by "the firm opacous globe / Of this round world" (3.418–19) – the spherical solid boundary dividing Cosmos from Chaos. Outermost within this boundary is the sphere of the stars – which in Scheiner's graphic of the ancient atomist scheme (p. 39) and in *Paradise Lost* appears as a region of considerable depth and (certainly for Milton) unimpeded by crystalline spheres – the cosmic glass ceilings of traditional Ptolemaic cosmology.

3.   Beneath the sphere of the stars is "the place of the planets and of Earth" (Scheiner), whose arrangement, including questions regarding Earth's possible movement(s), are discussed by Raphael and Adam in Book 8 of *Paradise Lost*. As Scheiner's diagram illustrates, however, questions about the interrelationships of the Sun, the Moon, Earth, and the planets – the main substance of debates regarding Ptolemaic, Copernican, and Tychonic cosmologies – although not trivial, can be seen on the scale of the Multiverse as concerning the organization of merely one local cosmic neighborhood.

CHAPTER 3

Copernicus and the cosmological bricoleurs

But to avoid these Paradoxes of the Earths motion, our later Mathematitians have rolled all the stones that may be stirred, and to salve
all apparances and objections, have invented new hypotheses, and
fabricated new systemes of the World. . . . In the mean time . . . they
tosse the Earth up and down like a ball, make her stand and goe at
their pleasures; one saith the Sun stands, another he moves, a third
comes in, taking them all at rebound. . . .

Robert Burton, *The Anatomy of Melancholy*[1]

But yet [the heavens'] various and perplexed course
Observ'd in diverse ages doth enforce
Men to find out so many Eccentrique parts,
Such divers downe-right lines, such overthwarts,
As disproportion that pure forme. It teares
The Firmament in eight and forty sheeres,
And in these constillations then arise
New starres, and old doe vanish from our eyes.

John Donne, *An Anatomie of the World*, 253–60[2]

. . . they come to model heav'n
And calculate the stars, how they will wield
The mighty frame, how build, unbuild, contrive
To save appearances . . .

Paradise Lost, 8.79–82

Much of the motivation for discarding the "Discarded Image" of the
Universe sketched in Chapter 1 was that model's inelegant, arbitrary,
and piecemeal character. Replacing it, however, was itself a highly complex
and often piecemeal process. What astronomers of the sixteenth and
seventeenth centuries – like most other human beings – sought but could
not quite achieve was coherence: a reliable *system* or worldview whose parts

[1] Robert Burton, *The Anatomy of Melancholy*, 1st edition (London, 1621), pp. 328–9.
[2] John Donne, *The First Anniversarie. An Anatomie of the World* (London, 1621), pp. 24–5.

satisfyingly, perhaps even beautifully, fit together. As indicated in his letter to Pope Paul III, which formed the preface to his *De Revolutionibus* in 1543, Copernicus himself was moved by annoyance at the ill-fitting, thrown-together components of the traditional picture of astronomy – and longed for something more unified and aesthetic:

> Your Holiness, ... what moved me to conceive a different model for explaining the motions of the universal spheres was merely my realization that the astronomers are not consistent among themselves regarding this subject. ... While some use only homocentric circles, others employ eccentrics and epicycles, from which however the desired results do not quite follow. Those relying on homocentrics, though they may use these for modeling diverse motions, nevertheless have not been successful in using them to obtain firm results in perfect accordance with the phenomena. Yet those who have invented eccentric circles, while they seem for the most part to have solved apparent motion in a manner that is arithmetically consistent, at the same time also seem to have introduced several ideas that contradict the first principles of uniform motion. Nor have they been able to discover or deduce by means of their eccentrics the main point, which is to describe the form of the Universe and the sure symmetry of its parts. Instead they have been like someone attempting a portrait by assembling hands, feet, head, and other parts from different sources. These several bits may be well painted, but they do not fit together to make up a single body. Bearing no genuine relationship to each other, such components, joined together, would compose a monster, not a man. ...
>
> Thus I pondered for a long time this lack of resolution within the astronomical tradition regarding the derivation of the motions of the universal spheres. It began to disgust me that the philosophers, who otherwise scrutinized so precisely the minutiae of this world, could not agree on a more reliable theory [*ratio*] concerning the motions of the system of the Universe, which the best and most orderly Artist [*Opifex*] of all framed for our sake.

The first part of this passage from Copernicus's letter sums up some of the difficulties with the Ptolemaic system described in Chapter 1: the less-than-successful attempts to save the phenomena by means of homocentrics and eccentrics, including the notorious equant. Copernicus is keenly aware of how these contrivances negotiate away supposedly basic principles, such as uniform motion. Still more importantly, however, the astronomers have failed to grasp "the main point," which is to produce a model coherent enough to befit something called a *universe*, whose components (Copernicus believes on theological grounds) must fit together in an orderly, unified, and symmetrical manner. The challenge for astronomers and for Copernicus is, therefore, to unfold a cosmology that is not an

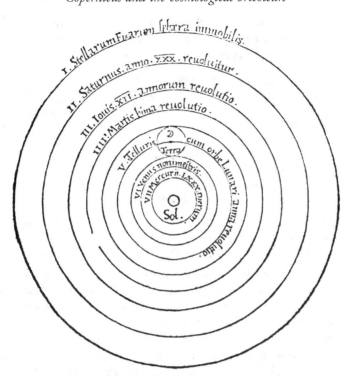

Figure 3.1   Copernicus, *De Revolutionibus*

inaesthetic hodgepodge like the thrown-together portrait referred to here but instead is a coherent picture befitting the skill of the *Opifex* who created the original.

But despite Copernicus's reputation for proposing a radical revision of Ptolemaic cosmology – and, of course, in some respects it was that – it is noteworthy in another respect how modest was the change he proposed. When the schematic drawings of Ptolemy's and Copernicus's planetary arrangements are compared, the similarities are clear. If we disregard the ninth and tenth spheres in Apian's graphic (the Crystallinum and the Primum Mobile; see Figure 1.2, p. 10), then the order of the next seven spheres from outer to inner – stars, Saturn, Jupiter (Jove), Mars, Sun, Venus, Mercury – correspond exactly to their revised order in Copernicus's diagram (Figure 3.1), with only one major geometrical modification: Earth changes places with the Sun (and, of course, the Moon stays with Earth, which, in addition, rotates). Copernicus sees the consequences of this transposition as being mathematically and aesthetically dramatic.

His brilliant and succinct conclusion to Chapter 9 of Book 1 prepares readers for the visual revelation – the now-famous cosmological graphic – that follows four pages later:

> If, granting immobility to the sun, we exchange earthly movement for solar movement, then the risings and settings of the constellations and the fixed stars that accompany morning and evening will appear just as they do. Furthermore, the stations as well as both the backward [i.e., retrograde] and forward motions of the planets will be seen not as their own motions but as earthly motion transmuted into apparent planetary motions. Finally, it will be accepted that the Sun occupies the center of the Universe. We learn all these things by discerning the order whereby the planets follow one another and by the harmony of the entire Universe.

That harmony – which Copernicus has presupposed because of the orderliness of the Creator – is now made manifest in his new depiction of the planetary arrangement, in which the periods of the planets are labeled: Mercury, 80 days; Venus, 9 months; Earth, 1 year; Mars, 2 years; Jupiter, 12 years; Saturn, 30 years. Copernicus's modest exchange of Earth and the Sun thus produces what mathematicians now call a *monotonic series*: The farther a planet is from the center, the longer is its period. Therefore, the apparent motions of the planets and the ordering of their spheres comport with the harmony of the whole – now encompassed by a starry sphere immobile and relieved of any necessity to whirl about us at an "incorporeal speed" once every twenty-four hours (*PL*, 8.37). In Copernicus's words: "In this orderly arrangement we discover the marvelous symmetry of the Universe and a firm harmonious connection between the motion and the size of the spheres such as can be discerned by no other means."

Again, we may note the relative modesty of Copernicus's grand cosmological proposal. It requires no relinquishing of crystalline spheres and no abandonment of the perfect circularity of planetary motion. And it proposes no boundless domain of stars, even though this would later come to be associated with Copernicanism. Nonetheless, the euphoric tone of Copernicus's summary of his cosmology should not blind us to a series of problems that it did create and that the best minds would continue to struggle with for a century and a half after his death. Some of them, mentioned here only in passing, we shall reencounter in subsequent chapters: the potential scandal of denying the Sun its planetary status and placing it in what had previously been considered by many to be the sump, the dead center, of the Universe; the granting of planetary status – literally star status – to Earth (which in the Ptolemaic system was never conceived to be a planet); the attributing to Earth of three different motions in a celestial realm where, before, natural motion had been held to be simple; the difficulty of comprehending, if Earth possessed those three motions, including diurnal rotation, why airborne things, such as clouds or arrows shot vertically upward, would not simply be blown away or off course or why heavy things would still fall toward Earth's center when it was no longer seen as residing in the universal center – toward which, according to Aristotle, heavy things tended. In Peter Barker's concise summation, "Copernicus's position clearly requires a new physics but does not provide it."[3]

Copernicus's cosmology faced still further obstacles that made it hard to accept. Most famously, perhaps, it strained human credulity by asserting terrestrial motion of at least two kinds:[4] It was making a daily (diurnal) rotation upon its axis and an annual revolution about the central Sun. Such motion, as Copernicus admitted in his letter to Pope Paul III, is flatly "contrary to the received opinions of astronomers and almost contrary to common sense" – indeed, "an absurd idea." Only a little historical imagination may suggest how surprising and counterintuitive the proposal of a moving Earth might have seemed to even intelligent, open-minded people who had never before encountered any such notion.

A further major problem – one that Copernicus was fully aware of – requires a greater degree of reflection than that of a moving Earth but might have been just as shocking. Ptolemy's was no cozy little universe. On the contrary, Ptolemy himself declared that the sphere of the fixed stars was immense – literally, immeasurably large – relative to Earth's globe or, conversely, Earth's globe was immeasurably small, "as a point," relative to the sphere of the fixed stars. Ptolemy had two elegant, observationally based proofs for this conclusion: (1) We can detect no diurnal parallax in the stars – that is, no noticeable alterations in the positions or appearances of stars, caused by the changing angles and distances between an earth-bound observer and those stars as they pass from horizon to overhead to horizon. The stars are simply too far away for any of these differences to be discernible. (2) "A plane drawn through the observer's line of sight at any point on earth – we call this plane one's 'horizon' – always bisects the whole heavenly sphere. This would not happen if the earth were of

---

[3] Peter Barker, "Constructing Copernicus," *Perspectives on Science* 10.2 (2002): 208–27 (p. 220).
[4] The "third terrestrial motion" postulated by Copernicus was Earth's retention of its axial orientation to the heavens while passing through its annual course about the Sun. For further discussion, see pp. 121–2.

perceptible size in relation to the distance of the heavenly bodies. In that case only the plane drawn through the center of the earth could exactly bisect the sphere."[5]

Put another way (with modern distance values superimposed on Ptolemy's geocentric system), Earth's roughly 8,000-mile diameter is perceptually reduced to nothing when set side by side with the great sphere of the fixed stars – a conclusion implying, again, that the starry sphere is immensely (immeasurably) large. In Chapter 6 of the first book of *De Revolutionibus*, Copernicus reiterates "the indescribable size of the heavens compared to that of the Earth." But in the heliocentric system that he proposed, there was not only no diurnal parallax but also no perceptible *annual* parallax. This implied in turn that the entire diameter of Earth's orbit – which Copernicus calls the *orbis magnus* and is today taken to be approximately 186 million miles across – is reduced to nothing relative to the sphere of the fixed stars. This was a whole new – and extraordinarily hard to believe – kind of "immeasurably large."[6] As Copernicus writes (if rather understatedly): "Even though [Earth] is not in the center of the universe, its distance from the center is nevertheless inconsiderable when compared to the distance of the sphere of the fixed stars."[7]

Before examining a range of responses to Copernicus, let us consider an actual historical and astronomical event that crucially informed the context of those responses: the appearance of the supernova of 1572. Danish

---

[5] Claudius Ptolemy, *Almagest*; quoted from *BOTC*, ed. Danielson, p. 72 (adapted from the translation of Toomer, p. 43). The great Protestant educator Philipp Melanchthon (among many others in the sixteenth century) repeated Ptolemy's arguments. See *Initia Doctrinae Physicae* (Wittenberg, 1549), fol. 51ʳ: *Sciendum ... , quod propter parvitatem collata ad coelum, habet se velut punctum, hoc est, non habet notabilem magnitudinem, ut multa illustria testimonia indicant, quia Horizon dividit coelum ubique in duo aequalia* ("It should be noted ... that because of [Earth's] smallness relative to the heavens, it is as a point, that is, it has no perceptible magnitude, as many clear evidences show, for the horizon everywhere divides the heavens in two equal parts").

[6] Francis R. Johnson argues "that when Copernicus suggested that not only the earth itself, but also its orbit about the sun, was but a point in comparison with the sphere of fixed stars, the change he introduced was merely one of degree rather than of kind. He simply made what was already infinitely small still more infinitesimal"; *Astronomical Thought in Renaissance England: A Study of the English Scientific Writings From 1500 to 1645* (1937; rpt. New York: Octagon Books, 1968), p. 109. However, Kepler, writing in the period 1618–21, clearly did consider it to be an impediment to the acceptance of Copernicanism: "But is not this amplitude of the sphere of the fixed stars unbelievable, for you make it to be 2,000 times greater than the sphere of Saturn, although among the ancients this sphere stood just above Saturn?" *Epitome of Copernican Astronomy*, trans. C. G. Wallis (New York: Prometheus Books, 1995), p. 43.

[7] This sentence appears at the end of Book 1, Chapter 6, of the manuscript of *De Revolutionibus* in a short section not included in the 1543 published version. Nonetheless, the implications of Copernicus's cosmology for the size of the Universe did not remain a secret.

astronomer Tycho Brahe (1546–1601) observed the phenomenon produced by the literal collapse of a star in our galaxy and his interpretation of that phenomenon would contribute to the final collapse of Aristotle's model of the Universe.

In the sixteenth century, before the advent of the telescope, humans could not observe galaxies beyond our own; indeed, the very existence of other galaxies remained controversial until the twentieth century. Nonetheless, every fifty years, on average, in a galaxy the size of ours, an aging star – one that is at least 1.4 times as massive as our Sun – suffers a gravitational implosion that triggers an explosion of the star's outer layers and produces a display of cosmic pyrotechnics whose luminosity for a short time can equal that of the rest of the stars in the galaxy combined. This is what earthly observers saw in 1572, although the radiance emitted from 10,000 light-years away had thus in galactic time been occasioned by an explosion taking place 10,000 years earlier than 1572. This event bears the technical name SN 1572, but popularly, it is known as Tycho's Supernova.

Tycho was actually not the first observer to spot it nor by any means the only one to write about it. On the evening of November 6, 1572, a little-known astronomer at the University of Wittenberg named Wolfgang Schuler was observing the constellation Cassiopeia and noticed the new star. Tycho first noticed it five days later, on Tuesday, November 11, 1572. The new star subsequently caused a sensation among astronomers all across Europe – from John Dee and Thomas Digges in England to Philip Apian and Michael Maestlin (later the teacher of Kepler) in Tübingen and Thaddeus Hájek in Prague. It also stirred up vigorous discussions in court circles, such as those of Wilhelm IV, Landgrave of Hesse, and Ludwig, Duke of Württemberg.[8] In Wittenberg, the star received comment by Schuler as well as by Caspar Peucer, who had been Tycho's first astronomy professor there in 1566.

But Tycho well deserves the honor implied by history's naming the new star after him. For in observing it and accounting for it, he not only set his own remarkable career path as an astronomer, but he also set a high standard by which all future astronomers would be measured. Tycho's initial narrative of the event (published in 1573) bypasses the scholarly debate about the new star and takes us back to the moment when the experience was fresh, not yet well known, and literally almost unbelievable.

---

[8] See Charlotte Methuen, "'This Comet or New Star': Theology and the Interpretation of the Nova of 1572," *Perspectives on Science* 5.4 (1997): 499–515.

He immediately startles his readers with the claim (quite credible in retrospect) that he has perfect knowledge of all the stars in the heavens – something, he adds parenthetically, with a touch of *sprezzatura*, that is not too hard to attain. Then, perhaps most important for his scientific reliability, he positively mistrusts his own eyes until their evidence can be corroborated by the observations of others. Having indicated his caution, the twenty-six-year-old Tycho gently spells out the long-held Aristotelian assumptions that his discovery is about to shatter:

> Last year [1572], on the eleventh day of November, in the evening, after sunset, while (as is my habit) contemplating the stars in the clear sky, I noticed, brighter than all the rest, shining almost directly over my head, a new and unusual star. And since almost from boyhood I have known perfectly all the stars in the heavens (for it is not too hard to acquire such skill), it was quite obvious to me that no star had ever previously existed in that location in the sky, even a small one, never mind a star of such conspicuous brightness. This thing filled me with such wonder that I was not ashamed to doubt the witness of my own eyes. However, observing that others, when the place was pointed out to them, could also see there was truly a star there, I was no longer in doubt. This was indeed a miracle. . . .
>
> For all philosophers agree, and facts themselves clearly declare, that in the ethereal region of the celestial world no change, neither of generation nor decay, takes place; but that the heavens and all the ethereal bodies they contain suffer no increase or decrease, no variation in number or size or luminosity or any other characteristic; that they remain always the same, like themselves in every respect, persisting without any wearing away of years. Moreover, skilled observations over thousands of years testify that all the stars have always retained the same number, location, order, motion, and size.[9]

Thus, Tycho's introduction clears the decks for the heart of his investigation. And the number one question – scientifically – was not what the new star meant or what it presaged but what and where it was.

In reviewing Tycho's account of the new star, as mentioned earlier in relation to Copernicus's claims about the immensity of the starry sphere, we recall that the main way of determining the distance of a heavenly object from Earth is to measure its *parallax* (Figure 3.2). One sights on the object at dusk and then six hours later at midnight by using a fixed star as a geometrical benchmark. If these two sightlines are found to be at an angle to each other, then one can perform some basic trigonometry by using that

[9] *Tychonis Brahe Dani Opera Omnia*, ed. J. L. E. Dreyer, 15 vols. (Copenhagen: Libraria Gyldendaliana, 1913–29), 3:97.

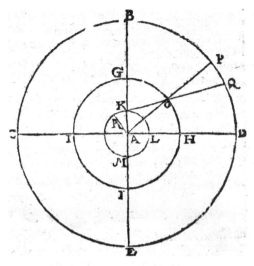

Figure 3.2 Tycho offers a diagram to show the triangle that *would* be created by
sightlines if the new star (o) were located at the Moon's height (circle GHFI) rather than
at the distance of the sphere of the fixed stars (BDEC). But no such triangle is created;
the star has *no* observable parallax. Therefore, Tycho concludes, the new phenomenon
is "a star shining in the firmament itself - one that has never previously been seen
before our time, in any age since the beginning of the world."

angle along with the length of Earth's radius (the length of the short side of
one's triangle) to determine how far away the object is from Earth. But if
those sightlines are found to be effectively parallel, then the object being
measured, like the fixed stars themselves, must be declared to stand at an
immeasurable distance from Earth.[10]

Tycho describes how he conducted this sort of measurement numerous
times – always finding that the angular distance from a given benchmark
star to the new star "was exactly the same, not varying by so much as a
minute." His conclusion, accordingly, is that the star is *super*lunary,
contrary to the opinions of Aristotelians, and furthermore that it is as
immeasurably distant as the fixed stars themselves: "I must place this star
not in the region of the element, below the moon, but far above, in an
orbit relative to which the earth has no perceptible size. . . . Therefore, this
new star is in the eighth sphere, among the other fixed stars."[11]

Tycho fully realized that the new star's mutability – its status as
something coming to be and passing away – had implications far beyond

[10] Tycho, *Opera Omnia* 3:104–5.   [11] Tycho, *Opera Omnia* 3:103, 105.

itself. The star must be made of something, which could not include the usual sublunary ingredients – earth, water, air, and fire. Indeed, to anyone so bold as to suggest that the star, being mutable, must be made of earthly elements, Tycho offers a satirically flavored knockdown argument: Because the new star is apparently "three hundred times bigger" than Earth, "what sublunary matter could be sufficient to the conformation of it?" Tycho suggests instead that the new star may have acquired its substance from the Milky Way itself. For "the very matter of Heaven, though it be subtile, . . . yet being compacted and condensated into one Globe . . . might give forme and fashion to this Starre." Logically, if the new star is in the grip of time, then its celestial building materials must also be "subject to dissolution and dissipation."[12] And thus do the foundations of the old "two storey" Universe begin to crack.

Another observer of the 1572 Supernova was Thomas Digges (1546–95), the leading English astronomer of his generation, whose work had significant connections with that of Tycho and Copernicus. Like Tycho, Digges studied the supernova of 1572 to determine whether that new phenomenon was sublunary or superlunary – whether it was truly stellar. And, like Tycho, he concluded on observational and trigonometric grounds that it genuinely was superlunary. In early 1573, Digges published (in Latin) a work with the short title *Alae* (*Wings*), whose longer title translates as *Mathematical Wings or Ladders Whereby We May Ascend the Highest Theater of the Visible Heavens*. Even though this important work on parallax and the application of trigonometry was not specifically about the new star of 1572, its prefatory dedication to William Cecil unambiguously declared the new phenomenon to be "far beyond the sphere of the moon."[13] Demonstrations that mutability exists in both domains – sublunary and superlunary – made it possible to begin imagining what else the two domains might have in common. In this way, the observation of the new star's coming to be and passing away inserted into human thinking the thin edge of a powerful analogy. Even allowing for great differences, it created grounds for adumbrating similitudes and

[12] In this paragraph, I quote the English translation offered in *Learned Tico Brahae His Astronomicall Conjectur of the New and Much Admired [Star] Which Appered in the Year 1572* (London, 1632), pp. 9–10.

[13] Thomas Digges, *Alae seu scalae mathematicae, quibus visibilium remotissima coelorum theatra conscendi* (London, 1573), sig. A.iii.ᵛ. Compare Thomas Hood's later summary of the state of the same question in *The Use of the Celestial Globe in Plano* (London, 1590): fol. 18: "The best Astronomers therefore concluded thus, that the new starre, whatsoever it was, had his place in the firmament . . . because none of them could observe in it any other motion then that, which usually they observe in all the fixed starres."

it raised a question, as Milton would express it (from the mouth of Raphael) almost a century later:

> ". . . what if Earth
> Be but the shadow of Heav'n, and things therein
> Each to other like, more than on Earth is thought?"
>
> (5.574–6)

In short, Tycho's and Digges's observations and measurements of change taking place in the realm of the stars began to erase the boundary between the lower and upper storeys of the Universe, so these no longer needed to be thought of as radically distinct or characterized by utterly dissimilar physics, substances, and beings. This realization was to have enormous consequences for almost every aspect of what was to prove a cosmological revolution in science and human imagination.

Even more significant than Digges's connection with Tycho is his contribution to Copernicanism. In *Alae*, Digges does not yet fully declare for heliocentrism, although he clearly perceives the stunning implications of observed changes in the heavens, openly praises Copernicus, and uses Copernican-flavored language to pour scorn on the inadequacies of traditional astronomy. The "heavenly spheres and universal machinery" offered by antiquity, he complains in the epistle to Cecil, are "inelegant, not to say monstrous," and accepted merely out of tradition, although now corrected and reformed "by that superhuman divine genius Copernicus."[14] Moreover, a much shorter publication from early 1573, an anonymous vernacular *Letter Sent by a Gentleman of England [Concerning] the Miraculous Starre Now Shyninge* – only recently attributed to Digges[15] – is similarly positive in its references to Copernicus, even if, like *Alae*, it stops short of expressly endorsing heliocentrism.

But within a few years, Digges distinguished himself as England's first open proponent of Copernicanism – fully two decades before Kepler or Galileo went public with their support – and in addition as Copernicus's

---

[14] Digges, *Alae*, sig. A4ᵛ (*à divino illo, ingenii plusquam humani Copernico*). As will become increasingly evident, Digges had intimate knowledge of Copernicus's work. Thanks to the sleuthing of Owen Gingerich, we know that Digges's own copy of *De Revolutionibus* is held by the Bibliothèque Publique et Universitaire de Genève. Sadly, it is but lightly annotated, although at the top of its title page is the three-word pronouncement *Vulgi opinio Error* ("the common opinion is wrong"), followed by Digges's signature. See Owen Gingerich, *An Annotated Census of Copernicus' De Revolutionibus* (Leiden: Brill, 2002), p. 215.

[15] Stephen Pumfrey, "'Your astronomers and ours differ exceedingly': the controversy over the 'new star' of 1572 in the light of a newly discovered text by Thomas Digges," *British Journal for the History of Science* 44.1 (March 2011): 29–60.

first (and only published sixteenth-century) translator. Digges's father, Leonard Digges, had repeatedly published versions of a perpetual almanac, or *Prognostication*, and in 1576, at age thirty, Thomas reissued his late father's work, offering an "addition" titled *A Perfit Description of the Caelestiall Orbes*, in which his Copernican partisanship is unmistakable. This work opens with a diagram that has become a standard illustration in any encyclopedia article or history-of-astronomy text on Copernicanism (Figure 3.3). Most famously, Digges's version of the Copernican universe indicates a starry realm – unlike the bounded sphere of *De Revolutionibus* – that continues "infinitely up." Despite this modification of Copernicus, the picture's dominant concentric circles do accurately reproduce the main structure of the Copernican system. Moreover, included in the same volume, Leonard Digges's *Prognostication* retains the standard graphic (based on Apian: Figure 1.2, p. 10) of the older Ptolemaic universe. Thus, at one level, Thomas Digges may be seen as merely (he implies) offering to a highly judicious readership alternative cosmologies.

Thomas Digges was not the first Englishman to outline Copernicanism in print. Robert Recorde, in a 1556 compendium of astronomical learning titled *The Castle of Knowledge*, presented a dialogue in which the Master informs the Scholar about the new cosmology:

> Master. . . . Copernicus a man of greate learninge, of muche experience, and of wondrefull diligence in observation, hathe renewed the opinion of Aristarchus Samius, and affirmeth that the earthe not only moveth circularlye about his owne centre, but also may be, yea and is, continually out of the precise centre of the world 38 hundreth thousand miles: but because the understanding of that controversy dependeth on profounder knowledge then in this Introduction may be uttered conveniently, I will let it passe tyll some other time.
>
> Scholar. Nay syr in good faith, I desire not to heare such vaine phantasies, so farr againste common reason, and repugnante to the consente of all the learned multitude of Wryters, and therefore lette it passe for ever, and a daye longer.
>
> Master. You are to yonge to be a good judge in so great a matter: it passeth farre your learning, and theirs also that are muche better learned then you, . . . and therefore you were best to condemne no thinge that you do not well understand: but an other tyme, as I sayd, I will so declare his supposition, that you shall not only wonder to hear it, but also peradventure be as earnest then to credite it, as you are now to condemne it.[16]

[16] Robert Recorde, *The Castle of Knowledge, Containing the Explication of the Sphere Both Celestiall and Materiall* (London, 1556), p. 165.

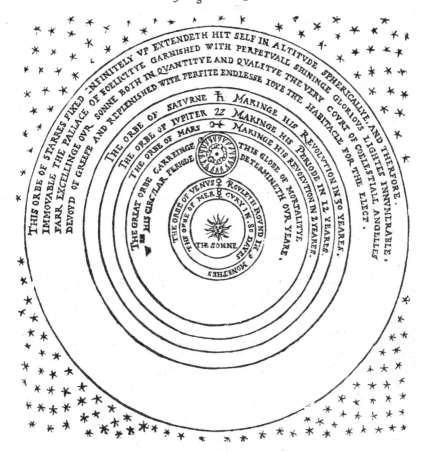

Figure 3.3 Digges's Cosmos

Still, despite Recorde's apparently open-minded approach, *The Castle of Knowledge* did not in fact endorse Copernicanism. The honor of being the first to do so in England would instead be claimed, twenty years later, by Thomas Digges.

In *A Perfit Description of the Caelestiall Orbes*, Digges's foreword "To the Reader" begins by mentioning the older model "according to the doctrine of Ptolemy, whereunto all universities . . . have consented" – but continues with this momentous announcement:

> But in this our age one rare witte (seeing the continuall errors that from time to time more and more have bin discovered, besides the infinite absurdities in their Theorickes, which they have bin forced to admit that woulde not confesse any mobilitie in the ball of the earth) hath by long studie, painfull practice, and rare invention delivered a new Theoricke or model of the world, showing that the Earth resteth not in the Center of the whole world, but onely in the Center of this our mortall world or Globe of Elementes which environed and enclosed in the Moones Orbe, and together with the whole Globe of mortalitie is carried yearely rounde aboute the Sunne, which like a king in the middest of all raigneth and geeveth lawes of motion to the rest, spherically dispearsing his glorious beames of light through al this sacred Caelestiall Temple. And the earth it selfe to be one of the Planets having his peculiar and strayinge courses tourning everye 24. houres rounde upon his owne Center whereby the Sun and great Globe of fixed stars seeme to sway about and tourne, albeit in deede they remaine fixed.[17]

This précis admirably conveys the substance and poetic flavor of Copernicus's "Theorick," or model of the world. Moreover, Digges discerns exactly the chief issues at the heart of the new model regarding its intent and the challenges one faces in promoting it. Whereas Copernicus, in his preface to Pope Paul III, uses the term *absurd* equally to describe the old cosmology and to anticipate how his own proposals will initially appear, Digges takes straight aim at the "infinite absurdities" of the traditional astronomy while speaking as if his audience comprises nothing but high-minded truth-seekers capable of dispassionate judgment. Accordingly, he continues in the same passage:

> I thought it convenient together with the olde Theorick also to publish this, to the ende such noble English minds (as delight to reache above the baser sort of men) might not be altogether defrauded of so noble a part of Philosophy. And to the ende it might manifestly appeare that Copernicus mente not as some have fondly excused him to deliver the grounds of the Earthes mobility onely as Mathematicall principles, fayned and not as Philosophicall truly averred.

Digges's assertion that Copernicus's model is "Philosophicall" crucially implies that it is not *merely* a model and not merely mathematical or hypothetical. Notoriously, when *De Revolutionibus* was published in

---

[17] Thomas Digges, *A Perfit Description of the Caelestiall Orbes* (London, 1576), sig. M.1ʳ.

Nuremberg in 1543, Andreas Osiander – without Copernicus's knowledge – inserted an anonymous two-page preface "Ad Lectorem" suggesting that "these hypotheses need not be true nor even probable." This reductively hypothetical or instrumental reading of Copernicus was widely accepted for a good number of decades and few ever learned how infuriated were those closest to Copernicus when, upon the book's publication, they saw Osiander's letter.[18] In copies that Copernicus's disciple Rheticus gave to friends, he carefully defaced the pages containing Osiander's letter. Copernicus's best friend, Tiedemann Giese, declaring the "Ad Lectorem" scandalous, wrote to the Nuremberg city council requesting (unsuccessfully) that Osiander be punished.[19] But Digges, unlike most sixteenth-century readers, has remarkably somehow grasped the realistic nature of Copernicus's cosmology – and emphasizes it with an enthusiastic triple pleonasm: "Philosophicall truly averred." Essentially, says Digges, Copernicanism is truly truly true.

While the Latin *Alae* had been aimed at a European audience, *A Perfit Description* is decidedly written for Digges's fellow Englishmen, perhaps especially – given the intellectual and ecclesiastical context of the 1570s – those with a taste for a return to pristine ancient doctrine that has long been corrupted and still stands in need of reformation. In keeping with this posture, the extended title of the English work reads *A Perfit Description of the Caelestiall Orbes, According to the Moste Aunncient Doctrine of the Pythagoreans, Latelye Revived by Copernicus.* Thus, the ancients, rather than being overturned, are to be a principal source of wisdom. Even in comments about Aristotle – "him selfe the light of our Universities" – whose celestial physics he must of course oppose, Digges speaks appreciatively, praising the Philosopher's "modesty" but complaining that "his disciples have not with like sobriety maintayned" his position. Any contest between theories must be settled, insists Digges, as if in harmony with Aristotle, "not with childish Invectives but with grave reasons Philosophicall and irreproveable Demonstrations Mathematicall."

In their addresses to their respective ideal audiences, then – Copernicus to Pope Paul III; Digges to "noble English minds" – both astronomers establish their seriousness and credibility by means of statements

---

[18] See Danielson, *The First Copernican: Georg Joachim Rheticus and the Rise of the Copernican Revolution* (New York: Walker, 2006), pp. 109–14. Typical of those who treated Osiander's "Ad Lectorem" as authoritative was Thomas Blundeville, who wrote: "Some also deny that the earth is in the middest of the world, and some affirme that it is moveable, as also Copernicus, by way of supposition, and not for that he thought so in deede"; *M. Blundevile His Exercises* (London, 1594), fol. 181ʳ.

[19] See Edward Rosen, *Copernicus and the Scientific Revolution* (Malabar, FL: Krieger, 1984), p. 197.

of principle ("grave reasons," etc.) and appeals to ancient authority. This posture, typical of much Renaissance and Reformation Christian Humanism, will be familiar to any reader of Milton. A further significant characteristic of Copernicus, Digges, and other early modern astronomers, however, warrants greater acknowledgment than historians of science have often granted it: not only the eclecticism of their rhetoric but also the "piecemeal engineering" aspect of the cosmologies they offer. Seen from a great distance, Ptolemy and Copernicus are easy to construe as adopting opposite positions. But examined up close – as when we set the diagrams of their planetary systems side by side – both accept a finite universe with circular celestial spheres, even though Copernicus's diagram crucially exchanges the positions of the Sun and Earth. One of the criticisms of astronomers on into the seventeenth century is that they behaved like tinkers.[20] But tinkering has always been a normal and legitimate driver of scientific and technological progress – in astronomy as well as in more familiar domains today, such as computer and automotive design. Relative to the cosmological revolution of the sixteenth and seventeenth centuries, I would suggest that *bricolage* may serve as a slightly more dignified term than tinkering or mere eclecticism, bespeaking a resourceful, pragmatic use of found materials, including a desire on the part of the bricoleur to build or rebuild a structure that is beautiful or useful. And despite Copernicus's charge that eclectic or piecemeal procedures in the case of the Ptolemaic system produced something "monstrous," the cosmological revolution that began but did not end with his own prodigious contribution is more a collective achievement of ingenious bricoleurs than is often recognized.

Thomas Digges was in fact a cosmological bricoleur par excellence and his bricolage has literary as well as natural-philosophical dimensions. While reveling in the science and the poetic flavor of Copernicus, Digges also noticeably retains, indeed reinserts, much vocabulary that he inherited from the system Copernicanism would eventually displace. In his account, for example, our "mortall world or Globe of Elementes . . . [is] environed and enclosed in the Moones Orbe, . . . together with the whole Globe of mortalitie." In *A Perfit Description*, such nods in the direction of contemporary commonplaces about the moral and spiritual meaning of cosmology are complemented by Digges's citations of a Latin poem by Marcellus Palingenius (an Italian also known by the toponym Stellatus) called the *Zodiacus Vitae*. This long poem was something of a bestseller in

---

[20] For example, Burton, *The Anatomy of Melancholy* (1621), p. 329.

Digges's day; the full Latin version was published in 1569 by Digges's own printer, Thomas Marsh, while Barnaby Googe's English translation of the full poem enjoyed at least three editions ranging from 1565 to 1588. So remarkable is the hybridity of Digges's discourse that it is worth quoting at length:

> The Globe of Elements enclosed in the Orbe of the Moon I call the Globe of Mortalitie because it is the peculiare Empire of death. For above the Moon they feare not his force but as the Christian Poet saith:

> Omne quod est supra lunam, aeternumque bonumque
> Esse scias nec triste aliquid Caelestia tangit.
> Quicquid vero infra Lunae convexa creavit
> Omniparens, natura, malum est, mortisque severas
> Perpetitur leges et edaci absumitur aevo.

> [All things are good and never fade above the Moone that dwell,
> Nor griefe can vexe those sacred states:
> But all that nature framed beneath the Moone, is nought, and ill,
> And lawe severe of death doth feele, and force of time to spyll.]

>   Againe.

> Omne malum est infra lunam, nox atra, procellae,
> Terribiles, frigus, calor, importuna senectus,
> Pauperies malesuada, labor, dolor, improbitas, Mors.
> Supra autem lunam, lucis sunt omnia plena,
> Nec non letitiae et pacis, non tempus et error
> Et MORS et senium est illic et inutile quicquam.
> Foelix o nimium foelix, cui sedibus illis
> Tam pulchris et tam iucundis tamque beatis
> Vivere concessum est, supreme munere Regis.

> [Beneath the Mone: as darksome night and stormes, and tempest mayne,
> Wyth colde and heate, and teasty age, dame neede of beggars hall,
> And labour, grief, and wretchednesse, and death that endeth all.
> Above the Mone continual light, wyth peace and joy remayne,
> No tyme, nor error, death nor age, nor any thing is vayne.
> O blest, and double blest agayne, that in so pleasaunt place,
> So fayre, so beautiful, to live of God obtayneth grace.]

>   And againe.

> Singula nonnulli credunt quoque sydera posse
> Dici Orbes, TERRAMque appellant sydus opacum
> Cui minimus Divum praesit etc.

[But some have thought that every Starre a worlde we well may cal,
The earth they count a darkned starre whereas the least of all
The God doth raine that underneath the clowdes hath placed his
  chaire. . . .]

In the midst of this Globe of Mortality hangeth this darck starre or ball of
earth and water balanced and sustained in the midst of the thinne ayer
onely with that propriety which the wonderfull workman hath given at the
Creation to the Center of this Globe with his magneticall force vehemently
to draw and hale unto it self all such other Elementall thinges as retaine the
like nature. This ball every 24. hours by naturall, uniforme and wonderfull
slie and smoth motion rouleth rounde, making with his Periode our
naturall daye, whereby it seemes to us that the huge infinite immoveable
Globe should sway and tourne about.[21]

It is hard at first to grasp how an astronomer who a few years earlier has,
like Tycho, studied evidence for mutability in the superlunary sphere
could still use language that Digges uses here. On the other hand, Palingenius's imagination is itself notably hybrid, encompassing not only traditional gloomy language about the sublunary sphere but also dropping not-
very-Aristotelian hints about the possibility of stars being other worlds – a
topic to which we shall return. Nonetheless, this immediate passage is
evidence that in order to accept Copernicus's account of the large-scale
structure of the universe, a sixteenth-century writer or reader need not
abandon the commonplace according to which Earth and the region below
the Moon are, in Digges's grim words, "the peculiare Empire of death."
Yes, Earth is to be reimagined as a planet, a wandering star, even one with
some magnetical system of attraction to keep things from flying off as it
takes its daily spin. But it remains for now a "darck starre" – complete with
the four Aristotelian elements and the sublunary physics that go along with
them. Again, Copernicus offered no live substitute for that physics. Thus,
hybrid as Digges's offered system may be, this lifeline to the old Aristotelian world picture appearing in the midst of his bold announcement of
Copernican cosmology would, it seems, only have enhanced his credibility
among his contemporary readers.

Beyond the preface, approximately twelve of the remaining thirteen
quarto pages of *A Perfit Description* comprise Digges's free translation of
chapters from *De Revolutionibus* itself – as mentioned, the first translation

---

[21] This entire passage appears on sig. M2ʳ of *A Perfit Description*. The English renderings of Palingenius
appearing here in square brackets are from Barnaby Googe's English translation, *The Zodiake of Life*
(London, 1565), in order of citation: Book 9, Sagittarius, sig. GG.vii.ʳ; Book 8, Scorpius, sig. CC.v.ᵛ;
Book 7, Libra, sig. Y.i.ʳ.

of Copernicus from Latin into any other language. In keeping with his taste for launching straight in, Digges begins with Book I, Chapter 10, the poetically and cosmologically most dazzling section of Copernicus's work, and only then proceeds to more technical matters: Aristotelian arguments for a stationary Earth and Copernicus's "Solution of These Reasons" – respectively, Chapters 7 and 8 of Book 1. Toward the end of the latter section, Digges also supplements his translation with three pregnant sentences from Chapter 9 of the same book containing Copernicus's preliminary but prescient comments about *gravitas*. Digges translates this as "gravity" – quite likely the earliest modern physical use of the term in English, predating the *Oxford English Dictionary*'s earliest citation of the word by forty-six years. This addition, together with the appeal to earthly magnetism in the preface, reveals Digges's awareness of the need to formulate a new physics accommodated to Copernican claims about a relocated and moving Earth.

In his translation, as in his graphic, Digges is thus unafraid of performing bricolage with found materials from disparate cosmologies while offering reflections and inferences of his own. Copernicus, in *De Revolutionibus* I.10, writes that "this whole domain encircled by the moon, with the center of the earth, traverses this *orbis magnus* amid the other planets in an annual revolution around the sun." Digges translates the Latin – *hoc totum, quod Luna praecingit* – as "this whole globe of Elements enclosed with the Moones sphere," even though Copernicus himself says nothing at all about elements. Moreover, Digges inserts the elements in the text and in his graphic. As already mentioned, earlier in Leonard Digges's *Prognostication* appears a Ptolemaic schema similar to Apian's (Figure 1.2, p. 10). In that depiction, one sees clearly the "elementary" hierarchy of the sublunary sphere, with earth and water together at the center, above which comes air (with clouds), followed finally by the sphere of fire. In Thomas Digges's diagram, however, if we visually zoom in, we notice that the Aristotelian/Ptolemaic "Globe of Mortality" is merely compacted and transposed – earth, water, air, and fire – into its new location in the Copernican system. Digges in effect photoshops the familiar if now pictorially miniaturized sublunary world onto the recently enlarged picture of the superlunary Cosmos offered by Copernicus.

Digges thus again combines or superimposes disparate cosmological elements – modifications that may have helped his readers keep their minds open to the new and staggering Universe being announced. Copernicanism was hard to accept because it required that so very many ingrained assumptions be set aside. This impediment is perhaps most succinctly and famously summed up by John Donne's lament, uttered thirty-five years after 1576, that the "new philosophy calls *all* in doubt, / The element of fire is quite put out." However, Digges, Copernican translator and cosmological bricoleur, scrupulously avoids putting out the element of fire or eliminating any of the other elements essential to Aristotelian sublunary physics – elements which to Digges's public would have seemed little more than common sense. In this way, his language and his graphic invite his audience to contemplate the encompassing Copernican cosmology without the trauma of having to jettison the "local arrangements" in which they understandably feel so at home.

At the same time, Digges does not minimize the astonishment one would have felt (and still feels) when contemplating the newly conceived immensity of the Universe. At the end of Book I, Chapter 10, of *De Revolutionibus*, Copernicus almost understatedly returns to one of his most stunning cosmological conclusions. Having explained the peculiar movements of the planets in relation to Earth's annual motion, he acknowledges that the same annual motion has no consequences whatsoever for the appearance of the fixed stars – "that none of these phenomena appears in the fixed stars proves that these are immensely distant, for which reason even the motion of the annual revolution, or the appearance thereof, vanishes from sight" – the same conclusion to which in the manuscript version of his treatise he had pointed at the end of Book I, Chapter 6. But Digges, much less given to understatement than Copernicus, inserts – as interpreter rather than merely as translator – this set of inferences at the end of the core statement of Copernican cosmology:

> Herein can wee never sufficiently admire thys wonderfull and incomprehensible huge frame of goddes woorke proponed to our senses, seing fyrst thys baull of the earth wherein we move, to the common sorte seemeth greate, and [yet] in respecte of the Moones Orbe is very small, but compared with *Orbis magnus* wherein it is caried, it scarcely retayneth any sensible proportion, so merveilously is that Orbe of Annuall motion greater then this litle darcke starre wherein we live. But that *Orbis magnus* beinge as is before declared but as a poynct in respect of the immensity of that immoveable heaven, we may easily consider what litle portion of gods frame, our Elementare corruptible worlde is, but never sufficiently be able to admire the immensity of the Rest. Especially of that fixed Orbe garnished with lightes innumerable and reaching up in Sphaericall altitude without ende.

Whereas Copernicus had dropped the merest hint of an infinite universe, Digges seizes upon the suggestion with great enthusiasm, endorsing the idea repeatedly in his text, as here, as well as in his famous diagram. Moreover, his enthusiasm proved influential. *A Perfit Description* appeared in at least seven editions from 1576 to 1605 and the infinite "sphere" of dispersed stars that it graphically offered came to be regarded in England, as Francis Johnson and Sanford V. Larkey indicate, "as part of the Copernican theory itself."[22]

In short, in a manner that does not detract from its status as the greatest English contribution to cosmology in the sixteenth century, one may read Digges's *A Perfit Description* as a magnificent piece of bricolage. Graphically and textually, the cosmology is modular: It offers the Copernican planetary system, with Mercury, Venus, Earth, Mars, Jupiter, and Saturn circling the central Sun. But it offers the terrestrial system – Earth with the Moon circling it – simply as a shrunken, simplified version of the ancient sublunary sphere – home of the familiar Aristotelian elements. And just as Digges neatly cuts and pastes those components of the Ptolemaic universe onto that of Copernicus, so in turn he quietly but dramatically drops Copernicus's finite Cosmos – what we now know simply as the solar system – into an infinite super-Cosmos of stars that "infinitely up extendeth itself in altitude spherically."

In England, before the advent of the telescope as well as after, the cosmological revolution continued to unfold as a work in progress performed by bricoleurs all at least partly aware that no matter how boldly or modestly they adjusted the machinery of their chosen "theorick," some problem remained. This was, of course, true on the Continent as well as in England. From the late fifteenth century on, one of the standard, oft-published academic texts on the arrangement and movement of the planets was Georg Peurbach's *Theoricae Novae Planetarum*. A new edition of this work appeared in Cologne in 1581 and enjoyed five further printings between then and 1610. But despite being a classic of Ptolemaic astronomy, this work contained a remarkably dyspeptic preface by a Frisian named Albertus Hero, also known as Snecanus, who complained:

> It is said that astronomy cannot do without theology, for the theologians' job is to prepare men's minds as much as possible for faith in things incomprehensible. And (without citing examples here) these things indeed teach that many experiences conflict with doctrine, no discipline being able

---

[22] Francis R. Johnson and Sanford V. Larkey, "Thomas Digges, the Copernican System, and the Idea of the Infinity of the Universe in 1576," *The Huntingdon Library Bulletin* 5 (April 1934): 69–117 (p. 117).

to offer more examples of this phenomenon than astronomy. To satisfy our experience, astronomers are accordingly constrained to arrange the celestial spheres into such a monstrous form that, if truth be told, nothing can be imagined more deformed than the heavens. ... And they ascribe to the noblest heavenly bodies deformities that reason cannot accept.[23]

The complaint has much of the flavor of Copernicus's preface to Pope Paul III in *De Revolutionibus* – downright embarrassment at what astronomers have produced – except that the book in which these words appear is no rejection of Ptolemaic astronomy but an exposition of it. Frustrated by the prospect of attributing monstrosity to the heavens or asserting "things incomprehensible," then, any self-respecting astronomer had little choice but to locate and adapt found materials in the hope that his chosen cosmological model might be rendered less incomprehensible.

For Tycho Brahe, the found materials were his own incomparable observations and components detached from the Ptolemaic and the Copernican cosmologies. Having pondered those two systems, Tycho did not exactly call down a plague on both houses; instead, he appropriated the foundation of the former (an immovable central Earth) and much of the superstructure of the latter (planets circling the Sun), with the aim of obviating the difficulties presented by both systems. Tycho's diagrammatic answer to Ptolemy and Copernicus (see Figure 3.4) appeared in 1588 in a book printed at Uraniborg (his own observatory on the island of Hven) and sent to a select number of astronomers and mathematicians around Europe. It was then reproduced and distributed more widely in Tycho's posthumously published *Progymnasmata* (1602, 1610).

In Chapter 1, we met with an array of the "Ptolemaic redundancy and awkwardness" to which Tycho refers in his caption. So far, in the present chapter, some of the possible absurdities of Copernicanism have been indicated, including the most obvious difficulty of imagining that the Earth beneath our feet is performing all at once a daily rotation and an annual revolution. We have also noticed the difficulty of conceiving the vastly increased disproportion between Earth's magnitudes and the sphere of the fixed stars that Copernicus's cosmology implies. But there was a

---

[23] Albertus Hero Snecanus, Preface to Georg Peuerbach, *Theoricae Novae Panetarum* (Cologne, 1581), sig. A6ʳ-A7ʳ: *Quin audio dicere, neque Theologiam Astronomia carere posse. Cum enim Theologi officium sit, animos hominum ad rerum incomprehensibilium fidem pro virili praepare, idque allatis exemplis, quae doceant etiam multas experientias cum ratione pugnare, nulla disciplina tantum poteris eiusmodi exemplorum suppeditare, quantum Astrologiae. Nam in hac, ut experimentis satisfaciant Astrologi, coelestibus orbibus tam monstrosam figuram affingere coguntur, ut, si verum dicerent, nihil caelo deformius cogitari posset. ... At qui nobilissimis coelorum corporibus talem attribui deformitatem ratio non admittit.*

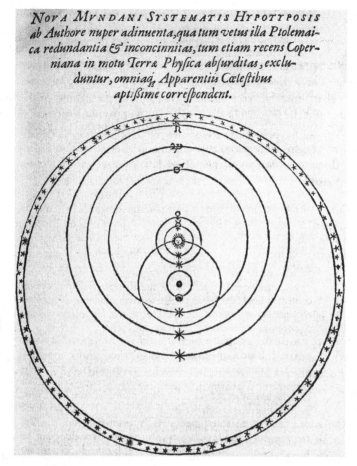

Figure 3.4 The caption reads: "A new description of the world system recently devised by the author, whereby are banished not only the longstanding Ptolemaic redundancy and awkwardness, but also the recent Copernican absurdity concerning the physical motion of the Earth, all of it corresponding most fittingly with the celestial phenomena."

further problem (like the latter, related to Earth's yearly revolution) that bothered Tycho and would plague Copernicanism on through the seventeenth century: stellar size.

Accepting that Earth made a grand annual circuit (*orbis magnus*) around the Sun, Copernicans nonetheless could not detect any annual stellar parallax. As already noted, this in turn entailed a vastly increased distance to the stars over estimates based on a geocentric model. But geometrically, those Copernican distances implied in turn – given that the stars have a measurable if small angular diameter – that each fixed star must be hugely, unimaginably larger than the Sun itself. Digges himself was aware of this problem. The script accompanying the frontispiece of *A Perfit Description* declares that those "glorious lightes" (the stars) far excel our Sun "both in quantitye and qualitye." He does not, however, draw further attention to this awkward inference. But Tycho, unembarrassed by a problem that only made his case for a geoheliocentric (and geostatic) system stronger, did indeed draw attention to it. He offered it as a *reductio ad absurdum* of heliocentrism:

> Indeed, it follows that if Earth moves through an annual circuit, then third-magnitude stars, which have a diameter of one minute, must equal that whole annual circle. That is, their diameter would encompass 2,284 semi-diameters of the Earth, and their distance away will be about 7,850,000 of the same unit. . . . Moreover, what if the eighth sphere were pushed higher, so that Earth's annual motion completely vanished? Figure it out geometrically and you will see how many absurdities . . . are entailed by this assumption [about Earth's motion].[24]

We shall return to the problem of star size, but for now, it is enough to acknowledge that Tycho had strong observational and scientific grounds for not accepting Copernicanism, that his proposed system was itself a piece of brilliant bricolage, and that nobody involved in what (with smug hindsight) we sometimes see as a unidirectional cosmological revolution could transcend the necessity of piecemeal model-making.[25]

Occasionally, however, when everything seems confusing, a well-chosen analogy can save the day. We have noticed how, with the decline of Aristotelian physics generally and particularly with its inability to account for a noncentral Earth's attraction of heavy things, Copernicus and, to a greater degree, Digges offer initial, nonsystematic attempts to describe the behavior of *gravitas*. Moreover, Digges, unlike Copernicus, also envisages

---

[24] Tycho Brahe, to Christoph Rothmann, 26 July 1589; in *Epistolarum Astronomicarum* (Nuremberg, 1601), p. 167. For further discussion, see Christopher M. Graney, "Regarding How Tycho Brahe Noted the Absurdity of the Copernican Theory Regarding the Bigness of Stars," *arXiv*:1112.1988v2; and Ann Blair, "Tycho Brahe's Critique of Copernicus and the Copernican System," *Journal of the History of Ideas* 51.3 (July–September 1990): 355–77. Tycho's scenario of "Earth's annual motion completely vanish[ing]" closely echoes Copernicus's acceptance of the same inference at the end of *De Revolutionibus*, Book 1, Chapter 10.

[25] For more on problems of star size and the question of scientific progress, see Dennis Danielson and Christopher M. Graney, "The Case Against Copernicus," *Scientific American* 310.1 (January 2014): 72–7.

Earth's center "with his magnetical force vehemently [drawing and haling] unto it self all such other Elementall thinges." It was exactly this analogy between the attractive forces of magnetism and what we now call gravity (although it was not then seen to be a mere analogy) that gave the new cosmologists some hope of a physical explanation – first for the behavior of the diurnally rotating Earth and later, particularly in the case of Kepler, for the motive powers of a central Sun. An account of the latter application can wait until Chapter 6. But the vision of Earth as something with attractive, magnetic powers had deep significance for the theory of terrestrial rotation independent of whether one's larger cosmological scheme was geocentric or heliocentric.

Theorizing about magnetism's cosmological relevance did have an early Copernican connection. An exploration of the nature of the lodestone had been conducted by thirteenth-century French scholar Petrus Peregrinus de Maricourt, whose manuscript *Epistola de Magnete* survived and was acquired by Achilles Gasser (1505–77), a learned Lindau doctor and polymath. In 1539, Gasser showed it to his friend and protégé Georg Joachim Rheticus, the twenty-five-year-old Wittenberg mathematics professor who went on to become the sole student and "apostle" of Copernicus. Although there is no indication in *De Revolutionibus* that Copernicus pondered any cosmological application of magnetism, it is possible that Rheticus told him about the work of Peregrinus. In any case, while residing with Copernicus, Rheticus wrote a short work on local geography for Duke Albrecht of Prussia in which he enthusiastically cited Peregrinus and described the cosmologically suggestive behavior of a spherical lodestone: "If the lodestone is shaped into a sphere, and hung up vertically upon its poles, that is, upon its north and south, ... then, in keeping with the property with which God has imbued it, it supposedly rotates once in twenty-four hours."[26] The analogy between the spherical, diurnally rotating lodestone and Earth must have seemed irresistible – at least to a budding Copernican. Before the end of the sixteenth century, such a stone would acquire the name *terrella*: a little Earth.

Gasser published Peregrinus's work in Augsburg in 1558, and in England it was read by William Gilbert (1544–1603), who conducted experiments in order to understand the properties of the terrella. Book 6,

---

[26] F. Hipler, "Die Chorographie des Joachim Rheticus, aus dem Autographon des Verfassers," *Zeitschrift für Mathematik und Physik*, 21 (1876): 125–50 (p. 149). For more on Gasser's interest in magnetism, see Danielson, "Achilles Gasser and the Birth of Copernicanism," *Journal for the History of Astronomy* 35.4 (Nov. 2004): 457–74.

Chapter 1, of his *De Magnete* (1600) is headed "Of the Globe of Earth as a Loadstone." And in Chapter 4 of the same book, Gilbert asserts: "this circular movement of the loadstone to its true and natural position shows that the whole earth is fitted, and by its own forces adapted for a diurnal circular motion. I omit what Petrus Peregrinus so stoutly affirms, that a terrella poised on its poles in the meridian moves circularly with a complete revolution in twenty-four hours." Gilbert adds that the weight of the stone probably makes an experimental test of Peregrinus's claim impracticable. But he clearly accepts the analogy as sound. It permits him to assert that "The earth moves by its primary form and natural desire" (thus undermining the Aristotelians' objection that Earth's movement would be "violent") and that "this is more probable than that those fixed luminous orbs, and the planets and the sun, ... should vainly circle around it."[27]

Although Gilbert was not a full Copernican, he certainly did assert Earth's diurnal rotation.[28] For present purposes, he thus illustrates not only the articulation of a demonstrated non-Aristotelian physical principle that promises to explain earthly motion but also the fact that Earth's diurnal motion, although one component of Copernicanism, could be (and often was) accepted by thinkers unable to accept heliocentrism.[29]

In short, Gilbert affords yet another example of a scientifically serious gatherer of found materials with which he hoped to theorize a more coherent world. He would not prove to be the last or even the greatest to do so. But Kepler himself was not ashamed to declare: "I build my

[27] William Gilbert, *De Magnete* (London, 1600), pp. 223–4; I quote P. Fleury Mottelay's translation (1893; New York: Dover, 1958), pp. 332–3.

[28] John L. Russell says that Gilbert "had no doubt about the diurnal rotation of the earth but he never clearly committed himself either for or against an orbital motion around the sun"; "The Copernican System in Great Britain," in *The Reception of Copernicus' Heliocentric Theory*, ed. Jerzy Dobrzycki (Dordrecht: Reidel, 1972), pp. 189–239 (p. 205).

[29] A notable medieval geocentrist who offered careful thought experiments probing the idea that Earth, rather than the starry sphere, turned about once every twenty-four hours, was Nicole Oresme. See his *Le Livre du ciel et du monde* (1377); in *Mediaeval Studies*, vol. 4, Toronto: Pontifical Institute of Mediaeval Studies, 1942 (excerpts translated in *BOTC*, ed. Danielson, Chapter 16). A further instance of someone Russell calls "a semi-Copernican" who gives no evidence of adhering to heliocentrism is the instrument-maker John Blagrave, who asserted: "it is the earth that whirleth about every 24 houres from West to East, of his owne propper nature allotted unto him, as most fit for the receptacle of all transitory things, being appointed in a place where nothing is to stay him from his continuall mooving"; *Astrolabium Uranicum Generale* (London, 1596), sig. F1ᵛ. In the seventeenth century, one of the most notable non-Copernican defenders of diurnal rotation, heavily influenced by Gilbert, was Nathanael Carpenter, whose *Geographie Delineated* (London, 1625), was subsequently attacked by the reactionary Aristotelian Alexander Ross.

whole astronomy upon Copernicus' hypotheses concerning the world, upon the observations of Tycho Brahe, and lastly upon the Englishman William Gilbert's philosophy of magnetism."[30] This pattern of cosmological bricolage remained, on into the seventeenth century, the norm rather than the exception.

[30] *Epitome*, trans. Wallis, p. 10.

CHAPTER 4

Milton and Galileo revisited (1): "Incredible delight"

But the opinion of which I am now speaking, which destroyed and
confounded *system*, was ... that the earth was a planet and movable,
and as it were one of the stars.

Francis Bacon, ca. 1612[1]

"Look downward on that globe whose hither side
With light from hence, though but reflected, shines;
That place is Earth the seat of man, that light
His day, which else, as th' other hemisphere
Night would invade, but there the neighboring moon
(So call that opposite fair star) her aid
Timely interposes ..."

Paradise Lost, 3.722–8

It is well known that Galileo alone among Milton's contemporaries is
mentioned by name in *Paradise Lost*. At some point during the young
poet's Grand Tour to Italy in 1638 and 1639, he met the aging astronomer,
then under house arrest. As Milton writes in *Areopagitica*: "I found and
visited the famous *Galileo* grown old, a prisner to the Inquisition, for
thinking in Astronomy otherwise then the Franciscan and Dominican
licencers thought."[2] Although I see no good reason for disbelieving
Milton's brief reference to that meeting,[3] it does not in fact tell us much
about astronomy. In context, Galileo stands as a symbol of Italian and
Romish conditions analogous to England's earlier "prelatical yoke," while
Milton holds up the standard of "philosophic freedom" that Englishmen
ought to enjoy, even if Galileo (on account of the Roman prelates) did not.

---

[1] *Works of Francis Bacon*, 10:420; italics added.
[2] *Complete Prose Works of John Milton*, ed. Wolfe et al., 2:538.
[3] Typical of (to my mind) tendentious efforts to cast doubt upon the veracity of Milton's claim that he
   met Galileo is George F. Butler, "Milton's Meeting With Galileo: A Reconsideration," *Milton
   Quarterly* 39.3 (2005): 132–9.

Nonetheless, there can be little doubt that Galileo had a greater influence on Milton than any other single astronomer.[4]

For present purposes, Galileo's role can be divided into three components: his observational achievements, his contributions to discussions (to oversimplify it) of scientific and religious authority, and his activity as a cosmological controversialist. All three afford insights into Milton's own engagement with astronomy and cosmology, although – perhaps ironically for someone who was blind – it is the first area of achievement that seems most to have caught Milton's poetic attention. Indeed, I would suggest that it is in his observational astronomy, particularly the *Sidereus Nuncius* (*Starry Messenger*, 1610), that Galileo himself is at his most poetic.

That extraordinary little book – although viewed from one angle it "was in effect a job application"[5] – offers itself to "all philosophers and astronomers." By specifying philosophers as well as astronomers, Galileo signals that he will be offering truth claims (one recalls Digges's phrase "Philosophicall truly averred") and not merely their mathematical coherence or capacity to save the appearances. Moreover, almost from the beginning of *Sidereus Nuncius*, Galileo shows he is aware that his credibility, like that of anybody employing a new invention, will not automatically be granted. Thus, he begins his story with a summary of how, in 1609, he heard "that a certain Dutchman [likely Hans Lippershey] had constructed a telescope, by means of which visible objects, although at a great distance from the eye of the observer, were seen distinctly as if nearby. Testimonies concerning its amazing powers were reported, but some believed these and others denied them."[6] Galileo continues with a review of his own efforts to construct and improve such a device and then launches straight into a more systematic account of how he observed first the Moon and "afterwards . . . both fixed stars and planets, with incredible delight." Despite the persistent naive assumption that he simply aimed his

[4] The literature on Milton and Galileo is copious. See, for example, Allan H, Gilbert, "Milton and Galileo," *Studies in Philology* 19.2 (April 1922): 152–85; and Marjorie Nicolson, *Science and Imagination* (Ithaca: Cornell Universitiy Press, 1956), especially Chapter 4, "Milton and the Telescope," first published in *ELH* 2 (1935): 1–32. For further comment on these and other critics who engage Milton and astronomy, see also Leonard, *FL*, Chapter 11. Malabika Sarkar, whose *Cosmos and Character in Paradise Lost* (Basingstoke: Palgrave Macmillan, 2012) came into my hands only after the present book was all but complete, offers yet another fascinating chapter on "The Galileo Question" (pp. 145–60).

[5] Owen Gingerich, "The Curious Case of the M–L *Sidereus Nuncius*," *Galilaeana: Journal of Galilean Studies* 6 (2009): 141–65 (p. 142).

[6] Galileo Galilei, *Sidereus Nuncius* (Venice, 1610), fol. 6ʳ; translation adapted from *The Sidereal Messenger of Galileo Galilei*, trans. E. S. Carlos (London, 1880). Most subsequent references to the *Sidereus Nuncius* will be given parenthetically in the text.

telescope at the heavens and showed that Copernicanism was correct, Galileo works hard in *Sidereus Nuncius* to offer testimony that will be philosophically credible and rhetorically delightful. His implicitly apologetical, forensic stance in the presentation of mediated sense experience may also render less surprising Milton's own careful distinction between an angel's perspicuous astronomical vision and "the glass / Of Galileo, less assured" (*PL*, 5.261–2). The need for epistemological caution having been conceded, however, Galileo boldly opens the full account of his lunar observations by addressing once more "all who love true philosophy" (*omnes verae Philosophiae cupidos*; fol. 7ʳ).

Famously, Galileo records that on the Moon's surface he can see spots (*maculae*) and he distinguishes the "great or ancient" ones visible to the naked eye from "other spots, smaller in size, but so thickly scattered that they sprinkle the whole surface of the Moon, especially the brighter portion of it." Hard on the heels of this assertion, however, before he goes on to cite more observational evidence, Galileo claims scientific precedence and draws a dramatic cosmological inference:

> These spots have never been observed by anyone before me; and from my repeated observations I have arrived at the following conclusion: that we undoubtedly do not perceive the surface of the Moon to be perfectly smooth, free from inequalities and exactly spherical (as a large school of philosophers believes concerning both the Moon and other heavenly bodies), but on the contrary to be full of inequalities, uneven, full of hollows and protuberances. It is like the surface of the Earth itself, which is everywhere varied with lofty mountains and deep valleys. (fol. 7ᵛ)

If this passage were merely a description of a new terrestrial location, then it might prove somewhat interesting but certainly would entail no full revision of one's cosmology. Galileo, however, knew he was offering a new picture of the Cosmos.

As Samuel Edgerton has shown, Galileo's capacity for interpreting the play of light on the Moon's surface derived from his combination of a strong mathematical grasp of linear perspective and his education in the painterly techniques of chiaroscuro.[7] It undoubtedly also helped that he was thoroughly familiar with the behavior of sunlight – be it at sunrise or sunset – upon nearby hills and mountains of the Apennines. His almost commonplace attention to that play of light upon something never before

---

[7] Samuel Y. Edgerton Jr., *The Heritage of Giotto's Geometry: Art and Science on the Eve of the Scientific Revolution* (Ithaca and London: Cornell University Press, 1991), Chapter 7, "Geometrization of Astronomical Space," pp. 223–53.

observed up close decisively shattered another element of the Aristotelian universe. Just as Tycho's Supernova had demonstrated change in the heavens, so did the recognition that the Moon's surface is rough, pock-marked, and mountainous – in short, earthlike – prove that at least one of the celestial bodies lacked the spherical perfection that celestial bodies were supposed to possess. Furthermore, as Edgerton also points out, "Christian dogma added to this euphoric image [of celestial perfection] by having the moon symbolize the Virgin's Immaculate Conception. 'Pure as the moon' became a commonplace expression for Mary, implying that the universe, like herself, was incorruptible, that God would not have created the moon or any other heavenly body in another shape" (p. 231). A demonstration of spots and mountains on the Moon, therefore, as Galileo saw clearly, had important consequences not only for astronomy but also for cosmology, culture, and perhaps religion. For the "upper storey" of the Universe could now no longer be seen as immaculate.

The metaphoric potential of Galileo's lunar probing must have been irresistible for a poet of Milton's imaginative capacity. Galileo's *macula* in Latin is quite properly translated as "spot." Although not always a pejorative term in English, "spot" can still today carry the suggestion of flaw or character blemish, as in a "spot on one's reputation" (cf. OED, "spotty" 1.b and Eph. 5:27, KJV – "spot" being the translation of σπίλος). Of course, the absence of any such blemish would return us to Galileo's lexicon: "immaculate." This overlapping of physical description and moral implication created an ambiguity that Milton happily exploits more than once in *Paradise Lost* – both times at Satan's expense. The first of these also offers the poem's first epic simile as well as its first direct allusion to Galileo. Following the initial dialogue of Satan and Beelzebub in Book 1, the poet continues:

> He scarce had ceased when the superior fiend
> Was moving toward the shore; his ponderous shield
> Ethereal temper, massy, large and round,
> Behind him cast; the broad circumference
> Hung on his shoulders like the moon, whose orb
> Through optic glass the Tuscan artist views
> At evening from the top of Fesole,
> Or in Valdarno, to descry new lands,
> Rivers or mountains in her spotty globe.
>
> (1.283–91)

The passage recalls accounts of other heroic shields – those of Achilles or Aeneas – shields forged by Hephaestus and Vulcan (Mulciber), respectively, especially in the latter case with hellish associations. By contrast, however, it is clear that Satan's shield has heavenly, not hellish, origins ("Ethereal temper"). The ostensible emphasis of the verse is on the shield's (potentially morally neutral) size and shape; its roundness is what creates the opportunity for the simile. Only "spotty" at the end of Milton's sentence leaves what might have remained pleasantly ethereal – a perfect orb or globe – less than immaculate. And, in turn, readers are left (especially if they have read Galileo) to ponder how and why it came to be thus.

Galileo's account of the earthlike structure of the Moon's surface furthermore creates a strong analogy between the "down here" and the "up there" – an analogy made more robust by the brilliant feat of calculating lunar elevations. Edgerton describes the simple geometry employed by Galileo to triangulate the height of a mountain whose top peeps up out from the Moon's shadow on the dark side of the terminator:[8]

> Since the moon's diameter was known to be two-sevenths of the earth's diameter, or about 2,000 miles, Galileo ... revealed by Pythagorean calculation that ... the mountain's height on center from its base reached more than four miles into the lunar sky! By applying a problem well known to students of Renaissance perspective, Galileo added yet another fact to his already wondrous revelations, that the mountains on the moon were more spectacular than the Alps here on earth.

The calculation is remarkable not only for Galileo's accuracy given the limitations of his equipment but also for the very fact that he was able to apply geometry – literally, "earth measure" – extraterrestrially. The implication, an anti-Aristotelian one, is that not only the landscape but also space itself is qualitatively the same up there as it is down here. Hence, as Edgerton calls this critical step in the new cosmology, the "geometrization of astronomical space."

The extraterrestrial application of geometry (etymologically, almost a contradiction in terms) is indeed well illustrated in *Sidereus Nuncius*, although as we have seen, it was also put to use in Digges's and Tycho's efforts to measure parallax in the 1572 supernova. Even before that, Copernicus's student Rheticus conceived of the astronomical applicability of geometry as symbolic (although not *merely* symbolic) of the unity of creation – just as Copernicus conceived of the Universe as possessing a fundamental symmetry (whose etymology again implies a common

[8] OED 2: "The line of separation between the illuminated and unilluminated parts of the disk of the moon or a planet."

measure). Thus, Rheticus – in a gentle echo of the Lord's Prayer – points to "God's geometry in heaven and on Earth"[9] And as noted in Chapter 3, that divinely given common measure *created* grounds for adumbrating similitudes – be they physical or poetic – and tended to emphasize what the "up there" and the "down here" have in common rather than what separates them, thus supporting Raphael's Miltonic conjecture:

> ". . . what if Earth
> Be but the shadow of Heav'n, and things therein
> Each to other like, more than on Earth is thought?"
> (5.574–6)

In any case, Galileo's successful employment of geometry as if it were a universal yardstick lent significant support to a vision of a single homogeneous Cosmos created by a sole geometer God. Little wonder, against such a backdrop, that in *Paradise Lost*, Milton should imagine Raphael measuring "things in heaven by things on earth" or God himself employing his eternal draftsman's tools – his "golden compasses" – to shape and "circumscribe / This universe" (6.893; 7.225–7). For as Kepler affirmed in response to *Sidereus Nuncius* (although undoubtedly he had thought so already): "geometry . . . shines in the mind of God."[10]

Galileo realized that Earth shines too. His observations of the play of light upon the Moon's surface revealed not only the geometrical and earthlike nature of that surface but also something of the reciprocal relationship between the Moon and Earth as astronomical companions. The importance of this finding can hardly be overstated, for an Earth previously thought to be qualitatively set apart – virtually quarantined within the "sublunary sphere" – indeed, considered to be no astronomical body at all. One recalls the ambivalence even of an early Copernican such as Digges, who did consider Earth an astronomical body and yet repeatedly referred to it as a "darcke starre." Galileo, by contrast, examining the Moon through his telescope, realized that something was subtly illuminating its dark side and that the illumination had to be created by sunlight reflected by Earth – just as our moonlight is actually sunlight reflected by the Moon.

This "earthshine" is an interesting enough phenomenon on its own, but its cosmological implications are stunning. For it entails a Cosmos

---

[9] Rheticus's letter to King Ferdinand (Krakow, 1557), in Karl Heinz Burmeister, *Georg Joachim Rhetikus, 1514–1574: Eine Bio-Bibliographie*, 3 vols. (Wiesbaden: Guido Pressler, 1967–68), 3:139.

[10] *Kepler's Conversation With Galileo's Sidereal Messenger*, trans. Edward Rosen (New York and London: Johnson Reprint Corporation, 1965), p. 43.

in which light travels a two-way street. Poetically, Galileo describes the phenomenon as constituting a kind of friendly commerce that also has immense consequences for humanity's conception of Earth's place and role in the Universe at large:

> The Earth, with fair and grateful exchange, pays back to the Moon an illumination like that which it receives from the Moon nearly the whole time during the darkest gloom of night. ... The benefit of [the Moon's] light to the Earth is balanced and repaid by the benefit of the light of the Earth to her. For while the Moon approaches the Sun about the time of the new Moon, she has in front of her the entire surface of that hemisphere of the Earth which is exposed to the Sun and vividly illumined with his beams, and so receives light reflected from the Earth. Because of this reflection, the hemisphere of the Moon nearer to us, though deprived of sunlight, appears of considerable brightness. ... This is the law observed between these two orbs: Whenever the Earth is most brightly enlightened by the Moon, that is when the Moon is least enlightened by the Earth, and vice versa.
>
> That is all I need say for now on this subject, which I will consider more fully in my *System of the Universe*, where many arguments and experimental proofs will be provided to demonstrate a very strong reflection of the Sun's light from the Earth – this for the benefit of those who assert, principally on the grounds that it has neither motion nor light, that the Earth must be excluded from the dance of the stars. For I will prove that the Earth does have motion, that it surpasses the Moon in brightness, and that it is not the sump where the Universe's filth and ephemera collect [*non autem sordium, mundanarumque fecum sentinam*]. (fol. 15^r–16^r)

Contrary to the persistent modernist myth that ancient and medieval geocentrism placed Earth and humankind in a position of supreme importance in the universe, Galileo's comment indicates that the center – as a place where heavy, gross things settle – was seen as a place of disrepute and that therefore Copernicanism literally entailed Earth's *exaltation*. There is much evidence in the writings of Galileo, Kepler, and other Copernicans (whom we shall revisit) that their version of heliocentrism in fact reconstrued Earth and the place of humankind as something dynamic and privileged rather than central and therefore low and ignoble – decidedly not a sump or *sentina*, the term Galileo uses to evoke the place in a ship below the lowest decks where bilge water collects. For him, Earth belongs not there but in the dance of the stars.[11]

[11] Noel Swerdlow asserts: "None of Galileo's discoveries provoked more hostility and more preposterous attempts at refutation than the rough surface of the Moon and the explanation of the secondary light, and with good reason because for none were the stakes as high"; *The Cambridge Companion to Galileo*, ed. Peter Machamer (Cambridge: Cambridge University Press, 1998), pp. 250–1.

In this respect, Milton – despite the Ptolemaism frequently attributed to him[12] – is robustly Copernican. In his series of astronomical what-ifs in Book 8 of *Paradise Lost*, Raphael clearly posits Earth's stellar character:

> "What if that light
> Sent from her [the Earth] through the wide transpicuous air,
> To the terrestrial moon be as a star
> Enlight'ning her [the Moon] by day, as she by night
> This Earth? Reciprocal . . ."
>
> (8.140–4)

Even beyond Raphael's hypotheticals, it is apparent in the universe of *Paradise Lost* that Earth is indeed a star and a participant in the starry dance. At the last stage of his journey to Earth, Satan must stop on the Sun to ask directions, for Earth *qua* planet is not astronomically unique; it is not obvious to a space-traveling observer which of the stars is humankind's habitation or even if these creatures are confined to a single planet. Satan asks:

> "In which of all these shining orbs hath man
> His fixèd seat, or fixèd seat hath none,
> But all these shining orbs his choice to dwell[?]"
>
> (3.668–70)

Even if some might doubt Satan's interpretation of his surroundings, Uriel, from his viewpoint on the Sun, offers an authoritative response that is thoroughly in keeping with Galileo's description of the starry commerce-in-reflected-sunlight between Earth and Moon:

> "Look downward on that globe whose hither side
> With light from hence, though but reflected, shines;
> That place is Earth the seat of Man, that light
> His day, which else as th' other hemisphere
> Night would invade, but there the neighboring moon
> (So call that opposite fair star) her aide
> Timely interposes, and her monthly round
> Still ending, still renewing, through mid-heav'n;
> With borrowed light her countenance triform
> Hence fills and empties to enlighten th' Earth,
> And in her pale dominion checks the night."
>
> (3.722–32)

---

[12] See, typically, *The Riverside Milton*, ed. Roy Flannagan (Boston: Houghton Mifflin, 1998), p. 325: Milton "makes the universe of *Paradise Lost* that of Galileo's Ptolemaic forebears, and Milton's cosmology is generally geocentric." Or *Paradise Lost*, ed. Kerrigan et al., p. xviii: "[I]n point of fact the design of the poem's universe is Ptolemaic."

Moving outward from Earth and the Moon, the twin wandering stars just discussed, Galileo in *Sidereus Nuncius* offers an account of what he saw when he examined the fixed stars through his telescope. At a stroke, his account lays the foundation for stellar astronomy and takes the first steps toward answering some of its central questions – in particular, the number of stars in the heavens and the nature of the Milky Way. For present purposes, his findings can be summarized relatively briefly.

Stellar magnitude, although often used loosely as a unit of apparent star size, is a measure of brightness: The brighter the star, the smaller is its assigned magnitude. Thus, first magnitude is brightest – down to sixth magnitude, which is the dimmest degree of brightness visible to the naked eye. Using a telescope, Galileo is able to extend this scale further downward, but first, he beautifully describes (and attempts to explain) a technical anomaly:

> The stars, fixed as well as erratic [i.e., the planets], when seen through a telescope, do not appear enlarged in the same proportion as are other objects, including the Moon. On the contrary, the stars appear much less magnified. Accordingly, if for example a telescope magnifies other objects a hundred times, you will find it magnifies the stars scarcely four or five times. But the reason for this is that, when stars are viewed with natural sight they do not, as regards their size, present themselves to us so to speak naked and unadorned but radiant with a certain splendor and fringed with a sparkling aura, especially as night wears on. Thus they seem much larger than they would if stripped of these inessential fringes, for apparent size within one's field of vision is determined not by the actual body of a star but by the luster with which it is circumfused. (fol. 16^r)

Among other things, the telescope's unreliability when it comes to measuring stars' true proportions underscores the need to interpret, not simply to "accept," what one sees. The anomaly here outlined would indeed pose a significant impediment to the acceptance of the new cosmology of which Galileo was becoming the foremost proponent.

With the aid of a telescope, however, Galileo was able to settle one question beyond any doubt: The stars are innumerable. From the time of ancient Babylon to early seventeenth-century Europe, there had been various estimates regarding the number of the stars, which were generally held to be uncountable (for practical reasons) but in reality finite in number – perhaps two or three thousand.[13] Of course, Digges, Bruno,

[13] As late as 1640, John Wilkins suggests the remarkably low number of 1,022 stars. See Wilkins, *Discourse Concerning a New Planet, Tending to Prove, That 'Tis Probable Our Earth Is One of the Planets* (London, 1640), p. 56.

and various atomists believed them to be infinite, but until the telescope, there was absolutely no empirical support for any such claim. As he composes *Sidereus Nuncius*, Galileo knows he is changing all that – and seeks to mitigate the shock by appealing to the (not yet actualized) firsthand testimony of his readers:

> But below stars of the sixth magnitude you will see through the telescope a host of other stars that escape natural sight – so many that it is almost unbelievable – more than six other degrees of magnitude, and the largest of them, which we can call seventh magnitude stars, or first magnitude invisible stars, appearing through the telescope larger and brighter than second magnitude stars seen with the naked eye.[14]

With a mixture of awe and triumph, Galileo continues to tell his audience what they will see when they also use a telescope – pointing it at the Milky Way – and what consequences their discovery will have for "disputes that have tormented philosophers for so many centuries": "The galaxy is nothing else but a mass of innumerable stars planted together in clusters. Point your telescope in any direction within the galaxy and at once a great mass of stars comes into view. Of these, many are fairly large and robustly conspicuous, but the number of small ones is utterly unfathomable."[15]

In *Paradise Lost*, Milton clearly accepted Galileo's conclusion, depicting Satan traveling through space, making "his oblique way / Amongst innumerable stars" (3.564–5). On the fourth day of creation, recounts Raphael, the Creator "sowed with stars the heaven thick as a field" (7.358). Moreover, when describing the (empyreal) heavenly road whereby the Son returns after his acts of creation, the angel does so by means of a simile rooted in this Cosmos: The Son traveled

> "A broad and ample road, whose dust is gold
> And pavement stars, as stars to thee appear,
> Seen in the galaxy, that Milky Way
> Which nightly as a circling zone thou seest
> Powdered with stars."
>
> (7. 577–81)

Raphael not only deftly unfolds the etymology of "galaxy" ("that Milky Way") but also speaks as if Adam can actually *see* that celestial phenomenon according to its articulated, starry nature. Whether Adam's sharp

---

[14] Unnumbered fol.[1]ʳ following fol. 16ᵛ.

[15] Unnumbered fol.[2]ʳ. Analogous to these observations of the Milky Way was Galileo's realization that "the stars which absolutely all astronomers until now have called *nebulous* are swarms of small stars astonishingly packed together" (unnumbered fol.[2]ᵛ).

prelapsarian eyes indeed perceive what the rest of humanity waited until 1609 to see or whether Raphael here is gently informing Adam concerning the stellar nature of the phenomenon (the "circling zone") is open to interpretation.

In any case, the picture of the galaxy conveyed by *Sidereus Nuncius* offered, in place of a semiopaque plane, a pattern of points and spaces or grains and voids. What had long seemed a coherent image was now understood to be, as it were, pixelated. The universe thus appeared through Galileo's telescope more and more as an array of discrete bits – as suggested by Donne's complaint that the new science left the world "all in pieces, all coherence gone"[16] – bits that shorn of their beams, deprived of their connective tissue, bereft of their crystalline spheres would urgently require a new force to hold them all together. It is perhaps little wonder that before a new physical principle (universal gravitation) was able to reestablish the physical world's coherence, Milton should be thinking about *creatio ex deo* and positing "one first matter" (5.472) that could lend unity to an apparently ever more atomistic and fragmented picture of the Universe.

Such centrifugal tendencies were reinforced by what *Sidereus Nuncius* offered as the greatest of Galileo's telescopic discoveries: the moons of Jupiter. Galileo considered this announcement more important than all the rest, and from a cosmological and Copernican viewpoint, it may well have been. In an unpublished manuscript known as the *Commentariolus*, circulated early in the sixteenth century, Copernicus had presented seven axioms outlining the cosmology he would later expound on in *De Revolutionibus*. The first axiom asserted that "there is no one center of all the celestial circles or spheres."[17] In observing the Jovian moons, Galileo knew he now had ocular support for that axiom: "We actually see four satellites circling about Jupiter, like the Moon about the Earth" (fol. 28^r).

Thus emerged a particular pattern in the history of astronomy. It had been assumed, in keeping with Aristotle's physics, that there was one center in the universe, but Galileo's observations now demonstrated that there were at least two. Furthermore, until his time, there was thought to be one moon – *the* Moon – but with Galileo's discovery of the Jovian satellites, humans could henceforth speak of *moons*. Other astronomical nouns similarly took on plural forms. Late in the sixteenth century, the

---

[16] *An Anatomy of the World: The First Anniversary*, line 213; John Donne, *The Complete English Poems*, ed. A. J. Smith (Harmondsworth: Penguin, 1971), p. 276.
[17] See Danielson, *The First Copernican*, pp. 60–4.

anti-Aristotelian Giordano Bruno extrapolated (contrary to Copernicus and not on observational grounds) an infinite Universe containing "innumerable suns, and likewise an infinite number of earths circling about those suns."[18] Earth and Sun thus acquired plurals too. Nor would that process cease. Late in the eighteenth century, "galaxy" likewise began to acquire a plural form, based on William Herschel's observations of the nebulae. And since the late twentieth century, in the wake of Big Bang cosmology, with its realization that the observable universe is not infinite in space or time, astronomers have also started theorizing about other *universes* – all encompassed within the *Multiverse*.

Milton participated in such "pluralization" of astronomical categories very much in the spirit of *Sidereus Nuncius*. Most straightforwardly, Raphael predicts that in the future, Adam may descry "other suns perhaps / With their attendant moons" (8.148–9). But as we shall see later, perhaps the most intriguing example of Milton's participation in the pattern is his use of the plural of *world*, which in the seventeenth century could mean either *Earth* or *Universe* – a Cosmos encompassing what in biblical language is called collectively "heavens and earth." Milton employs both of these distinct meanings in *Paradise Lost*, and in his hands, both appear in ways that are cosmologically adventuresome.

But to return to Galileo, with his observations of Jupiter's moons, he knew he was actually answering one of the toughest questions a Copernican had to answer: Given all previous assumptions about the uniformity of celestial motions, how can you assert that the Moon is circling Earth while Earth in turn circles the Sun? To observe the moons of Jupiter was to observe precisely this process in action. For one could now see that there are in this Universe (in the words of Copernicus) "numerous centers."[19] In short, Galileo had demonstrated the existence of a true epicycle – one that was no mere "device" contrived to save the appearances but rather itself an astronomical appearance – an orbit within an orbit. Thus, "no one can doubt that [the Medicean stars] make their revolutions about [Jupiter] while at the same time together completing twelve-year orbits about the center of the Universe" (fol. 28^r).

Back in 1541, when Copernicus was pondering the release of his heliocentric model – of which Galileo would become a principal proponent in the next century – he received a letter from Andreas Osiander, the Nuremberg

---

[18] Giordano Bruno, *De l'infinito universo et Mondi, 1584; reprinted in Le opere italiane di Giordano Bruno* (Göttingen, 1888). Quoted from *BOTC*, ed. Danielson, p. 144.

[19] *De Revolutionibus*, 1.9 (*Pluribus ergo existentibus centris . . .*); *BOTC*, ed. Danielson, p. 115.

theologian now notorious for having inserted his "Ad Lectorem" at the beginning of *De Revolutionibus* when it was published in 1543. In his 1541 letter to Copernicus, Osiander was already urging the astronomer to present his theory merely as a useful hypothesis: "I have always felt about hypotheses that they are not articles of faith but the basis of computation. Thus, even if they are false, it does not matter, provided that they reproduce exactly the phenomena of the motions. . . . It would therefore appear to be desirable for you to touch upon this matter somewhat in an introduction. For in this way you would mollify the peripatetics and theologians, whose opposition you fear."[20]

Because Copernicus considered his proposal that Earth revolves around the Sun to be more than just a hypothesis, he had been anxious about the reactions of two sorts of people: theologians (because some passages of Scripture, read literally, seemed to imply that the Sun moves and Earth stands still) and "peripatetics" – those Aristotelian philosophers who dominated the study of physics in the universities. Osiander, intending to be helpful, suggested a way of avoiding the difficulty and mollifying these critics – actually, from a purely diplomatic (rather than scientific) viewpoint, not a ridiculous suggestion. As he wrote to Rheticus, a preface offering Copernicus's work merely as a hypothesis rather than a physical proposal could in effect buy time for heliocentrism. Potential opponents would then "be diverted from stern defense and attracted by the charm of the inquiry; first their antagonism will disappear, then they will seek the truth in vain by their own devices, and go over to the opinion of the author."[21]

Rheticus, as defender and promoter of his teacher's work, took seriously both sorts of opposition mentioned by Osiander, although objections based on passages of Scripture were generally easier to dispel than were the philosophical kind. Rheticus composed his own small tract to demonstrate the absence of conflict between heliocentrism and the Bible, proposing, on the authority of St. Augustine, that any scientific obscurity should be tackled "by means of enquiry, not assertion" (*non affirmando, sed quaerendo*). He went on to make a distinction that is still part of the faith-science dialogue: In the Bible, the Holy Spirit's intention is not to teach science but to impart spiritual truths "necessary for our salvation." Moreover, whatever descriptions of nature do appear in the Bible are "accommodated to the popular

[20] Rosen, *Copernicus and the Scientific Revolution*, p. 193.
[21] Rosen, *Copernicus and the Scientific Revolution*, p. 194.

understanding."[22] This approach to harmonizing science and Scripture was relatively common in the sixteenth and seventeenth centuries. John Calvin, employing a similar hermeneutic in his *Commentary on Genesis* (1554), endorsed astronomers' proofs that (for example) Saturn is larger than the Moon – even though Genesis identifies the Sun and the Moon as being the "two great luminaries." Similarly, early in the seventeenth century, Kepler would defend heliocentrism by distinguishing between scientific and popular discourse. The Holy Scriptures "speak with humans in the human manner."[23] However, Rheticus never published his work on the compatibility of the Bible and Copernicanism, although it did appear anonymously in the Netherlands more than a century after its composition and was not discovered or identified as Rheticus's work until the 1980s.[24] Copernicus's best friend, Tiedemann Giese, who read it in manuscript, wanted it to be included in an improved second edition of *De Revolutionibus*[25] – but it was not. As for Copernicus himself, as indicated in his preface to Pope Paul III, what he offered possible opponents who raised Bible-based objections was not a counterargument but the back of his hand. He called them ignorant, "idle talkers" who distort and twist Scripture. He had "only contempt for their audacity."

Galileo, living in post-Council of Trent Italy and facing much more vigorous opposition than Copernicus ever had to worry about, in effect borrowed pages from the treatises of Rheticus and Copernicus: He attempted a rational, learned response to his critics while also exhibiting considerable contempt for those who would put him to the trouble. Galileo's principal statement regarding Copernican cosmology and its alleged conflict with Scripture is his *Letter to the Grand Duchess Christina*, written in 1615 but not published until 1636, after his 1633 appearance before the Inquisition. In this *Letter*, Galileo (like Rheticus) calls upon the authority of St. Augustine, who wrote that "we ought not to believe anything inadvisedly on a dubious point, lest in favor to our error we

---

[22] Rheticus, *De motu terrae*, pp. 1, 12, 40. This tract was published as an appendix to David Gorlaeus, *Idea Physicae* (Utrecht, 1651). The original text and literal English translation appear in Reijer Hooykaas, *G. J. Rheticus' Treatise on Holy Scripture and the Motion of the Earth* (Amsterdam: North-Holland Publishing, 1984). For further discussion, see Howell, *God's Two Books*, pp. 255–67. See also Noel Swerdlow's review of Hooykaas's edition in *Journal for the History of Astronomy* 17 (1986): 133–6.

[23] Calvin's and Kepler's comments are excerpted in *BOTC*, ed. Danielson, Chapter 20. Calvin's hermeneutic was transposed directly into the margins of the Geneva Bible (1560), which glosses the "two great lightes" of Gen. 1:16 thus: "To wit, the sunne and the moone; and here he speaketh as man judgeth by his eye: for els the moone is lesse then the planete Saturnus."

[24] For the account of Hooykaas's discovery, see Hooykaas, *Rheticus' Treatise*, pp. 17–19.

[25] Giese to Rheticus, 26 July 1543; in Rosen, *Copernicus and the Scientific Revolution*, p. 167.

conceive a prejudice against something that truth hereafter may reveal to be not contrary in any way to the sacred books of either the Old or the New Testament." As for Copernicus, says Galileo, "he did not ignore the Bible, but he knew very well that if his doctrine were proved, then it could not contradict the Scriptures when they were rightly understood." While clearly holding his opponents in less than high esteem ("they would have us altogether abandon reason and the evidence of our senses"), Galileo enunciates a sober position based on well-attested logical and hermeneutical principles.[26]

Like Rheticus, Calvin, and others, Galileo insists that not every word in the Bible should be taken literally, for the writers of Scripture accommodate their expressions "to the capacities of the common people." So do most other writers, Galileo points out – even great astronomers. For "Copernicus himself ... after he had first demonstrated that the motions which appear to us to belong to the sun or to the firmament are really not there but in the earth, he went on calling them motions of the sun and of the heavens when he later constructed his tables to apply them to use. He thus speaks of 'sunrise' and 'sunset,' of the 'rising and setting' of the stars, ... and so on." In any case, the Bible is not the right place to look for the full array of astronomical or physical truth. For that, "we ought to begin not from the authority of scriptural passages, but from sense-experiences and necessary demonstrations; for the holy Bible and the phenomena of nature proceed alike from the divine Word, the former as the dictate of the Holy Ghost and the latter as the observant executrix of God's commands."[27]

Galileo thus attempts to hold Scripture and nature at a safe distance from each other even while carefully insisting on their common authorship. The latter is a fundamental assumption of the traditional and potentially dynamic "two books" theme that we met with at the beginning of Chapter 1, in which Milton participates: "heav'n / Is as the book of God before thee set, / Wherein to read his wondrous works" (*PL*, 8.66–7). In Galileo's words, "the glory and greatness of Almighty God are marvelously discerned in all his works and divinely read in the open book of heaven." Moreover, the two books' common divine authorship guarantees their harmony with each other, presuming each is interpreted correctly. For, as Galileo puts it, "two truths cannot contradict one another."

---

[26] *Discoveries and Opinions of Galileo*, trans. Stillman Drake (New York: Doubleday, 1957), pp. 175–6, 179–80.
[27] *Discoveries and Opinions of Galileo*, pp. 181, 201–2, 182.

As Milton writes in *Areopagitica*: "To be still searching what we know not by what we know, still closing up truth to truth as we find it (for all her body is homogeneal and proportional), this is the golden rule in theology as well as in arithmetic."[28] This axiom concerning the homogeneal nature of truth forms a robust basis for pursuing what we now call scientific truth and for adjudicating possible apparent conflicts with Scripture. Citing Augustine, Galileo declares "that we must be no less careful and observant in reconciling a passage of the Bible with any demonstrated physical proposition than with some other biblical passage which might appear contrary to the first."[29]

In so asserting, Galileo is essentially extending a hermeneutical principle often designated "the analogy of Scripture" – much loved of such reformers as Luther and Calvin. As the Westminster Confession would express it: "The infallible rule of interpretation of scripture is the scripture itself; and therefore, when there is a question about the true and full sense of any scripture, it must be searched and known by other places that speak more clearly."[30] Milton endorses the principle a number of times in *De Doctrina Christiana*, underlining in one instance the standard premise that "clear things are not illuminated by obscure things, but obscure by clear."[31] The same principle theoretically ought to apply across God's two books – the book of his words and the book of his works – and also ought to guarantee the soundness of Galileo's claim that "a proposition cannot be both true and heretical." In practice, however, in both books there can be manifold degrees of clarity and obscurity – just as there can be different groups of people wielding authority in one domain or the other. As Galileo famously writes in *The Assayer* (1623): "Philosophy is written in this grand book, the universe, which stands continually open to our gaze. But the book cannot be understood unless one first learns to comprehend the language and read the letters in which it is composed. It is written in the language of mathematics, and its characters are triangles, circles, and other geometric figures without which it is humanly impossible to understand a single word of it."[32]

From a great distance, Galileo's words might well seem coherent and persuasive. Spoken in the Counter-Reformational political and ecclesiastical climate of early seventeenth-century Italy, however, they inevitably

---

[28] *Complete Prose Works of John Milton*, ed. Wolfe et al., 2:551.
[29] *Discoveries and Opinions of Galileo*, pp. 196, 186, 198.   [30] Westminster Confession I.9.
[31] Milton, *DDC*, pp. 86/87: *non enim clara obscuris, sed obscura claris illustrantur.*
[32] *Discoveries and Opinions of Galileo*, pp. 237–8.

resonated a challenge. For given his claims about "the mathematical language," no one could fail to see that Galileo thought himself, not the prelates, to be the fit interpreter of the book of God's works. As Ernan McMullin has commented, "here were the Copernicans ... dangerously close to the camp of the Reformers for whom the individual's right to interpret Scripture according to his or her own lights was paramount."[33] In this respect, Galileo may well have appeared frighteningly like a Protestant hermeneut: prepared and eager to read "the book" for himself. If so, Milton's political take on Galileo's plight, as expressed in *Areopagitica*, was admirably close to the mark.

Politics aside, however, many readers of *Paradise Lost* surely ask themselves, especially given the poem's repeated references to Galileo amid numerous other engagements with astronomy, why Milton (or Raphael in Book 8) is not more forthright in endorsing Copernicanism. Fabio Toscano may typify such readers in averring that "the poet addresses the Copernican issue without openly defending the heliocentric theory confirmed by Galileo's discoveries." Toscano goes on to ask: "Why, despite his tributes to Galileo, does the poet not explicitly pronounce himself in favour of the heliocentric theory?"[34] My response to Toscano's query – a claim to be fleshed out in subsequent chapters – is that Galileo's discoveries did *not* confirm the heliocentric theory despite how impressive and crucial they were astronomically and cosmologically.[35] But I wish to continue pointing out how richly Milton, short of an open proclamation of the heliocentric system, infuses his epic with powerful insights either implied or spun off by the achievements of Copernicus, Galileo, and other proponents of the new astronomy. In making these claims, moreover, I am not merely throwing up my hands and declaring, "Ah, well, Milton was a poet, not a scientist" (although that is true). For in withholding a full systematic endorsement of Copernicanism, Milton would in his own day have been in good company even among scientists.

As mentioned in the preface, perhaps the clearest instance of a seventeenth-century scientist who stopped short (much farther short than Milton) of endorsing Copernicanism is Francis Bacon. Bacon's main writings on astronomy – *Descriptio Orbis Intellectualis* and *Thema Coeli*

---

[33] *Cambridge Companion to Galileo*, p. 273.

[34] Fabio Toscano, "The Tuscan Artist: Images of Galileo in Milton's works," *Journal of Science Communication* 3.3 (Sept. 2004): 1–7 (pp. 1, 4).

[35] As Swerdlow puts it: "Galileo's celestial discoveries strengthened the case for Copernicanism but they fell short of being compelling"; *Cambridge Companion to Galileo*, p. 224.

(essentially, two parts of a single, apparently incomplete work) – were published posthumously in 1653. They were written, however, within a year or two of the publication of *Sidereus Nuncius*, which Bacon read, and the two names cited most often in these writings are those of Gilbert and Galileo.

Bacon repeatedly emphasizes a distinction already encountered in Digges, who attacked those who interpret Copernicus as delivering "the grounds of the Earthes mobility onely as Mathematicall principles, fayned and not as Philosophicall truly averred." Bacon, thirty-six years after Digges published those words, was deeply dissatisfied with everything that so far had presented itself as a "History of Celestial Bodies simple." For him, the purely hypothetical or mathematical theories are not enough, "for it is not merely calculations or predictions that I aim at, but philosophy" – "philosophy" here again implying something "actually and really true." Part of Bacon's frustration arises from the fact (he says) that "it is easy to see, that both they who think the earth revolves, and they who hold the *primum mobile* and the old construction, are about equally and indifferently supported by the phenomena." The same applies, he adds, to the recent system that makes "the sun the centre of the *secundum mobile*, as the earth of the *primum mobile*." Accordingly, if one wishes to choose among cosmological options offered by Ptolemy, Copernicus, and Tycho ("the author of the new construction" just referred to), then an appeal to the phenomena alone cannot decide the question.[36]

Bacon by no means diminishes Galileo's recently announced telescopic discoveries. He congratulates "both the industry of mechanics, and the zeal and energy of certain learned men, that now of late by the help of optical instruments, as by skiffs and barks, they have opened a new commerce with the phenomena of the heavens; an undertaking which I regard as being both in the end and in the endeavour a thing noble and worthy of the human race."[37] It is noteworthy, especially in retrospect, that Bacon's simile fleetingly envisages the "optical instruments" as admirable means of trade with and transportation to the extraterrestrial domain. But they do not get him to the destination he seeks, which is a *philosophy* in the sense of something with veracity, coherence, and completeness. For Bacon, "the first question therefore is, *whether there be a system?*" His philosophical

---

[36] *Works of Francis Bacon*, 10:413–16 (7:294–5, 297). I quote from the English translation appearing in vol. 10 but provide parenthetical references to the Latin original in vol. 7.
[37] *Works of Francis Bacon*, 10:416 (7:297).

opponents in this quest are principally the atomists: "Democritus and Epicurus boasted that their founders had overthrown the walls of the world." However, some of the ancients whom Copernicus and Galileo claimed as ancestors, "who believed that the earth was a planet and moveable, and as it were one of the stars," are also seen as destroyers of "system."[38] What most bothers Bacon, it seems, is the multicentrism of the atomists, of Copernicus, and of Tycho because for Bacon, the denial of a single center also threatens a denial of system.

Bacon therefore displays little patience with Copernicus. Although he has read *Sidereus Nuncius*, he clearly does not feel that Galileo's observations have (to echo Toscano) "confirmed" heliocentrism at all – certainly not as a philosophy or a system:

> In the system of Copernicus there are found many and great inconveniences; for both the loading of the earth with a triple motion is very incommodious, and the separation of the sun from the company of the planets ... is likewise a difficulty, and ... making the moon revolve about the earth in an epicycle ... are the speculations of one who cares not what fictions he introduces into nature, provided his calculations answer. But if it be granted that the earth moves, it would seem more natural to suppose that there is no system at all.[39]

Bacon is less harsh with Gilbert than with Copernicus because the *rotation* only of Earth or of individual stars would not entail a loss of the kind of "systematic" order Bacon holds up as an ideal. Accordingly, "as ... suggested by Gilbert, [the stars] may revolve each round its own centre in its own place, without any motion of the centre, as the earth itself does; if only you separate that diurnal motion of the earth from those two suppositious motions which Copernicus superadded."[40] Bacon is provisionally willing, with reference to Tycho and Galileo, to ponder "whether there be many different centres in the system, and as it were many dances."[41] In the end, however, he is at a loss to see how any available system is truly a system in the philosophical sense, so his default position includes a stationary Earth "(for that I now think the truer opinion)" – one that does not so much as rotate.[42]

---

[38] *Works of Francis Bacon*, 10:419–20 (7:299–300).   [39] *Works of Francis Bacon*, 10:422–3 (7:303–4).
[40] *Works of Francis Bacon*, 10:424 (7:306–7).
[41] *Works of Francis Bacon*, 10:431 (7:313: *utrum sint plura et diversa centra in systemate, et plures tanquam choreae*).
[42] *Works of Francis Bacon*, 10:469, 478 (7:350, 358). A geostatic position, it should be remembered, is in principle consistent with the Ptolemaic and the Tychonic systems.

Despite Bacon's falling back on a provisionally geostatic cosmology, his recognition that the Tychonic and Copernican systems entail "many dances" is intriguing against the backdrop of the long history of the term *system*. Of course, a system can be either "first order" – a reality or thing itself, such as the Universe (or an organized entity within the Universe) – or "second order," naming or representing or modeling the first-order thing. It is in the latter sense that one speaks of the Ptolemaic, Copernican, and Tychonic systems. What Bacon and probably most other natural philosophers desire is a system in this second sense: a model – but one that maps accurately and comprehensively onto the Universe or other real entity. Part of the satire directed against astronomers arises when they appear to forget that they are "making worlds" only in the second-order sense. Among examples of such satire are Melanchthon's complaint about "that Polish astronomer who moves the Earth and immobilizes the Sun" (Chapter 1, ref. 6), Burton's humorous account of "our later Mathematitians" who "tosse the Earth up and down like a ball" (epigraph to Chapter 3), and Raphael's reference in *Paradise Lost* to future astronomers who will "come to model heav'n" and attempt to "wield / The mighty frame" (8.79–80). But again, astronomers' and in particular cosmologists' efforts are quite properly directed toward making a model – a second-order system – that is accurate, comprehensive, and consistent.

Moreover, although Bacon seems to drop the idea almost as soon as he mentions it, the image of a dance can complement a system's desired accuracy, comprehensiveness, and consistency by enabling us to imagine it also as something dynamic. The parallel artistic metaphor historically associated with the idea of a system is musical. Ptolemy himself, in the second century, employed *system* in exactly this way when he wrote about harmony: "The name '*systēma*', unqualified, is given to a magnitude put together out of concords, just as a concord is a magnitude put together out of melodics, and a *systēma* is, as it were, a concord of concords."[43] The musical analogy (and it may be more than an analogy) shares with the metaphor of the dance a recognition that the whole may have components that are dynamically (to borrow a term coined by Milton) *intervolved*. And as Michel-Pierre Lerner has shown in his scholarly history of the concept of "world system," it was the

[43] Ptolemy, *Harmonics*, Book 2, Chapter 4; in *Greek Musical Writings*, 2 vols., ed. Andrew Barker (Cambridge: Cambridge University Press, 1984), 2:323.

early Copernicans who appropriated and developed it for their new astronomy and cosmology.[44]

The idea flows naturally enough from the notion that creation is God's composition (*systasis*). And in the first published announcement of Copernicanism, the *Narratio Prima* (1540), Rheticus complains that heretofore astronomers have "fashioned their theories and devices for correcting the motion of the heavenly bodies with too little regard for the rule which reminds us that the order and motions of the heavenly spheres agree in an absolute system." It would be much better, he says, "to imitate the musicians who, when one string has either tightened or loosened, with great care and skill regulate and adjust the tones of all the other strings, until all together produce the desired harmony."[45] Even though Copernicus himself does not use the term *system* in *De Revolutionibus*, Rheticus's advance notice of his teacher's heliocentric model proclaims that

> if anyone desires to look either to the principal end of astronomy and the order and harmony of the system of the spheres or to ease and elegance and a complete explanation of the causes of the phenomena, [then] by the assumption of no other hypotheses will he demonstrate the apparent motions of the remaining planets [i.e., those besides Earth] more neatly and correctly. For all these phenomena appear to be linked most nobly together, as by a golden chain.[46]

In this way, the concept of a system, including its potentially dynamic musical and choreographical connotations, became part of the cosmological revolution. Tycho Brahe announced his model under the heading *Nova Mundani Systematis Hypotyposis* (Figure 3.4, p. 73). Kepler famously expounded his *Harmony of the World* (*Harmonices Mundi*, 1619). And Galileo, as we have seen, gestured toward Copernicanism's inclusion of Earth in "the dance of the stars."

Galileo's comment about this dance occurs in a passage in which he promises to expand on the same ideas in his *System of the Universe*. That work did not in fact appear in quite the form Galileo may have led his readers to expect in 1610 nor did it appear soon. But more than two decades later, he did publish his system in the form of a conversation: *Dialogue Concerning the Two Chief World Systems*

---

[44] Michel-Pierre Lerner, "The Origin and Meaning of 'World System,'" *Journal for the History of Astronomy* 36 (2005): 407–41 (pp. 410–13).

[45] Rheticus, *Narratio prima; in Three Copernican Treatises*, trans. Edward Rosen, 3rd edition (New York: Octagon Books, 1971), p. 138.

[46] *Three Copernican Treatises*, pp. 164–5.

(*Dialogo Sopra i Due Massimi Sistemi del Mondo*, 1632), to which we shall return in Chapter 5.

As for Milton, he seems to avoid the word and the concept of *system* altogether – with one exception: Early in the prefatory epistle to the *De Doctrina Christiana*, he says he has surveyed "Theologorum Systemata."[47] In *Paradise Lost*, the word appears not at all. Perhaps one can only speculate why it does not, especially given the astronomical dialogue that unfolds between Adam and Raphael in Book 8. But I would venture a suggestion: I suspect that, cosmologically, Milton was satisfied at the second-order level with a bricoleur's best effort – one that left plenty of open questions and honest loose ends – something that would never have satisfied Bacon. Milton certainly believed in, even if he did not systematically envisage, a first-order Cosmos composed not by astronomers or poets but by Copernicus's *Opifex*, the Creator God – the one who also beyond all others enjoys this Universe's dynamism and music. Thus, cosmologically speaking, in *Paradise Lost*, there is no system, but there are dances, with the ones taking place in this Cosmos resembling those performed in highest Heaven. For right after the primordial moment in the epic – the exaltation of the Son in Book 5 – as Raphael tells Adam in words that unify and compress the choreographical and musical themes just considered:

> "That day, as other solemn days, [the angels] spent
> In song and dance about the sacred hill,
> Mystical dance, which yonder starry sphere
> Of planets and of fixed in all her wheels
> Resembles nearest, mazes intricate,
> Eccentric, intervolved, yet regular
> Then most, when most irregular they seem,
> And in their motions harmony divine
> So smooths her charming tones, that God's own ear
> Listens delighted."
>
> (5.618–27)

---

[47] Milton, *DDC*, p. 4.

CHAPTER 5

Milton and Galileo revisited (2): "What if?"

I do not want to hide from the reader that not long ago a certain instrument was brought from Belgium. It has the form of a long tube in the bases of which are set two glasses, or rather lenses, by which objects far away from us appear very much closer. ... When the moon is a crescent or half full, it appears so remarkably fractured and rough that I cannot marvel enough that there is such unevenness in the lunar body. Consult the reliable little book by Galileo Galilei, printed in Venice in 1610 and called *Sidereal Messenger*, which describes various observations of the stars first made by him.

Far from the least important of the things seen with this instrument is that Venus receives its light from the sun as does the moon, so that sometimes it appears to be more like a crescent, sometimes less, according to its distance from the sun. ...

Since things are thus, astronomers ought to consider how the celestial orbs may be arranged in order to save these phenomena.

Christoph Clavius, 1611[1]

Whether the Earth move or stand still hath been a Problem, that since Copernicus revived it, hath much exercised the Wits of our best modern Astronomers and Philosophers, amongst which notwithstanding there hath not been any one who hath found out a certain manifestation either of the one or the other Doctrine. The more knowing and judicious have for many plausible reasons adhered to the Copernican Hypothesis: But the generality of others ... have rejected it as a most extravagant opinion. ... For such Persons I cannot suppose that they should understand the cogency of the Reasons here presented. ... Tis not here my business to instruct

---

[1] Christoph Clavius, Commentarium in Sphaeram Joannis de Sacro Bosco; in *Operum Mathematicorum* (Mainz, 1611), 3:75; this was among the last published comments on Sacrobosco (and Ptolemaic cosmology) made by Clavius before his death in 1612. Translation of this passage is from Lattis, *Between Copernicus and Galileo*, p. 198. The original of the final sentence reads: *Quae cum ita sint, videant Astronomi, quo pacto orbes coelestes constituendi sint, ut haec phaenomena possint salvari.*

them in the first principles of Astronomy, ... But rather to furnish
the Learned with an *experimentum crucis* to determine between the
Tychonick and Copernican Hypotheses.[2]

As indicated in Chapter 4, Milton nowhere explicitly offers a cosmological
"system" such as that longed for by Francis Bacon or proposed by either
Tycho or Galileo. Indeed, as hinted in Chapter 3, truly systematic cosmologies were the exception rather than the rule, even among genuine scientists. Looking back across the centuries, we may perceive Copernicus's
heliocentric model, for example, as a single system without noticing its
fusion of separate components, each of which aimed at solving – almost
independently – separate problems. Copernicanism asserted a diurnal
rotation of Earth upon its axis and an annual revolution of Earth about
the Sun. The former addressed the problem of why the greatest and most
distant sphere of all (that of the fixed stars) should seem to circle the
Universe once every twenty-four hours, whereas the latter explained
why the planets are ordered as they are and appear to move as irregularly
as they seem to.

However, there was nothing to stop cosmological bricoleurs (if not
systematizers) from opportunistically picking and choosing which
devices they preferred for solving particular problems. A rotating Earth
could be and was asserted by various cosmologists wishing to solve the
"whirling starry sphere" problem but unwilling to accept heliocentrism
as such with its implication of a planetary Earth. But as we have seen, the
avid Copernican Thomas Digges imported a Ptolemaic-looking sublunary sphere into his otherwise thoroughly heliocentric system. On the
other hand, Christoph Clavius, the late sixteenth century's foremost
defender of the Ptolemaic system, came to accept the corruptibility of
the heavens on evidence such as that of Tycho's Supernova of 1572 and
thus similarly engaged in a measure of cosmological bricolage. Still other
certifiably non-Copernican figures would abandon further components
of classic Ptolemaism, such as the solid celestial spheres. Robert
Bellarmine, for example, opted instead for a stoically inflected
"fluid heaven" account whereby the planets move "like birds in the air,
or fish in the sea."[3]

---

[2] Robert Hooke, *An Attempt to Prove the Motion of the Earth From Observations* (London, 1674), pp. 1–2.
[3] For more on the fluid-heaven theory, see Lattis, *Between Copernicus and Galileo*, pp. 94–102, and
Galileo Galilei and Christoph Scheiner, *On Sunspots*, ed. and trans. Eileen Reeves and Albert Van
Helden (Chicago: University of Chicago Press, 2010), pp. 44–5.

What all this implies for a reading of cosmological debate in the late sixteenth and seventeenth centuries is that, in general, we are not justified in jumping to conclusions about a particular figure's allegiance based merely on a single component of his astronomy or cosmology. Digges's repeated references to the sublunary sphere as a "Globe of Mortalitie" do not mean he was a Ptolemaist. Gilbert's belief in Earth's diurnal rotation does not imply he was a Copernican. Nor does any writer's expression of doubt or tentativeness about a particular cosmological assertion sufficiently warrant a claim that he was a dogmatic, backward-looking, or timid adherent of a default traditional model. Without denying the monumental strides made by science in the period from Copernicus to Newton, one may assert that the details of cosmological ferment in the period – critically examined – offer little support for a simplistic, Whiggish picture of "progress," its champions, and its opponents.

Nowhere is the tension between genuine cosmological progress and simplistic triumphalism more of a problem than in an assessment of Galileo and his influence. Such is his prestige as a hero or supposed "martyr" of science – and as a defender of Copernicanism – that even present-day debates pertaining to the history of science do well to acknowledge Galileo's continuing "presence" rhetorically as well as scientifically, including the persistence of some of the potentially misleading binaries he employed so effectively. A particular hazard in this connection, perhaps ironically, is that anyone offering a critique of Galileo may appear to fall afoul of one of those binaries, as if in league with the dogmatic or backward-looking Simplicio of the *Dialogo*. But it is a risk worth taking. For Galileo's work is so full of brilliant insights and yet so marked by a few seductive oversimplifications that the best appreciation of that work and influence will combine admiration and critical awareness – the more so in the case of the *Dialogo* itself, Galileo's most popular work, and also the one that led to his trial before the Roman Inquisition.

While there can be little doubt that Milton knew the *Dialogo*, his precise use of it and his absorption of its lessons are of course debatable, as is the question concerning what version or versions of it he knew. Nothing precludes his having read the Italian original (1632), although a translation soon appeared in Latin (1635). In addition, an English rendering of the *Dialogo* – translated by Thomas Salusbury – was published in 1661, so Milton in fact could also have *heard* the great work in his native tongue, although not, on account of his blindness, actually have seen it.[4]

---

[4] I will favor Salusbury for citation purposes, although I have consulted the Italian original – *Dialogo sopra i due massimi sistemi del mondo* (Florence, 1632) – as well as Galileo, *Dialogue*

Before we focus on the specifically cosmological content of this work, it is worth noticing some of the epistemological claims and assumptions Galileo's *Dialogo* puts on display – ones that might well have interested Milton. As already remarked, in *Paradise Lost*, at the beginning of the dialogue on astronomy, Raphael endorses the "two books" hermeneutic ("heav'n / Is as the book of God"), along with the concept of God as "the great Architect" (8.66–7, 72). At the portal of the *Dialogo*, the dedication to the Grand Duke of Tuscany likewise invokes the themes of the "gran libro della Natura," in which we read of the works "d'Artefice Onnipotente." In the *Dialogo*, Galileo also appears to employ a distinction acknowledged, if qualified, by Milton. Galileo's spokesperson, Salviati, discussing mathematical knowledge, asserts that our understanding "proceedeth by ratiocination [*con discorsi*], and passeth from conclusion to conclusion, whereas [God's] is done at one single thought or intuition" (Salusbury, p. 87; *Dialogo*, p. 97). Milton's Raphael distinguishes two forms of reason: "Discursive, or Intuitive"; "discourse / Is oftest yours [humans'], the latter most is ours [angels'], / Differing but in degree, of kind the same" (5.487–90).

The latter qualification, however ("Differing but in degree"), is consistent with Milton's aversion to the kind of sharp binary to which Galileo often seems attracted. One of the most notable of these polarities shows itself in Salviati's egregious (but still-commonplace) distinction between the humanities and the natural sciences as to their purchase on truth. In "Law, or other part of the Studies called *Humanity*," he says, "there is neither truth nor falshood." Instead, it is "the acutenesse of the wit, readinesse of answers, and the general practice of Writers" that make an offered "reason more probable and plausible." But "in Natural Sciences, the conclusions ... are true and necessary, and ... the judgment of men hath nothing to do [*né vi ha che far nulla l'arbitrio umano*]" (Salusbury, p. 40; *Dialogo*, pp. 45–6). I do not know that Milton offers any single, direct refutation of this exaggerated binary, although his sensitivity to how apparent opposites might differ "but in degree" – not to mention *Areopagitica*'s vision of Truth: dynamic, beleaguered, and embodied – gives one confidence that he might have done so.

Regarding another kind of relativity, however, Milton offers a picture strikingly consonant with one sketched by Galileo in the *Dialogo*: relativity not of truth but of size and distance. As indicated in Chapter 3,

Concerning the Two Chief World Systems, trans. Stillman Drake (1953; Berkeley: University of California Press, 1967).

Copernican heliocentrism entailed a many-orders-of-magnitude increase in the size of the sphere of the fixed stars over the already immeasurably great magnitude implied by geocentrism. Ptolemy had asserted that Earth is "as a point" relative to the sphere of the fixed stars, but Copernicanism implied that Earth's entire annual orbit – the *orbis magnus* – is as a point in comparison to the stellar sphere. Galileo, like Kepler but unlike Thomas Digges before him and many Copernicans after him, continued to assert the finitude, albeit immensity, of that sphere. But in response to objections against Copernicanism's allegedly extravagant expansion of stellar sizes and cosmic distances, Galileo offers a thought experiment summed up by a marginal gloss in the *Dialogo*: "The whole starry sphere beheld from a great distance might appear as small as one single star." Salviati's words fill in the details of the scene:

> Do not you call a fixed star very small, I mean even one of the most apparent, and not one of those which shun our sight; and do we not call them so in respect of the vast space circumfused? Now if the whole Starry Sphere were one entire lucid body; who is there, that doth not know that in an infinite space there might be assigned a distance so great, as that the said lucid Sphere might from thence shew as little, yea lesse than a fixed star, now appeareth beheld from the Earth? From thence therefore we should *then* judg that self same thing to be little, which *now* from hence we esteem to be immeasurably great.[5]

In *Paradise Lost*, Milton actualizes and dramatizes this theoretical scenario, populating it with two sets of characters and superimposing Salviati's "*then*" and "*now*." At the end of Book 2, Satan, having journeyed from Hell across Chaos, comes within light's sphere of influence as he approaches Heaven itself:

> And fast by hanging in a golden chain
> This pendant world, in bigness as a star
> Of smallest magnitude close by the moon.
> (2.1051–3)

Numerous commentators have mistakenly read "world" to mean Earth[6] – but no, it is our entire Universe, through whose outer shell Satan at this

---

[5] Salusbury, *Mathematical Collections and Translations* (London, 1661), p. 335. I will cite this translation of the *Dialogo* hereafter as "Salusbury." John Wilkins draws attention to this passage of the *Dialogo* in his *Discourse Concerning a New Planet* (1640), p. 121: "If all this eighth sphaere (saith Gallilaeus) as great as it is, were a light body, and placed so farre from us that it appeared but as one of the lesser Starres, we should then esteeme it but little."

[6] Leonard cites Patrick Hume, Joseph Addison, and Richard Bentley: *FL*, pp. 711, 716, 720. See also Maria Mitchell, (infra: Appendix, pp. 207–8). Compare Zachary Pearce's 1733 recognition that "[t]his pendant world" is indeed not Earth but our entire Universe (Leonard, *FL*, p. 726).

juncture has yet to pass. And while the principal viewpoint conveyed by these lines is Satan's, Milton's use of the deictic "this" deftly includes us in the scene. For Satan, so far out in Chaos that the immensity of our Universe appears as but a point, it is still surely *that* world. Only for us, its inhabitants, is it *"This* pendant world." This striking fusion of cosmic perspectives – the character's and the readers' – thus transforms Galileo's theoretical thought experiment by means of a dramaturgy that simultaneously actualizes roles for Satan and us.

As Leonard points out, this scene springs a surprise on readers. The opening of *Paradise Lost* indicates that "the distance between Heaven and Hell is thrice the radius of our universe" ("As from the center thrice to the utmost pole"; 1.74) and, taken literally (in Bentley's words), "The Distance is much too little." But Satan, in his voyage through Chaos, has clearly traversed distances far exceeding mere multiple radiuses of the pointlike Cosmos he catches sight of at the end of Book 2. Leonard is surely right that we ought not to "impose a spurious consistency" on the epic's scale of distances and also probably right that Milton may even have surprised himself "by discovering, in the process of composition, just how much space his poem needs" (*FL*, p. 721). Such "need for space" is certainly one of the inferences drawn by the Jonathan Richardsons (father and son) in 1734, who rightly see the comparison as offering a measure of how far Satan must already have traveled:

> What a Vast Imagination! what an Idea of Distance, the Distance from Hell to where *Satan* Now is! He is as it were at his Journeys End, and yet So Remote as that the New Creation, the Immense Heavens wherein are plac'd the Fix'd Stars; This Vast Globe, to which our Earth is but a Point, an Atom, appears as the Smallest Star. if to be at This Distance from it is, compar'd with the Journey, to be as it were in the Neighbourhood of the New Creation, What must That be through which the Devil has pass'd on his *Bad Errand!*[7]

In that quietly audacious simile, which also renders the relative smallness of our Cosmos ("in bigness as a star / Of smallest magnitude"; 2.1052–3), "magnitude" is technically a measure of brightness and "smallest" implies a traditional magnitude of 6, the dimmest star visible to the naked eye – "one of those which shun our sight" (in Salusbury's felicitous rendering of Galileo).[8] The main implied contrast is thus

---

[7] Jonathan Richardson and Jonathan Richardson, *Explanatory Notes and Remarks on Milton's "Paradise Lost"* (London, 1734), p. 88; quoted by Leonard, *FL*, p. 727.

[8] Salusbury, p. 335; *Dialogo*, p. 362: "che fuggono la nostra vista."

between our Universe's smallness and dimness relative to the size and brightness of Heaven. In *Sidereus Nuncius*, Galileo had referred to a similar relative contrast between Venus, an exceptionally bright star, and the Sun: "stars emerging at sunset in the first coming on of twilight, even stars of the first magnitude, appear very small. Indeed, even Venus, whenever she is visible in broad daylight, seems so small as scarcely to equal a little star of the least magnitude."[9] Milton's simile thus evokes a maximal contrast of luminosities while at the same time permitting us – inhabitants of a yet more minuscule "punctual spot" deep *within* the (to Satan) barely visible and immensely distant Universe – a poignant, momentary sense of being suspended between Pascal's "two abysses of the Infinite and Nothing," although terrifyingly closer to the latter end of this scale.[10]

Whereas Galileo brilliantly hypothesized an "infinite space" – something he did not actually believe existed – in which "there might be assigned a distance so great, as that the said lucid Sphere [of stars] might from thence shew as little, yea lesse than a fixed star," in *Paradise Lost* the comparison is actual, not hypothetical. Moreover, it is experiential, not merely mathematical. The experience, if we take it up, offers us a profound, humbling, exhilarating taste of a paradox that the most advanced twenty-first-century cosmology has only reinforced: Infinitesimally small cosmic life-forms though we are, we know with certainty that we are not nothing and we sense – hopefully, anxiously, perhaps faithfully – that our presence, our role, must have some significance in the larger story of the Universe. Thus, as we read Milton's jewel-like simile at the end of Book 2, our experience of contingency is heightened further still. For the "bad errand" of that distant malevolence now zeroing in from afar intends our world's and our own destruction. We, along with our home Universe, are cosmically "pendant" creatures indeed.

While Galileo's *Dialogo* is probably the single most illustrative astronomical work for a reading of *Paradise Lost* as well as among the most accessible primers on Copernicanism, we need to acknowledge how badly Galileo and his interpreters have skewed the popular picture of the cosmological

---

[9] Galileo, *Sidereus Nuncius*; *BOTC*, ed. Danielson, p. 151.
[10] As John Leonard has reminded me in private conversation, Galileo with his telescope discovered "below stars of the sixth magnitude … a host of other stars that escape natural sight" (*Sidereus Nuncius*, fol. 17ʳ: … *naturalem intuitum fugientium*). That the vocabulary of the *Sidereus Nuncius* corresponds with the later Italian of the *Dialogo* (see last footnote but one) strengthens the case for interpreting the contrast implied by Milton's simile as even more radical than mere naked-eye observation would suggest.

revolution itself. In Chapter 4, I cited Toscano's recent suggestion that Milton "addresses the Copernican issue without openly defending the heliocentric theory confirmed by Galileo's discoveries."[11] An innocent reading of the *Dialogo* might well lead one to believe that Galileo confirmed heliocentrism – although, in truth, he did not. To understand Galileo's skewing of the historiography of science, one must begin with the very title of his great work: *Dialogo ... sopra i due Massimi Sistemi del Mondo Tolemaico, e Copernicano – Dialogue ... on the Two Great Systems of the Universe, the Ptolemaic and the Copernican.*

This title posits a binary that by 1632 was actually obsolete and scientifically insupportable. Already for at least two decades, no serious student of astronomy had defended the "Discarded Image" outlined in Chapter 1; it had indeed been discarded. To treat the cosmological contest as if it were a struggle between Ptolemy and Copernicus was thus to hand an easy, unearned, bogus victory to the latter. But much history of science and much commentary on Milton have uncritically assumed Galileo's simplistic antithesis. Allan H. Gilbert's lengthy 1922 article on "Milton and Galileo" typically falls into the trap of Galileo's binary, assuming at each turn that an astronomical or cosmological passage in *Paradise Lost* must hold to Ptolemy or hold to Copernicus or else waver between those two poles. Among such passages in the epic, Gilbert writes: "Some are neutral, neither Ptolemaic nor Copernican, many clearly Ptolemaic, and a less, though considerable, number as clearly Copernican."[12] Ignoring *other* systems (such as those mentioned in Chapters 3 and 4) permits Gilbert to infer, for example, that when Adam speaks about the Sun's motion ("Scarce the sun / Hath finished half his journey," etc.; 5.558–9), he must be speaking as "a Ptolemaic."[13] Even if Adam's locution were in fact astronomical in its intent, the most one could say about it is that it is geostatic, an adjective that does not equate with Ptolemaic. Of course, at the risk of stating the obvious, one may add further that even today, most of us when speaking nontechnically still refer to the Sun rising or setting or being high in the sky without worrying that someone will therefore identify us as adherents of a cosmology all but abandoned four centuries ago.

But four centuries ago, there were certainly more than two "great systems" available for educated Europeans to choose from. Various scholars have enumerated them differently. Leaving aside Fracastoro's

---

[11] Toscano, "The Tuscan Artist," p. 1.
[12] Gilbert, "Milton and Galileo," *Studies in Philology* 19.2:156.
[13] Gilbert, "Milton and Galileo," *Studies in Philology* 19.2:157.

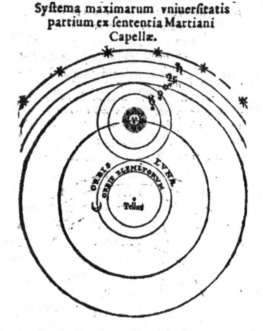

Figure 5.1   The Capellan (or Egyptian or Heraclidean) system according to Valentina Naiboda, *Primarum de Coelo et Terra Institutionum* (Venice, 1573), fol. 41ʳ.

"homocentric spheres" (1538) mentioned in Chapter 1, one can distinguish at least six different systems current by the early seventeenth century:

1. The Ptolemaic (geocentric, geostatic)
2. The Capellan, also sometimes called the Egyptian (geocentric, geostatic), derived from Martianus Capella (fl. 410–39), who adumbrated a version of the system of Heraclides of Pontus, according to which Mercury and Venus revolve not around the Earth but around the Sun[14] while the other planets circle Earth (Figure 5.1)
3. The Copernican (heliocentric): Earth has diurnal and annual motions
4. The Gilbertian (geocentric but not geostatic): Earth has a diurnal motion
5. The Tychonic (geocentric, geostatic): the Sun circles Earth while serving as the center of the planetary orbits (except for that of the Moon)
6. The Ursine (geocentric but not geostatic): very similar to the Tychonic model, but Earth has a diurnal motion

[14] See *BOTC*, ed. Danielson, pp. 78–80.

Some commentators identify the Keplerian model with its elliptical orbits as a seventh alternative, although for present purposes, Kepler can be fairly categorized as a Copernican. One might also further distinguish varieties of Copernicanism depending on whether the fixed stars lie in a bounded sphere, as implied in *De Revolutionibus*, or are dispersed "infinitely up," as in Digges's *A Perfit Description* and likewise later by John Wilkins. There were also semi-Tychonic versions of Tycho's system in which Jupiter and Saturn traced their circles about Earth, not the Sun.[15]

In any case, by about 1611, among these cosmological systems, the most highly favored alternative to the Copernican was not the Ptolemaic but the Tychonic. In the absence of compelling empirical, observational, or commonsense reasons to accept either Earth's motion or Earth's cosmic eccentricity, any system that held to a central, unmoving Earth possessed a huge advantage. This criterion narrowed the field in favor of the Ptolemaic, the Capellan, and the Tychonic systems. In practical terms, the Capellan got conflated with the Tychonic (as for example in Riccioli), so it was the Tychonic system – possibly with semi-Tychonic adjustments but retaining a stationary Earth – that by default became the flagship of geocentrism once telescopic observation placed a final nail in Ptolemy's coffin.

On 5 December 1610, Benedictine mathematician Benedetto Castelli wrote to Galileo, asking him a crucial question relating to observation and the arrangement of the Cosmos:

> Since (as I believe) the opinion of Copernicus that Venus revolves around the Sun is correct, it is clear that she would necessarily be seen by us sometimes horned and sometimes not. ... Now I would like to know from you if you, with your wonderful spyglasses, have noticed such an appearance, which, without doubt, will be a sure means of convincing any obstinate mind.[16]

Galileo had indeed been pursuing this question telescopically. On December 11, 1610, he sent the Tuscan ambassador in Prague an anagram, intended for Kepler's eyes, containing the heart of his discovery, which, he averred, would offer "a strong argument for the Pythagorean and

---

[15] For varying enumerations of systems, see Michael F. Flynn, "The Great Ptolemaic Smackdown," *Analog: Science Fiction and Fact* (Jan./Feb. 2013): 14–27, and Kerry V. Magruder, "Jesuit Science After Galileo: The Cosmology of Gabriele Beati," *Centaurus* 51 (2009): 189–212.

[16] Galileo, *Opere*, Edizione Nazionale, 20 vols., ed. Antonio Favaro (Florence: Barbera, 1890–1909, rpt. 1929–1939), 10:481–482; excerpted and translated in *Sidereus Nuncius*, ed. and trans. Albert Van Helden (Chicago: University of Chicago Press, 1989), p. 106.

Copernican arrangement"[17] and which, by the first day of 1611, he was able to disclose by unraveling his anagram: "*Cynthiae figuras aemulatur mater amorum*, that is, 'the mother of love [Venus] emulates the figures of Cynthia [the Moon].'"[18] In somewhat less cryptic language, he assured Castelli:

> Know therefore that about 3 months ago I began to observe Venus with the instrument, and I saw her in a round shape and very small. Day by day she increased in size and maintained that round shape until finally, attaining a great distance from the Sun, the roundness of her eastern part began to diminish, and in a few days she was reduced to a semicircle. She maintained this shape for many days, all the while, however, growing in size. At present, she is becoming sickle-shaped, and as long as she is observed in the evening her little horns will continue to become thinner, until she vanishes.[19]

In the Ptolemaic system, according to which the epicycle of Venus always lies between the Sun and Earth, it must likewise always be the case that the Sun's light illuminates more of the surface of Venus that faces away from Earth and less of the surface of the planet that faces Earth. In other words, if the Ptolemaic model were accurate and if an earthling observer had a sharp telescopic view of Venus, then from that standpoint the planet would *continuously* appear as a crescent, although the crescent's thickness would vary. By contrast, the Copernican and Tychonic models posit that Venus revolves about the Sun and thus periodically appears opposite the Sun. The latter is the stage at which Venus will appear smallest (because it is farthest from Earth) and most nearly full or circular (like a full Moon). As Venus in its orbit approaches Earth, however, it moves from full to gibbous to half to crescent (again, like the Moon) and accordingly also appears larger and larger in diameter. As it then again recedes from Earth, the process reverses itself, as illustrated by Galileo's own sketch (Figure 5.2). As this line of reasoning should make clear, moreover – although in Galileo's telescopic study of Venus, it is the horns of the planet that often seem most observationally interesting – it is in fact Venus's gibbous and full phases that are cosmologically of greatest significance, for these are what disconfirm predictions implied by a Ptolemaic model.

---

[17] Galileo, *Opere* 10:483; quoted and trans. Stillman Drake, "Galileo, Kepler, and the Phases of Venus," *Journal for the History of Astronomy* 15 (1984): 198–208.

[18] *Sidereus Nuncius*, ed. and trans. Van Helden, p. 107.

[19] *Opere* 11:12; *Sidereus Nuncius*, ed. and trans. Van Helden, pp. 107–8.

Figure 5.2   Galileo's sketch of the phases of Venus, from *Il Saggiatore* (Rome, 1623)

In *Paradise Lost*, Raphael's narrative of the fourth day of creation describes the Maker's placing "by far the greater part" of light "In the sun's orb." But hence (that is, from the Sun), says Raphael, "the morning-planet gilds her horns" (7.359–66). The reference is interesting and beautiful and does suggest that Venus depends exclusively on the Sun's light for her light – apparently unlike some of the other stars, "from human sight / So farr remote," mentioned in the following lines, which possess a "small peculiar [light]" (7.368–9). Nonetheless, the reference to the horns of Venus, while it is evidence of an awareness of telescopic observations of Venus, cannot count as evidence of Milton's or Raphael's Copernicanism because a Ptolemaic model would equally predict from an earthly perspective that Venus should appear as horned.

Galileo's observations of Venus's gibbous and full phases, however, did indeed rule out fundamental aspects of the Ptolemaic system – something confirmed and recognized almost immediately even by non-Copernicans as being cosmologically significant. Christoph Scheiner, Galileo's opponent in the sunspots controversy, had already in 1612 enumerated some of the implications:

> When Galileo observed horned Venus above several Italian cities, other mathematicians in Rome admired it and indeed discovered in it the same horned, bisected, and gibbous shape. From this incredible phenomenon [*incredibili Phaenomeno*] we have two ineluctable arguments. The first is that Venus, just like the Moon, is without light of its own. . . . The second is that, according to the same phenomenon, Venus goes around the Sun. Since all phenomena thus agree and all reasons are in concert, the prudent man will scarcely dare to doubt it in the future.[20]

---

[20] Scheiner, *Tres Epistolae de Maculis Solaribus* (Augsburg, 1612), p. 15; the translation of this passage appears in *On Sunspots*, ed. and trans. Reeves and Van Helden, p. 196.

Among the mathematicians to whom Scheiner refers was Christoph Clavius, doyen of Ptolemaic astronomy at the Jesuit Collegio Romano, who, approaching the end of his life, similarly acknowledged that as "seen with this instrument," Venus sometimes "appears to be more like a crescent, sometimes less" – and that now, "astronomers ought to consider how the celestial orbs may be arranged in order to save these phenomena."[21] Christoph Scheiner and his student Johan Georg Locher, in their *Disquisitiones Mathematicae* of 1614, showed exactly how the orb (or orbit) of Venus must be rearranged in order to save the phenomena (Figure 5.3): Venus must be reconceived as circling the Sun. Their depiction accords precisely with the Tychonic Universe and with Galileo's observations of the phases of Venus – and leaves little doubt about why an informed historian of science might describe Clavius, who died early in 1612, as "the last major Ptolemaic astronomer."[22]

In the *Dialogo*, some two decades after the death of Clavius, Salviati reprises Galileo's own account of the phases of Venus with precision and verve – complete with an explanation of how the telescope divests a planet of its "adventitious rayes" (Salusbury, p. 306; *Dialogo*, p. 330) and thus offers a truer impression, based on apparent size, of the planet's distance from the observer. After hearing Salviati's account and its implicit demolition of a major component of the Ptolemaic model, Sagredo exclaims: "Oh, Nicholas Copernicus, how great would have been thy joy to have seen this part of thy Systeme, confirmed with so manifest experiments!" (Salusbury, p. 307; *Dialogo*, p. 331). As fascinating and profoundly significant as Galileo's "manifest experiments" were and as capable (in Castelli's words) of convincing obstinate minds, their precise effect was in fact convincingly to *dis*confirm Ptolemaism, not to confirm Copernicanism. Things would have been different had there truly been only two viable "great systems of the Universe"; in such a case, logically, to negate one option would be to affirm the other. But to conclude as Sagredo does is to ignore the viability of the Tychonic system, which harmonized perfectly well with Galileo's telescopic discoveries yet retained the philosophical and commonsense advantages of a geocentric and geostatic model. Copernicus's joy would have been premature, as indeed was Galileo's.

---

[21] See this chapter's first epigraph. In his published correspondence with Galileo, Scheiner draws explicit attention to Clavius's near-deathbed call for "another system of the world"; *On Sunspots*, ed. and trans. Reeves and Van Helden, p. 229.

[22] Magruder, "Jesuit Science After Galileo," *Centaurus* 51: 191.

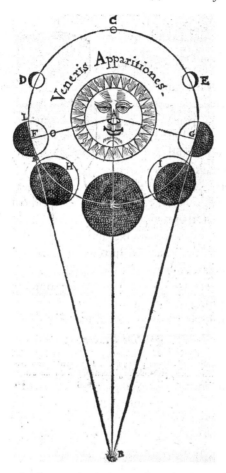

Figure 5.3   Locher and Scheiner's sketch showing how the phases of Venus will appear from the perspective of an observer on the central, unmoving Earth of the Tychonic Universe, from *Disquisitiones* (Ingolstadt, 1614)

Formerly stalwart adherents of Ptolemy, such as Clavius and Scheiner, in acknowledging the cosmological force of the observed phases of Venus, bear witness to their own openness to experimental evidence (their minds were not as "obstinate" as Castelli or Galileo might suggest) and to a widespread reasonable disinclination to accept the Ptolemaic/Copernican binary. For, as indicated, there was an attractive geocentric and geostatic alternative to Copernicanism even given the "death of Ptolemy" – and its advantages over the discarded image were many. The Tychonic system's observational equivalence to Copernicanism relative to the planets has already been mentioned. Moreover, unlike the classic Ptolemaic model, Tycho's dispensed with solid crystalline spheres. Robert Burton in 1621 summarized this position in his *Anatomy of Melancholy*, noting that Tycho and some of his contemporaries are of the same opinion about the "matter of Heavens, that it is not hard and impenetrable, as Peripateticks hold ... but that it is penetrable and soft as the ayre it selfe is, and that the Planets move in it as Birds in the ayre, fishes in the sea." Meanwhile, Tycho, his followers, and others have exploded "those *Eccentricks* and *Epicycles*. Which howsoever Ptolomy, Alhasen, Vitello, Maginus, Clavius, and many of their associats stiffely maintaine, to be reall orbs, excentricke, concentricke, circles aequant etc. are absurd and ridiculous. For who is so mad to thinke that there should be so many circles, like subordinate wheeles in a clock, al impenetrable and hard, as they faine[?]" In this way, even a nonspecialist such as Burton appears receptive to a considerable range of models from various Copernicans and non-Copernicans – but *not* from the Ptolemaics, who alone among contemporary cosmologists are dismissed as proponents of absurdities.

Copernicanism itself, however, could likewise appear to imply absurdities and not only those directly related to the counterintuitive claim that *terra firma* beneath our feet is in motion. Mention has already been made of the incredible increase in the implied distance to the fixed stars – and thus also of the diameter of the sphere of the fixed stars – implied by the heliocentric premise of Earth's annual motion combined with the fact that no annual stellar parallax was observable. As Tycho wrote to Rothmann in 1589, "what if ... Earth's annual motion [as proposed by Copernicus] completely vanished? Figure it out geometrically and you will see how many absurdities ... are entailed by this assumption [about Earth's motion]."[23]

Moreover, as indicated in that same letter to Rothmann, the Copernican conundrum of cosmic size entailed a still further daunting problem: that of stellar size. Rhetorically and scientifically, Copernicanism made much of the Sun's predominant, even divine role while at the same time encouraging the notion that the stars might be "other suns." The latter phrase appears not only in Bruno but also in Galileo's *Dialogo* (Salviati: the fixed stars "are so many Suns" [Salusbury, p. 300]) and in *Paradise Lost* (Raphael: "other suns perhaps" [8.148]). The dilemma for Copernican heliocentrism was thus that on the one hand it offered an asymmetry

---

[23] Tycho to Rothmann, 26 July 1589; see Chapter 3, note 23.

between Sun and stars – echoed in Satan's observation that at the sight of the Sun, "all the stars / Hide their diminished heads" (4.34–35) – while on the other, it undercut solar supremacy by suggesting solar/stellar equivalency.

But as indicated, Tycho realized that, much worse, Copernicanism must still more drastically diminish the Sun's size and status relative to the fixed stars. Nor did the advent of the telescope solve this problem. In 1631, Peter Crüger, a former student of Tycho and Kepler, expressed his exasperation with the problem of star size even in light of observations made with the telescope:

> How should they [the stars of varying magnitudes] through a telescope all appear confusedly as mere points? For have not Galileo and others, by means of the telescope, discerned stars of a further six magnitudes otherwise invisible to natural sight? So surely, one must admit that, even through a telescope, the stars have an apparent diameter. Take only a tiny star, one whose diameter is merely a quarter of a minute, or 1/120th that of the Sun. . . . From Kepler's calculation that there are 60,000,000 Earth-radii between the center and the firmament, it therefore follows . . . that the true diameter of such a tiny star is 2,181 Earth-diameters. . . . Now, also according to Kepler, the Sun has a diameter of 15 Earth-diameters. So from this it follows that the diameter of the tiny star I mentioned must be more than 145 times greater than the diameter of the Sun, and likewise (by the authority of Euclid, book 12, proposition 18) the body of the same star must be 3,048,624 times as great as the Sun. Indeed, moreover, if a tiny star had a visible breadth even of a mere 60th of a minute, then according to the above hypothesis its true thickness would be more than nine times that of the Sun, and its volume 730 times greater. I therefore do not understand how the Pythagorean or Copernican *Systema Mundi* can survive. How can the Sun, given its size, prevail over all the other stars? I simply cannot fathom it! If anyone else does, I pray that he teach me how.[24]

As earlier noted, a Copernican such as Thomas Digges, although his work preceded even that of Tycho, was likewise aware of and accepted this

---

[24] Peter Crüger, *Cupediae Astrosophicae* (Breslau, 1631), Sig. Jj i[r]. For further discussion of the problem, see Christopher M. Graney, "The Work of the Best and Greatest Artist: A Forgotten Story of Religion, Science, and Stars in the Copernican Revolution," *Logos: A Journal of Catholic Thought and Culture* 15.4 (Fall 2012): 97–124. As Graney points out (p. 120, n. 11): "One minute of space is one sixtieth of a degree, or approximately one thirteenth the apparent size of the Sun or Moon." This figure differs from the one used by Crüger by roughly 100%, although the difference is not large enough to alter the fundamental problem Crüger sketches. Historian of science Albert Van Helden asserts that the logic of Tycho and his followers "was impeccable; his measurements above reproach. A Copernican simply had to accept the results of this argument"; *Measuring the Universe: Cosmic Dimensions From Aristarchus to Halley* (Chicago: University of Chicago Press, 1985), p. 51.

geometrical reasoning concerning star size. The script on the frontispiece of *A Perfit Description* asserts that those "glorious lightes" (the stars) far excel our Sun "both in quantitye and qualitye." Such implications, based on Copernicanism's implied cosmic scale and consistent even with Crüger's post-telescopic reasoning, not only beggar belief but also undercut the plausibility of seeing the stars as "other suns." Or else, even if the Sun is a star, surely it must be the smallest and most inconsiderable of the lot. And what then becomes of Digges's claim, echoing that of Copernicus, that "the Sunne . . . like a king in the middest of all raigneth and geeveth lawes of motion to the rest"?

What *would* have solved the star-size problem for the Copernicans is a recognition that stars do in fact appear as mere points of light, not as light sources with measurable diameters – but this recognition emerged decisively only with George Biddell Airy's 1835 account of stars' illusory appearance as discs when viewed through the telescope. Galileo himself repeatedly confirmed stars' spherical appearance, typically asserting that "stars, whether they are fixed or wandering, are always observed to maintain their shape, and that shape is circular."[25] In the *Dialogo*, Salviati acknowledges the problem of star size, mentioning Tycho by name, but argues that "stars of the first magnitude have diameters of 5 seconds of arc at most, and claims that this telescopically observed size, combined with the assumption that stars are suns, fully answers any objections to Copernicus arising from the absurdity of the distance and physical sizes of the fixed stars."[26] However, as Graney has shown, "the argument does not work." "Only if the stars are true points will they not be a problem for Copernicus," as Simon Marius, based on his own calculations and published telescopic observations, argued in 1614.[27]

Giovanni Battista Riccioli, perhaps the most prominent Italian astronomer of the mid-seventeenth century, offered in his *Almagestum Novum* (1651) thoroughgoing observations and calculations also consistent with the case earlier articulated by Tycho, Marius, and Crüger – but again contrary to Copernican cosmology and the claims of Galileo, whom Riccioli

---

[25] *On Sunspots*, ed. and trans. Reeves and Van Helden, p. 101. Other examples, along with invaluable discussion of the "Airy disc" problem, are provided by Christopher M. Graney, "The Telescope Against Copernicus: Star Observations by Riccioli Supporting a Geocentric Universe," *Journal for the History of Astronomy* 41 (2010): 453–67 (pp. 454–6). See also Graney, "Seeds of a Tychonic Revolution: Telescopic Observations of the Stars by Galileo Galilei and Simon Marius," *Physics in Perspective* 12 (2010): 4–24.

[26] Graney, "The Telescope Against Copernicus," p. 455; cf. Salusbury, pp. 325–6.

[27] Graney, "The Telescope Against Copernicus," pp. 456, 462. Graney refers to Marius's *Mundus Jovialis* (Nuremberg, 1614).

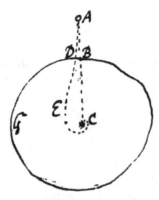

Figure 5.4   Riccioli argued that a rotating Earth must produce certain observable phenomena, which were in fact *not* observed. For example, a heavy ball dropped from high above Earth should fall straight to Earth if Earth is immobile but should deflect to the East if Earth rotates. This illustration of this supposed effect (the large circle is Earth; path A to B is the vertical fall of a dropped ball; path A to D, and so on, is the path of the ball if Earth rotates counterclockwise toward G) was produced not by Riccioli but a generation later by Isaac Newton in a letter to Robert Hooke in which Newton made the same argument.

considers unreliable on this topic. One of Riccioli's more concise summations of the star-size argument is this: "If the Earth circles the sun, then the stars must be exceedingly, vastly, hugely voluminous. They must be huge compared to the Earth, huge compared to the sun, even huge compared to the annual orb. It is not merely the most prominent star that is huge, but also even the least of the stars. But this is absurd and incredible."[28]

A further cogent category of argument against Copernicanism had to do not with Earth's annual motion but with Earth's alleged diurnal motion. Riccioli claimed that if Earth were rotating, one ought to be able to detect certain deflections in the trajectories of projectiles and falling bodies. Tycho had also said that a rotating Earth should produce observable effects. Isaac Newton would later propose the deflections discussed by Riccioli as a means of detecting Earth's rotation (Figure 5.4). But such experiments would in fact not be successful until the nineteenth century. Today, this kind of deflection is understood as resulting from the

---

[28] Riccioli, *Almagestum Novum* (Bologna, 1651), 2:461: *Si Terra moveretur per orbem Annuum, non solum prime, sed etiam infima magnitudinis Stellae Fixae haberent molem nimis magnam, seu Sole et Orbe ipso Annuo seu caelo Solari maiorem. Hoc autem est absurdum et incredibile.* The translation is that of Christpher M. Graney, "Further Argument Against the Motion of the Earth, Based on Telescopic Observations of the Stars," *arXiv*:1011.2228v1.

"Coriolis force," named for the French scientist Gaspard-Gustave de Coriolis (1792–1843), who worked out a full mathematical description of such effects.[29]

The picture that emerges from the details of seventeenth-century cosmological debates, contrary to Whiggish narratives whereby forward-looking true scientists gradually gained ground against backward-looking dogmatic geocentrists, is more complex and more interesting than the simplistic binary that Galileo's *Dialogo* reinforced in his own day and beyond. Instead, observation, logic, and examination of evidence continued to be wielded by a variety of natural philosophers of varying persuasions. Even by the end of Milton's life, Copernicanism was not yet an established victor over geocentrism – although it was Tychonic apologists, not Ptolemaic ones, who continued to carry the flag of geocentrism.

The state of that debate in the year of Milton's death is indicated by Robert Hooke's *An Attempt to Prove the Motion of the Earth From Observations*, cited in this chapter's second epigraph. Hooke's rhetoric in that work strongly suggests that his opponents are idiots: He "cannot suppose that they should understand the cogency of the Reasons here presented." One wonders, of course, why Hooke might need to attempt a proof of Earth's Copernican annual motion if the contrary geocentric and geostatic cases were as contemptible as he indicates. Nonetheless, in his opening pages, he coins the phrase *experimentum crucis* and proposes a decisive measurement of annual parallax that might serve as "a certain manifestation," settling once and for all the debate "between the Tychonick and Copernican Hypotheses." Not incidentally, Hooke's experiment failed and nobody convincingly recorded annual stellar parallax until Friedrich Bessel did so in 1838. For our purposes, however, Hooke's ingenious proposal serves as a reminder of the still open nature of the cosmological debate in 1674 and of how the main (although not sole) alternative to a Copernican model was Tychonic rather than Ptolemaic – as indeed it had been for more than half a century.

The obvious question for a study of *Paradise Lost*, therefore, is how Milton could have constructed the world of his epic according to the Ptolemaic model – or, more accurately, how generations of his readers could come to

---

[29] See Graney, "Giovanni Battista Riccioli's Seventy-Seven Arguments Against the Motion of the Earth: An English Rendition of *Almagestum Novum* Part II, Book 9, Section 4, Chapter 34, Pages 472–7," *arXiv*:1011.3778.

believe that he did so. I hope that the staleness, flatness, and unprofitability of the Ptolemaic allegation might be something the present study helps to expose. But the meme of Milton's Ptolemaism is a potent reality that must be acknowledged. Fortunately, for serious Milton readers, the heavy work of tracing and critiquing the meme has recently been performed by John Leonard's magisterial *Faithful Labourers* (Chapter 11, "The Universe"). What Leonard convincingly shows is that a mere three lines of *Paradise Lost* "come up again and again in arguments for Milton's Ptolemaic conformity" (*FL*, p. 705) – lines routinely interpreted with disregard for their context or irony. The scene is the parodic "Paradise of Fools" account, in which the superstitious fools themselves hope, on the strength of the clerical costumes they wear, to rise from their deathbeds into heaven "disguised" (3.480):

> They pass the planets seven, and pass the fixed,
> And that crystalline sphere whose balance weighs
> The trepidation talked, and that first moved.
>
> (3.481–3)

Leonard's conclusion concerning these lines, which do indeed incorporate Ptolemaic vocabulary, is best summed up by the Richardsons, whose perceptive comments Leonard reintroduces into the Miltonic conversation. They wrote in 1734:

> It is to be Observed Here that this Crystalline Sphere, this *Primum Mobile*, are no more parts of *Milton*'s System of the new Creation than the Wicket Gate in the next line; That must be Sought for in the short account of it at the Latter end of This Book and the Beginning of the Seventh. He very Poetically says These were Some of the Reveries of the Philosophers and Astronomers, *Quaint Opinions* to be Laught at, as VIII. 78. he says This by flinging them into the Paradise of Fools.[30]

But so many have read the infamous three lines uncritically (without an ear for Milton's humor) – and so often have their hasty inferences been scribbled over the epic as a whole – that the blot on Milton's cosmological contribution has become almost indelible to the point where he has been left appearing a cosmologically "backward looking" writer.

That is certainly not where he deserves to be left. Leonard's is a powerful rescue mission, declaring "a simple, startling truth: there are no spheres in *Paradise Lost*" (*FL*, p. 709). I will therefore not attempt to re-scour the reception landscape so effectively worked over in *Faithful Labourers*,

---

[30] Richardson and Richardson, *Explanatory Notes*, pp. 122–3; quoted by Leonard, *FL*, p. 707.

although since 1970 (Leonard's *terminus ad quem*) not a great deal has changed. From Lawrence Babb's "The world of *Paradise Lost* is obviously Ptolemaic" to the (among other editions) Milton Reading Room's inference that *Paradise Lost* presents a universe with "nine concentric spheres" (based merely on Milton's mention of Satan's removal from Heaven "As from the center thrice to th' utmost pole" [1.74]),[31] the meme of Milton's Ptolemaism has continued to reproduce itself.

In attempting to replace the meme with something more satisfying and critically responsible and before returning to the seventeenth century, I would like to consider briefly two critics who knew a great deal about the history of astronomy but whose comments on Milton fall far short of being helpful or even fair. The first is Grant McColley, whose major contribution, as Leonard avers, "has been to discredit the idea that Milton had just two world systems from which to choose" (*FL*, p. 760). Nonetheless, across a series of articles published in the 1930s, McColley's commentary on Milton and astronomy grew more and more dyspeptic, in the end alleging views of the poet that aligned him with the truly backward-looking Alexander Ross.[32] Moreover, having rightly denied that someone in Milton's situation had a stark choice between "two rival systems, the Ptolemaic and Copernican,"[33] McColley denigrates Milton for omitting any "direct reference" or even "indirect allusion to the geo-heliocentric theory."[34] It is undeniably true that Milton refrained from mentioning Tycho Brahe in *Paradise Lost*. But he also undeniably refrained from mentioning Ptolemy – except indirectly, as we have seen, by means of a more general implied critique (8.66–84) of those who strive "to model heav'n / And calculate the stars." But it was not only Ptolemaics who sought to "save appearances." McColley was in perhaps a preeminent position to realize that Adam's initial geocentric and geostatic assumptions are as consistent with Tycho's model as they are with Ptolemy's. And surely there is little point in banishing Galileo's

[31] Lawrence Babb, *The Moral Cosmos of Paradise Lost* (East Lansing: Michigan State University Press, 1970), p. 80; Milton Reading Room, note to *PL*, 1.74 <http://www.dartmouth.edu/~milton/reading_room/pl/book_1>. Much closer to Leonard's reading of this section is that of David Quint, "'Things Invisible to Mortal Sight': Light, Vision, and the Unity of Book 3 of *Paradise Lost*," *Modern Language Quarterly* 71.3 (Sept. 2010): 229–69 (p. 255).

[32] McColley, "Milton's Dialogue on Astronomy: The Principal Immediate Sources," *PMLA* 52.3 (Sept., 1937): 728–62. I shall return to the Wilkins-Ross debate in Chapter 7.

[33] McColley, "The Theory of the Diurnal Rotation of the Earth," *Isis*, 26.2 (March 1937): 392–402 (p. 392).

[34] McColley, "The Astronomy of *Paradise Lost*," *Studies in Philology* 34.2 (April 1937): 209–47 (p. 234).

bogus binary but then proceeding as if "geocentric and geostatic" merely equate with "Ptolemaic."

Such neglect of detail similarly leads Francis R. Johnson, in his otherwise highly informative study of *Astronomical Thought in Renaissance England*, to patronize Milton with the comment that we should (he implies "merely") "read the cosmological passages in *Paradise Lost* as great poetry."[35] In his review of Johnson's book, McColley noted favorably the title of the final chapter – "The Two Chief Systems of the Universe: The Tychonic and the Copernican" – and endorsed Johnson's "valuable point that scholars 'who support the view that Milton was deeply learned in the astronomical science of his day' must explain why the poet failed to discuss the Tychonic system."[36] Johnson – having, like McColley, putatively banished the binary – nonetheless attaches Milton to one pole of it, principally on the strength of Milton's prescribing of ancient astronomy texts in *Of Education* in 1644. But Galileo had also taught Ptolemaic astronomy in his early career, writing his own commentary on Sacrobosco's *Sphaera Mundi*.[37] It is hard not to conclude that McColley and Johnson assemble impressive material that could profitably be applied to a reading of *Paradise Lost* – but, as Leonard says of Johnson, simply do "not bother to question the received wisdom" (*FL*, p. 780).

In the same review, McColley repeats his earlier charge against Milton that "a writer who seriously discussed in 1663–1665 the triple motion of the earth had not followed the development of technical astronomy after 1630."[38] McColley here refers to Copernicus's claim in Book 1, Chapter 11, of *De Revolutionibus* that Earth possesses three different motions: a diurnal rotation, an annual revolution, and a further annual "motion" whereby Earth maintains its axial orientation to the sphere of the fixed stars rather than to the ecliptic. Thus, the Sun appears higher or lower above the southern horizon depending on the time of year and the cycle of the seasons, but the fixed stars appear continuously at the same elevation. Copernicus seems to have considered this a motion because, given the older conception of a planet being carried about in a transparent spherical shell, Earth's axis (without some "motion" of planet Earth relative to that shell) would tilt continuously in a single orientation to the Sun – instead of, as it actually does, maintaining its continuous orientation to the stars.

---

[35] Johnson, *Astronomical Thought in Renaissance England*, p. 287.
[36] McColley, untitled review of Johnson, *Isis* 28.2 (May, 1938): 514–16.
[37] See Lattis, *Between Copernicus and Galileo*, p. 38.
[38] McColley, untitled review of Johnson, *Isis* 28.2: 516; cf. McColley, "The Astronomy of *Paradise Lost*," *Studies in Philology* 34.2:232, and Leonard, *FL*, p. 772.

In the *Dialogo*, Salviati asserts that in fact "the third is no motion," although he helpfully describes the phenomenon Copernicus intended to account for: namely, that

> the Axis of the diurnal motion doth always remain parallel to it self; so that if we imagine that same Axis to be continued out until it reach the fixed stars, ... the said Axis describeth the superfices of an oblique Cylinder. ... And this same cylinder is oblique to the Plane of the Ecliptick, according to the inclination of the Axis that describeth it, which we have said to be 23 degrees and an half. (Salusbury, pp. 344–5)

However, Raphael in *Paradise Lost*, in the course of sketching a tentative Copernican model, asks "what if ... the planet Earth ... three different Motions move?" (8.128–30).

McColley is of course correct that Raphael's summary is outdated as a piece of technical astronomy. But promoting an appreciation of Milton's creative engagement with the cosmological revolution entails neither an attempt to mine *Paradise Lost* for the (in 1667) latest technical scientific theory nor the need to paper over astronomical inconsistencies in Milton's work when we encounter them. Earth's triple motion, as indicated, might have come straight from Copernicus himself, although it also appeared in some popular summations of heliocentrism. Burton, for example, commented that the Copernicans "ascribe a triple motion to the Earth, the Sunne immovable in the Center, and salve all apparances better then any other way whatsoever."[39] Considerably more interesting, however, than Raphael's inconsistency with mid-seventeenth-century technical heliocentrism is the inconsistency between Earth's hypothesized third motion and the prelapsarian premises of *Paradise Lost* itself.

Milton's account of the cosmological consequences imposed on the world after the fall betrays that inconsistency. A pair of mutually exclusive alternatives is sketched – the first heliocentric; the second geocentric (be it Ptolemaic or Tychonic), although having the same result:

> Some say, [God] bid his angels turn askance
> The poles of Earth twice ten degrees and more
> From the sun's axle; they with labor pushed
> Oblique the centric globe: some say the sun
> Was bid turn reins from th' equinoctial road
> Like distant breadth to Taurus with the sev'n
> Atlantic Sisters, and the Spartan Twins,
> Up to the Tropic Crab; thence down amain

---

[39] Burton, *Anatomy of Melancholy* (1621), p. 326.

By Leo and the Virgin and the Scales,
As deep as Capricorn, to bring in change
Of seasons to each clime; else had the spring
Perpetual smiled on Earth with vernant flow'rs,
Equal in days and nights ...

(10.668–80)

Thus, if one's model is heliocentric, then Earth's axis after the fall is seen to have been adjusted so our planet attained its familiar 23½-degree inclination relative to the ecliptic; if the model is geocentric, then the ecliptic itself must have been tilted the same number of degrees. In either case, *before* the fall, the Sun's and Earth's paths are such that day and night are continuously equal ("equinoctial") and Earth's axis stands perpendicular to the celestial equator and the plane of the planetary orbits.[40] Raphael's heliocentric what-if in Book 8 is therefore in this respect anachronistic regarding the mentioned "three different motions," for the third of these has utterly no role to play if the celestial equator and the planetary orbits are coplanar. In short, on this point, Raphael's cosmology in Book 8 gets seriously ahead of itself, although Milton seems not to notice.

On the other hand, Raphael's side of the astronomical conversation with Adam offers a rich feast of cosmological themes that were variously discussed before and after the advent of Copernicus. If Raphael's what-ifs exhibit less boldness than we might wish Milton had exhibited regarding the new astronomy – certainly less boldness than Galileo in general reflected in his own *Dialogo* thirty-five years before the first publication of *Paradise Lost* – then at least some of the evidence displayed in the present chapter indicates that hesitations about heliocentrism were in Milton's day grounded in responsible science, not merely in dogmatism, timidity, or a hankering after dead ideas. Moreover, as Leonard puts it, "If Milton were indifferent to astronomical questions, he could have ignored them. But they keep arising" (*FL*, p. 758). Indeed, interest in cosmological issues shines forth from the epic undimmed by expressions of caution or pious decorum. It is true, of course, that the angel tells Adam: "Heaven is for thee too high / To know what passes there; be lowly wise" (8.172–3). But then again, even Galileo's Salviati endorses what he calls Simplicio's "truly Angelical Doctrine," according to which "it would be an extravagant boldnesse for any one to goe about to limit and confine the

---

[40] See Fowler's stimulating comments on this aspect of prelapsarian cosmology, *The Poems of John Milton*, ed. John Carey and Alastair Fowler (London: Longman, 1968), p. 449; cf. Leonard, *FL*, pp. 809–10.

> Hinc è regione in Angulo, qui Borrhapelioten respicit, ferrea quædã for-
> nax sub conveniente testudine, ita ut nihil in Hypocausto occupet spatij, posi-
> ta est, ut eius beneficio tempore Obfervationũ hybernalium frigus arceatur.
>   Superiùs autem sub ipsâ, quâ Hypocaustum contegitur, fornice, depi-
> ctaest T y c h o n i s neoterica inventio Hypothesium cœlestium, eâ, quam
> ipsa testudo capere potest, magnitudine. Proximè verò sub hâc, ad parietem
> paulò inferiorem, verfus Septentrionem, ubi eius Imago repræsentatur:
> manu alterâ surfum monstrans, habet intra binos digitos pictam schedam, in
> qua hæc inscriptio.
>
> ‖ QVID SI SIC? ‖
>
>   Quasi antiquioribus istis & circûm depictis Astronomis dicat: Quid de
> hac inventione vobis videtur?   Ex Hypocausto hoc itur, ordinariâ Ianu-
> arum dispositione, hinc inde, in reliquas Cryptas, ubi Instrumenta locantur.

Figure 5.5   An excerpt from Tycho Brahe's *Astronomical Letters* (Nuremberg, 1601)

Divine Power and Wisdome to some one particular conjecture of his own." Salviati's final words of the *Dialogo* offer a doctrine

> in like manner divine, which whilst it giveth us leave to dispute, touching
> the constitution of the World, addeth withall … that we cannot find
> out the works made by his hands. Let therefore the Disquisition permitted
> and ordain'd us by God, assist us in the knowing, and so much
> more admiring his greatnesse, by how much lesse we finde our selves
> too dull to penetrate the profound Abysses of his infinite Wisdome.
> (Salusbury, p. 424)

Neither in Galileo nor in Milton, therefore, does astronomical inquiry presuppose impious audacity any more than do pious expressions concerning the limits of human knowledge preclude disputations "touching the constitution of the World." Moreover, by means of his apparently tentative what-ifs, Raphael places himself symbolically among a handful of the most prominent astronomers of the cosmological revolution. Tycho Brahe depicted himself under the arches of his observatory at Stjerneborg, gesturing with his hand toward his own cosmological system, accompanied by a caption extending from his fingers that read: *Quid si sic?* ("What if [it be] thus?"; see Figure 5.5).[41] Tycho's question may strike us – because it is not an outright statement of fact – as somewhat modest or scientifically tentative. However, in the eyes of his most bitter opponent, imperial mathematician Nicolai Reymers Baer (better known as Ursus), it was anything but modest; rather, in his self-portrait, Tycho was "arrogating to himself with shameless effrontery his

[41] Tycho Brahe, *Epistolarum Astronomicarum* (Nuremberg, 1601), p. 246.

Figure 5.6   Frontispiece to Kepler's *Rudolphine Tables* (1627)

QUID SI SIC and vainly putting forth as his own handiwork his new discovery of hypotheses."[42]

Kepler, who publicly defended Tycho against Ursus, remembered the phrase years later when he designed the frontispiece for his *Rudolphine Tables* (Figure 5.6). This famous graphic offers an emblem of the history of astronomy progressing from background to foreground, with the strength or weakness of particular astronomical systems symbolized by the quality of the pillars associated with them, ranging from wooden and

---

[42] Ursus, *De Astronomicis Hypothesibus* (Prague, 1597), sig. Dii^r, translated in Nicholas Jardine, *The Birth of the History and Philosophy of Science: Kepler's A Defence of Tycho Against Ursus* (Cambridge: Cambridge University Press, 1984), p. 55.

incomplete to roughhewn stone to brick to two of polished marble at the front of the picture. The stars, of course, form the observational foundation for all the astronomers presented in the graphic, but on the ceiling is depicted the schematic of the Tychonic geoheliocentric system. The two most prominent astronomers, each adjacent to his own polished marble column, are Copernicus and Tycho, the latter pointing up at the geoheliocentric system while ascending from his mouth are the words *Quid si sic?*[43] Among other things, of course, Kepler's graphic offers still further evidence against the implicit claim of Galileo's title five years later that the "due massimi sistemi del mondo" were the Ptolemaic and the Copernican.

Tycho's three-word query retained its geoheliocentric association for at least one other astronomer whom we have already met. Peter Crüger long taught the advantages and disadvantages of the Ptolemaic, Tychonic, and Copernican systems – for example, in his textbook *De Hypothetico Systemate Coeli* (Gdańsk, 1615). But his own preference for the cosmology of Tycho appears in the margin of one of the copies of *De Revolutionibus* that he owned. Next to Copernicus's famous compassed sketch of the heliocentric universe, Crüger painstakingly drew in the Tychonic system and captioned it in his own hand with the phrase *Quid si sic?*[44]

In England, however, the phrase would jump cosmological parties. John Wilkins's Copernican writings on the Moon and on planetary Earth were published together in 1640, accompanied by a frontispiece (Figure 5.7) by William Marshall, engraver of Milton's portrait for his *Poems* five years later. Embodying Wilkins's enthusiasm for new cosmological directions is Copernicus, depicted standing on the left of the title page and pointing to his heliocentric system – here supplemented by the endless diffusion of stars that had entered English heliocentrism with Thomas Digges in 1576. It is Copernicus who now succeeds – or supersedes – Tycho Brahe by taking the words out of his mouth: *Quid si sic?* Copernicus is supported, of course, by his pair of astronomical assistants, Galileo and Kepler, each of whom adds a three-word phrase of his own. Galileo, telescope firmly in hand, declares *Hic ejus oculi*

---

[43] For a fuller interpretation of Kepler's frontispiece, see Barbara Becker's excellent commentary at <http://faculty.humanities.uci.edu/bjbecker/ExploringtheCosmos/lecture6.html>

[44] Crüger's copy, now in the Russian State Library in Moscow, was the 1566 edition, with Copernicus's graphic appearing on fol. 9ᵛ; see Gingerich, *An Annotated Census of Copernicus' De Revolutionibus*, pp. 190–1.

Figure 5.7 Wilkins's Frontispiece for his *Discourse Concerning a New World and Another Planet* (1640)

("Here be his eyes"), while the mathematician Kepler adds *Utinam et alae* ("Yes, and his wings").[45] The picture's cheerful suggestion, it would

---

[45] The metaphor of arithmetic and geometry as the two wings enabling astronomy reaches back through Digges's *Alae* (1573) to Rheticus and even to Plato; see Danielson, *The First Copernican*, pp. 25–6.

seem, is that observation and mathematics indeed combine to confirm Copernicus's model.[46]

For Milton, there is no such confirmation – and, as indicated in this chapter, for good reason. And yet for him, *Quid si sic?* retains its validity and its Copernican expansiveness. It remains, as it does for Wilkins, a question leading readers upward and outward into a Cosmos waiting to be understood, wondered at, and explored. Moreover, in *Paradise Lost*, the question, although still properly tentative, is fully authorized – to be heeded and pondered even more than anything uttered by Tycho or Copernicus. For here, it is voiced by an angel, asking Adam and asking us "What if?"

---

[46] For much more on the frontispiece, see N. Kaoukji and N. Jardine, "'A frontispiece in any sense they please'? On the significance of the engraved title-page of John Wilkins's *A Discourse concerning A NEW world & Another Planet*, 1640," *Word & Image* 26.4 (Oct.–Dec. 2010): 429–47. See also Gudula Metze, "Die Entwicklung der Copernicus-Porträts vom 16. Jahrhundert bis zum 18. Jahrhundert," Dr.Phil. diss. University of Munich, 2004, pp. 124–5.

CHAPTER 6

The Sun

"According to generally accepted principles of astronomy ... all celestial appearances are directed by the mean motion of the Sun, and the whole harmony of the celestial motions is constituted and preserved by his government. Thus the ancients called the Sun 'director' [χορηγός], governor of nature, and king. ... And now my learned teacher [Copernicus] declares that the rejected account of the Sun's rule in the realm of nature must be revived. ... For he sees [among other things] that in human affairs the Emperor need not himself hasten from city to city to perform the duties God has assigned him. ... While our common theories gave us no clue about this rule of the Sun in the realm of nature, we disregarded most of the ancients' *encomia* of the Sun as if they were merely poetry."[1]

Georg Joachim Rheticus, 1540

"Behold, in the midst of all resides the Sun. For who, in this beautiful temple, would set this lamp in another or a better place, whence to illuminate all things at once? For aptly indeed do some call him the lantern – and others the mind or the ruler – of the Universe. Trismegistus calls him the visible god, and Sophocles' Electra 'the beholder' of all things. Truly indeed does the Sun, as if seated upon a royal throne, govern his family of stars as they circle about him."[2]

Nicolaus Copernicus, 1543

"O thou that, with surpassing glory crowned,
Look'st from thy sole dominion like the God
Of this new world; at whose sight all the stars
Hide their diminished heads; to thee I call,

---

[1] Rheticus, *Narratio Prima* – the first-ever Copernican publication – (Gdańsk, 1640), sig. Civ^{r-v}. Rpt. in Leopold Prowe, *Nicolaus Coppernicus*, 2 vols. (1883–4; rpt. Osnabrück: Zeller, 1967), 2: 320–1. The original of the final phrase reads: *pleraque Veterum Solis* ἐγχώμια *tanquam poëtica negligebamus.*
[2] Copernicus, *De Revolutionibus* (Nuremberg, 1543), I.x.

> But with no friendly voice, and add thy name,
> O Sun, to tell thee how I hate thy beams
> That bring to my remembrance from what state
> I fell, how glorious once above thy sphere."
>
> Satan, *Paradise Lost*, 4.32–9

In religion, in astronomy, and in poetry, there is surely no more dominant heavenly body than the Sun – and no celestial phenomenon that more readily blurs distinctions among religion, astronomy, and poetry. The technical name, of course, for the cosmological model proposed by Copernicus in the sixteenth century is *heliocentrism*, although from the beginning, as this chapter's first two epigraphs indicate, the justification of this Sun-centered system also employed the language of devotion and of poetry. In a typical Renaissance maneuver, Rheticus – Copernicus's only student and the first writer to expound heliocentrism in print – calls upon the ancients for support: They acknowledged the Sun's governing role in nature and gave him names, such as *chorēgos* ("director"), that had theatrical and literary as well as political connotations. As Rheticus suggests, astronomers should have paid more attention to poetry all along, for the poets' praises of the Sun pointed to his actual cosmological role and rule – if only one had listened more carefully.

Copernicus also famously pulls out the poetical stops in arguing for the appropriateness and orderliness of his new/old Sun-centered cosmology. Having already declared in his preface to *De Revolutionibus* that the Universe was framed by God, "the best and most orderly Artist of all," here, adjacent to his likewise famous diagram (Figure 3.1, p. 53), the astronomer underlines the elegance and efficiency of the Artist's having placed the Sun in the center. In fact, Copernicus somewhat fumbles his literary references to the Sun as "visible god" and as Sophocles' "the beholder."[3] Nonetheless, by means of his own diction, Copernicus reinforces the literary case for the Sun (*Sol*) being located upon a central, royal throne (*solium*) – a pun perhaps echoed by Satan, who, while "revolving," refers enviously to the Sun's "sole dominion" (4.31, 33). Furthermore, for Copernicus, the Sun functions as *pater familias*, encircled by his entire family of stars: *Astrorum familiam* (not merely "planets," as in most modern translations). Copernicus's is certainly a friendlier image

---

[3] Edward Rosen details elements of confusion in Copernicus's allusion to "Trimegistus" [*sic*] and his slip in citing Sophocles (he should have referenced *Oedipus at Colonus*, not *Electra*). See his "Was Copernicus a Hermetist?" in *Historical and Philosophical Perspectives of Science*, ed. Roger H. Stuewer; *Minnesota Studies in Philosophy of Science* 5 (Minneapolis: University of Minnesota Press, 1970): 163–71.

than that of Satan's predominantly political construal, in which – cringing, as it were – "all the stars / Hide their diminished heads" (4.34–5). For his part, Galileo would express discomfort at such a high level of figurative language. As Salviati comments in the *Dialogo*:

> Copernicus admireth the disposition of the parts of the Universe, for that God hath constituted the grand Lamp, which is to give light all over his Temple in the centre of it, and not on one side. . . . But let us not mix these Rhetorical Flowers with solid Demonstrations, rather let us leave them to the Orators, or if you will to the Poets, who know how in their drolling way to exalt by their prayses things most sordid, yea and sometimes most pernicious. (Salusbury, p. 241)

Galileo's objection is somewhat surprising, given his own displays of rhetorical skill. But it is worth pondering why Copernicus might so exert himself poetically when discussing the Sun and its position in the Universe, especially because he is today often misunderstood in this regard. In Chapter 7, we will examine the process of reimagining Earth as a planet and see how heliocentrism, contrary to the common cliché, cosmologically exalted (not demoted) Earth. For, put simply, the dominant Aristotelian and pre-Copernican conception of the universal center was that it served as a kind of cosmic sump where heavy – and, by extension, *ignoble* – things collected. As Pico had expressed it, the center represented "the excrementary and filthy parts of the lower world."[4] Copernicus's poetic effusions about the Sun's new position are best read against this background. He knew that his ideas could be seen by his contemporaries as removing the Sun from the heavens and depositing it in the lowest, least exalted place: in the "dead center" of the Universe. Indeed, the first semiofficial response to *De Revolutionibus* – written by a Dominican friar only a year after its publication and framed in transparently Aristotelian terms – complained that "Copernicus puts the indestructible sun in a place subject to destruction."[5] In short, Copernicus anticipated the charge that he was relegating the Sun to the cosmic basement and he therefore took pains, rhetorically, to renovate the basement.

Such was his success in reimagining the center that we no longer dream of the Sun as occupying a place of dishonor. But Copernicus's

[4] Giovanni Pico, *Oration on the Dignity of Man*, in *The Renaissance Philosophy of Man*, ed. Ernst Cassirer et al. (University of Chicago Press, Chicago, 1948), p. 224. The original phrase is *excrementarias ac foeculentas inferioris mundi partes; Opera Omnia Ioannis Pici* (Basel, 1493), p. 314.

[5] Giovanni Maria Tolosani, writing in June 1544, "Tolosani's Condemnations of Copernicus' *Revolutions*," in Rosen, *Copernicus and the Scientific Revolution*, p. 189.

cosmological model did imply a repudiation of the Sun's planetary status and a recent analogy might convey a taste of the emotional impact of that change. In 2006, the International Astronomical Union, meeting in Prague, voted to downgrade Pluto (discovered in 1930) to the status of "dwarf planet." Widespread objections ensued in the press, in state legislatures, and among admirers of Pluto's discoverer, Clyde Tombaugh. The American Dialect Society subsequently named "plutoed" as its word of the year for 2006: "to pluto is to demote or devalue someone or something, as happened to the former planet Pluto."[6] All this reaction concerned mere nomenclature, as it pertained to a celestial object never seen except by a minuscule proportion of the human race and discovered only seventy-six years before its "demotion." How much more of a shock must it have entailed, then, for Copernicus to pluto the Sun – of all the visible objects in the Universe the one that for millennia and across countless cultures had been an object of highest honor, if not outright worship. If early Copernicans' rhetoric on this point strikes us as somewhat energetic, we might therefore keep in mind how much credibility they had to lose should they appear to show insufficient respect for the Sun's role, dignity, even divinity. To seek to diminish the Sun's glory might make them appear hateful and satanically overreaching indeed.

Historically and theologically, however, such perilous overreaching can be taken in two opposite directions. If one extreme involves an improper or impious diminution of a magnificent component of creation, such as the Sun, the opposite danger is to forget that the object deserving one's respect or veneration is a created thing: to fall into idolatry or, in the words of St. Paul, to worship and serve "the creature more than the Creator" (Rom. 1:25). This distinction seems to have informed biblical theology right from its beginnings – also in connection with astronomical phenomena. The text of Genesis, in the well-known account of the fourth day of creation, avoids names for the Sun and the Moon altogether, referring to them only as "lights," created "to give light upon the earth" – a "greater light" and a "lesser light" (1:14–16). Some have suggested that biblical writers avoided the Hebrew noun for the Sun – *shemesh* – because it "was too reminiscent of the Canaanite and Mesopotamian sun god, Shamash."[7] Similarly, in the Book of Job, the title character "judges it necessary to profess that he never raised his hand in homage to the sun or

---

[6] See: <http://www.americandialect.org/plutoed_voted_2006_word_of_the_year>
[7] Stuart S. Miller, "'Epigraphical' Rabbis, Helios, and Psalm 19," *The Jewish Quarterly Review*, New Series, 94.1 (Winter 2004): 27–76 (p. 61).

the moon" (Job 31:26–7), although he also avoids *shemesh*, employing instead the same word for "light" used in the first chapter of the Bible.[8] However, the Genesis text clearly marks the obliquely-referred-to Sun and Moon as having a kind of governmental function: created "to rule over the day and over the night" (1:18). But as Calvin asserted concerning this verse:

> [Moses] doth not ascribe any such rule to the Sunne and Moone, as may diminishe any thing of the power of God [*Non adscribit soli et lunae dominium quod ex Dei imperio quicquam vel delibet*]: but bicause the Sunne doeth governe the day by compassing the earth about, and the Moone the night in like manner: therefore he attributeth unto them, rule. And let us remember that this principalitie is such, that the Sunne is nevertchelesse a servant. . . . Let us content our selves with this simple exposition, that God doeth governe the dayes and nightes by the service of the Sunne and Moone: because they are as it were his charriotes, which give convenient light to everie time.[9]

Thus, biblically and in the exegetical tradition, the Sun occupies a God-given place or role of honor – but one that is properly subservient.

In *Paradise Lost*, in contrast to that normative tradition, Satan would seem to err in two different directions almost simultaneously. His idolatrous address ascribes to the Sun precisely "such rule" (*dominium*) – "sole dominion like the God / Of this new world" – as Calvin says the Genesis account excludes. As David Quint rightly points out, it is fundamental for Milton that one acknowledge "works" – created things – so as "to distinguish them from their divine Creator, God, the 'great work-master' (3.696)."[10] But Satan utterly fails (or refuses) to make this distinction. Thus, in his soliloquy to the Sun in Book 4, he in effect addresses Shamash rather than *shemesh*. Still, his characteristically resentful response to divinity immediately turns his attitude to rivalry and hostility. He reads the stars' response to the Sun in terms of competition – at his sight, they "Hide their diminished heads" – and later, he will employ the same competitive calculus in his encounter with Gabriel, belittling him as a "Proud limitary Cherub" (4.971). Likewise, here in his soliloquy, in his hatred toward the Sun and the enlightenment it seems to force upon him, Satan boasts that his own former state – "glorious . . . above

---

[8] E. Lipínski, "Shemesh," *Dictionary of Deities and Demons in the Bible*, ed. Karel van der Toorn et al., 2nd ed. (Leiden: Brill, 1999), pp. 764–8.

[9] Calvin, *A Commentarie . . . upon . . . Genesis*, trans. Tymme, sig. C.iii.ᵛ; *Commentarii Joannis Calvini in Quinque Libros Mosis* (Geneva, 1573), p. 7.

[10] David Quint, "'Things Invisible to Mortal Sight': Light, Vision, and the Unity of Book 3 of *Paradise Lost*," *Modern Language Quarterly* 71.3 (Sept. 2010): 229–69 (p. 230).

thy sphere" (4.39) – in fact surpassed the Sun's "surpassing glory." Within eight lines, he thus manages to idolize and then to depreciate one of the Creator's most excellent works.

For Satan, there is indeed something about the Sun that is repulsive and attractive, and, of course, even before his soliloquy in Book 4, it catches his eye. I shall return to the passage in Book 3 that traces Satan's space journey from the edge of our Universe toward the Sun and then Earth, but here, let us simply observe Milton's diction as he describes the fallen angel catching sight of the Sun among other celestial objects: "above them all / The golden sun in splendor likest Heaven / Allured his eye" (3.571–3). "Above," as in the soliloquy's "above thy sphere," is not a spatial designation of height but an indication of preeminence – an issue Satan is repeatedly much concerned with. The affinity between the Sun and Heaven, signaled by "likest," will again be pertinent in the Book 4 soliloquy, for it is what reminds Satan whence he fell. The most telling piece of diction in these lines, however, is "Allured." Allurement is like temptation in that it can mark not only the (possibly evil) intention of the tempter but also, or instead, the moral disposition of the agent receiving the allurement or temptation. Milton almost always uses the word in this way, most notably in *Paradise Regained*, when the Son of God, responding to the "Kingdoms of the World" temptation, declares that the grandeur of Rome does *not* "allure mine eye, / Much less my mind" (4.112–13). By injecting into Satan's (we might think) mere perception of the Sun a tincture of moral and spiritual danger, *Paradise Lost* reminds us again that there is no neutral territory – that, as in the *shemesh/* Shamash ambiguity, the perils of idolatry are never far from our eyes, including when we view heavenly bodies.[11]

And yet, among heavenly bodies, the Sun is a symbol without peer. Raymond B. Waddington has sketched some of the many literary and philosophical threads that weave together in admiration for the Sun and what it represents, among them Orphic, Platonic, and, of course, Christian.[12] The epithet "eye of the world" (Ovid, *Metamorphoses* 4.228: *mundi oculus*) finds resonance in Shakespeare (Sonnet 18: "the eye of

---

[11] On idolatry, see also Quint, "'Things Invisible to Mortal Sight,'" *Modern Language Quarterly*, 257–63. Quint indicates that Milton's main source for knowledge of ancient Sun worship was John Selden, *De diis syris* (London, 1617). For more on Milton, Selden, and pagan gods, see Jason P. Rosenblatt, *Renaissance England's Chief Rabbi: John Selden* (Oxford: Oxford University Press, 2006), Chapter 3, "Selden and Milton on Gods and Angels" (pp. 73–92).

[12] Raymond B. Waddington, "Here Comes the Son: Providential Theme and Symbolic Pattern in *Paradise Lost*, Book 3," *Modern Philology* 79.3 (Feb. 1982): 256–66.

heaven") and Kepler (*veluti oculus mundi*)[13] as well as in Milton (*PL*, 3.578: "lordly eye"). Moreover, the main Christian tradition finds no contradiction (despite the presence of danger) in honoring the Sun, reading it symbolically, and acknowledging it as a divine "work" – a balance nicely summarized by Ambrose: "Do not . . . without due consideration put your trust in the sun. It is true that it is the eye of the world, the joy of the day, the beauty of the heavens, the charm of nature and the most conspicuous object in creation. When you behold it, reflect on its Author. When you admire it, give praise to its Creator."[14]

Milton's newly created and unfallen Adam follows this prescription precisely in the scene that completes the Satan/Adam diptych in which both characters address the midday Sun, although with contrasting results. We have already considered Satan's response in Book 4. But Adam's response, in his first moments of consciousness, is to address the Sun as part of the wider fabric of creation, within which he situates himself:

> "'Thou sun,' said I, 'fair light,
> And thou enlightened earth, so fresh and gay,
> Ye hills and dales, ye rivers, woods, and plains,
> And ye that live and move, fair creatures, tell,
> Tell, if ye saw, how came I thus, how here?
> Not of myself; by some great Maker then,
> In goodness and in power pre-eminent;
> Tell me, how may I know him, how adore[?]'"
> (8.273–80)

Instinctively knowing himself and his surroundings, including the Sun, as *creatures*, Adam is led by ineluctable logic toward the Creator. Adam and Eve together – later in time but earlier in the poem – similarly address their morning psalm to all created things, including the Sun, calling them to join in worshipping the Creator: "Thou sun, of this great world both eye and soul, / Acknowledge him thy greater, sound his praise" (5.171–2). Of course, these utterances are informed by the speakers' sinless assumption that far from being in competition with their implied audiences and certainly not coerced or threatened by the creatures they address, they are partners in a shared enterprise of adoration and worship.

---

[13] Johannes Kepler, *Epitome Astronomiae Copernicanae* (Linz, 1618–22), p. 439.

[14] Ambrose, *Hexameron*, trans. John J. Savage, Book 4, the Fourth Day (Sixth Homily), 1.2; in *The Fathers of the Church* 42 (New York: Fathers of the Church, 1961): 127. See also Walter Clyde Curry's chapter "The Lordship of Milton's Sun," *Milton's Ontology, Cosmogony and Physics* (Lexington, KY: University of Kentucky Press, 1957), pp. 114–43.

At the beginning of his influential work *On the Sun* (*De Sole*, 1593), Florentine neoplatonist Marsilio Ficino emphasizes that his book is "allegorical and anagogical rather than dogmatic." There is no doubt that writings on the Sun by Ficino and also Kepler have – in keeping with those categories of "allegorical and anagogical" – a strong mystical flavor. Nonetheless, as implied by Rheticus's disapproving comment about the habit of reading "the ancient *encomia* of the Sun as if they were merely poetry," we may also similarly interpret the Sun's role in Milton and other early modern authors without undue concern for the separation of theology, astronomy, and poetry. For all these areas share a concern for decorum or fitness that can lead to fruitful insights and connections and did so for Ficino and Kepler.

For all their differences, Ficino and Kepler saw the Sun as in the deepest sense theologically *significant* – in Ficino's words: "Above all the Sun can show you God himself [*tibi significare potest*]. The Sun will give you signs. Who dares call the Sun false?"[15] However, this recognition, which includes a verbatim borrowing from Virgil's *Georgics*, need entail no idolatry. Ficino underlines this point by immediately echoing the language of Romans 1:20: The process of signification effected by the Sun and other elements of creation allows the invisible things of God – "his eternal power and Godhead" – to be clearly seen.[16] Moreover, that theological function leads Ficino directly to an inference about the Sun's dominant cosmological role: "The Sun, manifestly lord of the sky, rules and governs all heavenly things. . . . It implants light into the stars, whether these have some small light of their own (as some suppose) or none at all (as believed by many)."[17] The latter technical uncertainty concerning whether the stars' light is their own or, like the Moon's, merely reflected sunlight reappears in *Paradise Lost* in Raphael's account of the Sun's creation, "great palace . . . of light," which functions as the wellspring of luminosity for "other stars" (7.363–4):

> "By tincture or reflection they augment
> Their small peculiar, though from human sight
> So far remote, with diminution seen."
>
> (7.367–9)

---

[15] Marsilio Ficino, *De sole* (Florence, 1493), sig. a iii^r, quoting Virgil, *Georgics*, 1.463–4: *Sol tibi signa dabit: Solem quis dicere falsum audeat?*

[16] *De sole*, sig. a iii^{r-v}: *invisibilia Dei . . . conspiciuntur: per Solem vero sempiterna quoque Dei virtus atque divinitas.*

[17] *De sole*, sig. a iii^v: *Sol tanquam manifestus caeli dominus omnia prorsus caelestia regit et moderatur. . . . lumen stellis omnibus inserit: Sive nativum illae per se lumen exiguum habeant (ut nonnulli suspicantur): sive nullum (ut plurimi putant).*

Ficino's meditation on the Sun resonates in an intriguing way with another aspect of seventeenth-century thought that deserves mention. Having repeated the Orphic designation of the Sun as "eye of heaven" (*caeli oculus*), Ficino draws attention to a further corporeal analogy: "The Sun was named by the old physicians 'heart of heaven,' and by Heraclitus 'fountain of heavenly light'" (sig. a vii^v). The heart metaphor may be "only poetry," but it affords an analogy not at all incompatible with heliocentrism. Moreover, every analogy has two sides, and William Harvey would take full advantage of the ready-made parallel between world and body – macrocosm and microcosm – declaring in his *De Motu Cordis* (1628): "The heart . . . is . . . the sun of the microcosm, even as the sun in his turn might well be designated the heart of the world; for it is the heart by whose virtue and pulse the blood is moved."[18] This cardiac correspondence is a reminder that the cosmological revolution pertained to the microcosm as well as the macrocosm. We observe, once more, that analogy serves as more than "merely poetry."

This was a lesson Kepler learned well – perhaps directly from the writings of Rheticus, whose *Narratio Prima* was included as an appendix to Kepler's own first Copernican treatise: the *Mysterium Cosmographicum* (1596). In his *Epitome of Copernican Astronomy* (1618–22), Kepler asserts, "most rightly is the sun held to be the heart of the world and the seat of reason and life . . .; and these praises [*encomia*] are true in the philosophic sense, since the poets honour the sun as the king of the stars."[19]

Moreover, what Kepler calls the "philosophic" sense (we might say "physical" or "cosmological") extends to the actual mechanics of the Universe. In Ficino, the analogy of the cosmic and the divine culminates in an anagogical lesson:

> All heavenly things appear to turn back toward one Sun as to a single governor and measurer of the heavens, and so we are reminded that all things in heaven, and beneath the heavens, and above the heavens likewise return to that one beginning of all things – considering which, finally, let us at least worship him with such honor as those heavenly things do the Sun.[20]

[18] William Harvey, *Movement of the Heart and Blood in Animals*, trans. Kenneth J. Franklin (Oxford: Blackwell, 1957), p. 49.

[19] Kepler, *Epitome*, trans. Wallis, p. 16; cf. *Epitome Astronomiae*, pp. 440–1.

[20] Ficino, *De sole*, sig. c i^r. As David C. Lindberg points out, although Ficino touches on cosmological themes, his main focus is Neoplatonic philosophy, not cosmology. See Lindberg, "The Genesis of Kepler's Theory of Light: Light Metaphysics From Plotinus to Kepler," *Osiris*, 2nd series, 2 (1986): 4–42 (p. 24).

Although Kepler was not averse to drawing such spiritual lessons, as a natural philosopher he pursued astronomical more than anagogical conclusions. The Sun's language becomes, for him, an explanation – although overflowing with what Galileo called "Rhetorical Flowers" – of how the physical Universe operates. Although his description of the worshipful orbiting of the planets about the Sun may accordingly be highly figurative, its substance is cosmological:

> This positioning of the six primary spheres round the Sun, honoring him with their perpetual revolution, and, so to speak, adoring him . . . and this special matter of the harmonies which is now added to that consideration, a very clear trace of the highest providence in the affairs of the Sun, wrings from me the following confession. Not only does light go out to the whole world from the Sun, as from the focus or eye of the world, as all life and heat does from the heart, all motion from the ruler and mover; but in return there are collected at the Sun from the whole cosmic province, by royal right, these, so to speak, repayments of the most desirable harmony.[21]

Various affinities between Kepler and Milton have been proposed by Anita Lawson.[22] The astronomer and the poet were particularly fascinated by the Sun's celestial dominance, by its light, and by its symbolic richness. One of Kepler's assertions, as in the passage just quoted, is that commerce between the Sun and the rest of the Universe is a two-way affair. Perhaps supported by Galileo's discovery, reported in *Sidereus Nuncius*, that the Moon and Earth actually engage in a "fair and grateful exchange," Kepler also uses the language of financial transactions – repayments, as it were, collected "from the whole cosmic province" – to describe what the Sun receives back from the recipients of its light. Milton hints at a similarly "commercial" relationship between the Sun and other celestial bodies – except that he imagines the relationship as involving a recirculation of vaporous nutrients: "The Sun that light imparts to all, receives / From all his alimental recompense / In humid exhalations" (5.423–5).

A more significant affinity, cosmologically, is Milton's well-known echo of Kepler's proposed physical mechanism for the movements of the planets and stars now that the Ptolemaic solid spheres had been discarded. As noted at the end of Chapter 3, Kepler claimed William Gilbert's "philosophy of magnetism" as one of the pillars of his cosmology and he saw the

---

[21] Johannes Kepler, *The Harmony of the World*, trans. E. J. Aiton et al. (N.p.: American Philosophical Society, 1997), p. 492.

[22] Anita Lawson, "'The Golden Sun in Splendor Likest Heaven': Johannes Kepler's *Epitome* and *Paradise Lost*, Book 3," *Milton Quarterly* 21.2 (May 1987): 46–51.

Sun, like Earth, as a great magnet – one that served as "the first cause of the movement of the planets and the first mover of the universe."[23] Moreover, Kepler held up this physical hypothesis – to which he saw no reasonable alternative – as a further reason for accepting heliocentrism, for "there is only one solar body, which is situated at the centre of the whole universe, and to which this movement of the primary planets around the body of the sun can be ascribed."[24] As we know, Milton nowhere explicitly endorsed heliocentrism, although in offering Satan and us a first glimpse of the Sun in *Paradise Lost*, he comes close to doing so. In Book 3, Satan passes downward from the edge of our Universe among the stars, above all of which

> The golden sun in splendor likest Heaven
> Allured his eye: thither his course he bends
> Through the calm firmament; but up or down
> By center, or eccentric, hard to tell,
> Or longitude, where the great luminary
> Aloof the vulgar constellations thick,
> That from his lordly eye keep distance due,
> Dispenses light from far; they as they move
> Their starry dance in numbers that compute
> Days, months, and years, towards his all-cheering lamp
> Turn swift their various motions, or are turned
> By his magnetic beam, that gently warms
> The universe, and to each inward part
> With gentle penetration, though unseen,
> Shoots invisible virtue even to the deep:
> So wondrously was set his station bright.
>
> (3.572–87)

Typically, Milton carefully avoids firm cosmological claims because so much about the world is indeed "hard to tell." The phrase "station bright," as Kerrigan, Rumrich, and Fallon note regarding line 587, "suggests a sedentary sun, as in the Copernican system, ... [but] could also refer to the fixed sphere or course of the sun in the Ptolemaic cosmos." Moreover, the conspicuously Keplerian "magnetic beam" whereby the Sun activates or animates the parts of the "starry dance" is preceded by a Miltonic "or" and accordingly needs to be read as a merely possible, although distinct,

---

[23] Kepler, *Epitome*, trans. Wallis, p. 15.
[24] Kepler, *Epitome*, trans. Wallis, p. 55; cf. *Epitome Astronomiae*, p. 513: *solum et unicum esse corpus Solare, situm in medio totius universi, cui motus iste primatiorum planetarum circa corpus Solis, possit asscribi*. See also Thomas Kuhn, *The Copernican Revolution: Planetary Astronomy in the Development of Western Thought* (Cambridge, MA: Harvard University Press, 1957), pp. 247–9.

physical explanation of how the *machina mundi* actually works.[25] None-theless, mention of the "magnetic beam" certainly encourages an active engagement with solar physics, not only symbolism – an engagement the poet pursues in subsequent lines with a remarkably keen imaginative sense of the physical and the concrete.

One early seventeenth-century debate, however, that entailed a collision of physical and symbolic cosmological elements concerned the interpretation of sunspots. Galileo, with some justification, receives much credit for discovering this solar phenomenon, but Christoph Scheiner also deserves recognition for his observational and interpretive contribution, even if in most respects he came out the loser in the controversy. In 1611, having taken up a telescope and begun observing spots, *maculae*, on the Sun's face early that year, Scheiner wrote three letters on the subject (*Tres Epistolae de Maculis Solaribus*), offering a preliminary account of his observations. He sent these to his friend Marc Welser in Augsburg, who published them under the pseudonym "Apelles" and sent them to Galileo for his response. From the beginning of the letters, one notices respectful references (not unlike those of Ficino and others) to the Sun as a "source of illumination and the commander of heavenly bodies."[26] But only a few sentences farther along, Scheiner identifies the problem. As he was using the "optical tube" to measure the Moon's and the Sun's magnitudes, he writes, he "noticed on the Sun some rather blackish spots like dark specks [*nigricantes quodammodo maculas, instar guttarum subnigrarum*]" (p. 61; sig. A2r).

In Chapter 4, we reflected on the shared, potentially negative connota-tions of English "spot" and Latin *macula*; in a moral context, both words can carry the sense of flaw or character blemish. If this sense of the word entailed a problem for Galileo's account of the Moon's surface, then for Scheiner, it seemed even more disturbing as applied to the Sun. For this reason – because it seemed to him "unfitting [*inconveniens*] that on the

---

[25] Such open-mindedness about magnetic forces sets Milton decisively apart from, for example, the reactionary Aristotelian Alexander Ross, who scoffs that "Keplar's *opinion that the Planets are moved round by the Sunne, and that this is done by sending forth a magneticke vertue, and that the Sunbeames are like the teeth of a wheele, taking hold of the Planets*, are senselesse crotchets, fitter for a wheeler or miller, then a Philosopher: This magneticke vertue is a salve for all sores, a pin to stop every hole"; Ross, *The new planet no planet, or, The earth no wandring star, except in the wandring heads of Galileans* (London, 1646), p. 112.

[26] Christoph Scheiner, *Tres epistolae de maculis solaribus* (Augsburg, 1612); *On Sunspots*, ed. and trans. Reeves and Van Helden, p. 59. In-text page references are to this translation and signature numbers align with the original *Tres epistolae*.

most lucid body of the Sun there would be spots" (p. 62; sig. A3^r) – Scheiner interprets the appearances not as something actually on the solar surface but instead as stars (i.e., planets) circling about in the Sun's "sky," analogous to the Medicean "stars" that Galileo in early 1610 discovered orbiting Jupiter. In the third letter, Scheiner returns to the theme of championing the Sun's honor by means of a planetary interpretation of the spots: "It pleases me to liberate the Sun's body entirely from the insult of spots [*macularum injuria*]" (p. 67; sig. A4^v). Nor was he alone in expressing shock – as much moral and symbolic as cosmological – at the possibility that the glorious Sun's face might not be immaculate. In a jocular but perceptive letter dated January 4, 1612, Tuscan poet Alessandro Allegri acknowledged that the "Flemish glass" was being used to reveal "filth on the cheeks of the Sun."[27]

For his part, Galileo resolutely – and, from a scientific viewpoint, admirably – refused to let this rhetorical or symbolic dimension of the discussion interfere with his treatment of the evidence. In his response to Welser, publisher of the Scheiner's *Tres Epistolae*, he carefully rejects *a priori* assumptions concerning where sunspots might actually be located:

> The author [of the letters], having established that the observed spots are not illusions of the lens or defects of the eye, seeks to determine something general about their location, showing that they are neither in the air nor on the solar body. . . . But the hypothesis that they cannot be on the solar body does not appear to me to have been fully and necessarily determined. For it is not conclusive to say, as he does in the first argument, that because the solar body is very bright it is not credible that there are dark spots on it, because as long as no cloud or impurity whatsoever has been seen on it we have to designate it as most pure and most bright, but when it reveals itself to be partly impure and spotted, why shouldn't we call it both spotted and impure [*macolato e non puro*]? (*On Sunspots*, p. 91)

Galileo was of course correct to pinpoint the fallacy – the circular reasoning – in Scheiner's approach to the problem of sunspots, their nature, and their location. The revulsion Scheiner expressed regarding the possibility of a besmirched Sun is nonetheless instructive. In other areas of astronomy, he was actively revising his position in the face of new evidence, citing with approval the near-deathbed call by Christoph Clavius in 1611 that astronomers, "on account of . . . new and hitherto invisible phenomena [such as the telescopically revealed Moon-like phases of

---

[27] *On Sunspots*, ed. and trans. Reeves and Van Helden, p. 77; Alessandro Allegri, *Lettere di Ser Poi Pedante* (1613; rpt. Cassalmaggiore, 1850), p. 21: "luridumi delle gote del Sole."

Venus], . . . must unhesitatingly provide themselves with another system of the world."[28] Moreover, Galileo commended Scheiner's openness to evidence: The author of the *Tres Epistolae* "begins to lend his ear and approval to the true and good philosophy, and especially in the matter concerning the constitution of the universe, but . . . he cannot yet totally free himself from those fancies previously impressed on him, fancies to which his intellect still returns from time to time, habituated to assent by long custom" (p. 95). If Scheiner could wield a telescope, make accurate observations of sunspots, and revise his cosmology (albeit in a Tychonic direction) – yet still not countenance conclusions positing *maculae* and "filth" on the Sun's face – then his position stands as a sharp reminder of the more-than-astronomical honor in which the Sun was held, and not only by neoplatonists such as Ficino.[29]

At the end of Book 3 of *Paradise Lost*, in his most detailed description of the Sun, Milton weaves together a number of prominent stylistic, thematic, epistemological, and imaginative threads. In Chapter 4, we noticed the characterization of Satan's shield, by means of epic simile, as displaying a surface like that of the Moon's telescopically observed "spotty globe" (1.291). In Book 4, Galileo and his instrument are evoked again, although here, the simile is given and then taken away:

> There [on the Sun] lands the fiend, a spot like which perhaps
> Astronomer in the sun's lucent orb
> Through his glazed optic tube yet never saw.
>
> (4.588–90)

In Chapter 2, we observed how Milton wields the postponed negative – the just-in-time volta – that changes everything – as for example in the long description of the atomist abyss of Chaos, whose elements "must ever fight, / *Unless* th' Almighty Maker them ordain / His dark materials to create more worlds" (2.914–16). The poet employs a similar technique in describing Raphael's first glimpse from afar of Earth, "as when by night the glass / Of Galileo, less assured, observes / Imagined lands and regions in the moon" (*PL*, 5.261–2). Here, the crucial modifications appear in the middle of the clause and at the turn of the lines ("less assured,

---

[28] *On Sunspots*, ed. and trans. Reeves and Van Helden, p. 229. For more on Clavius's final published comments on "another system of the world," see the first epigraph to the previous chapter as well as Lattis, *Between Copernicus and Galileo*, pp. 198–9.

[29] For a helpful summary of Galileo and Scheiner's debate on sunspots, see (besides *On Sunspots*, ed. and trans. Reeves and Van Helden) the Galileo Project: http://galileo.rice.edu/sci/observations/sunspots.html.

observes / Imagined ... "), thus rendering the comparison of the two elements more contrast than similarity – as to both their subject (Raphael's clear angelic sight versus Galileo's fallible human sight) and their object (our earthly lands and regions, unlike the lunar ones, not being merely imagined). In Book 4, the astronomical simile conjures up sunspots (their nature and ontological status themselves subject of controversy); adds further uncertainty with "perhaps"; and then still further undercuts the reality of the compared items with "yet never saw."

These readings certainly support Amy Boesky's magisterial discussion of "Milton, Galileo, and Sunspots" with its emphasis on epistemology and on Galileo as "an overdetermined figure for Milton, representing both the powers of mortal vision and its fallibility."[30] Just as significant, however, are this short scene's moral and cosmological implications. Rightly recognizing the common meaning of "spot" as moral impurity, Boesky generalizes this sense, apparently leaving no use of the term untainted: "In Milton's writing ... 'spots' signify a stain or blemish, or are suggestively associated with sites (spots) of temptation" (p. 28). But surely, to the contrary, Milton's sunspots simile effectively supports the distinction between spots that are just spots and spots that are truly evil. If Christoph Scheiner were, hypothetically, to encounter this scene, perhaps he would realize he need not worry about the solar spots he and Galileo observed – or even about other signs of mutability in the heavens, such as comets or supernovae. For these things are simply part of a good and universally coherent, dynamic Cosmos in which change occurs – change not threatening to the creation's or the Sun's glory and integrity. Instead, what we humans ought to worry about is "spottedness" that threatens from without, blemishes not aesthetic but moral and metaphysical, evils that are spiritually extraneous, malevolent, malignant – like which no observer by means of any mere optical device, not even Uriel, "The sharpest sighted spirit of all" (3.691), yet ever saw or could see.

The spiritual dimension of cosmology adumbrated by Uriel's presence on the Sun also has biblical and possibly Keplerian connections. Milton makes the former explicit with his reference to Uriel (whose name means "light of God") as "The same whom John saw also in the sun" (3.623). The affinity with Kepler is more speculative but nonetheless noteworthy. Milton's account of the "magnetic beam" whereby the Sun activates the

---

[30] Amy Boesky, "Milton, Galileo, and Sunspots: Optics and Certainty in *Paradise Lost*," *Milton Studies* 34 (1997): 23–42 (p. 23). This article is also extremely useful for its references to other scholarly engagements with the topic of Milton and Galileo.

"starry dance" is, as we have seen, Keplerian in substance. For his part, Kepler, in his own discussion of the behavior of sunspots, points to their consonance with the Sun's rotation: They appear to move across the solar face because the Sun itself is turning. Moreover, the Sun's rotation is in Kepler's eyes evidence that contrary to a merely mechanical conception of the Universe, there is an inherent dynamism in things he calls "soul." The world and its components are animated and the Sun itself "seems to continue this movement by the reinforcement of a motor soul."[31] What Kepler appears to aim at is a conception of the world that is in some sense incarnational: on the one hand not mechanistic and on the other not dualistic or merely referential, as for Plato or Ficino. Milton's conception, as is well known, is philosophically materialist but neither Hobbesian nor mechanistic. Stephen Fallon has called Milton's position "animist materialism"[32] and it is best illustrated by the angelology of *Paradise Lost*, in which those spiritual beings have bodies, eat heavenly and earthly food, and (after their own manner) copulate. In short, there is no radical separation of nor contradiction between the physical and the spiritual. Similarly with the Sun, Milton gives us an imaginatively concrete description of at least some aspects of its physics in a manner harmonious with the interangelic scene – the spiritual drama – that unfolds on the physical celestial body that Adam and Eve will call "of this great world both eye and soul" (5.171).

The physical scene Milton sets has conspicuously earthly components:

> The place he found beyond expression bright,
> Compared with aught on Earth, metal or stone;
> Not all parts like, but all alike informed
> With radiant light, as glowing iron with fire;
> If metal, part seemed gold, part silver clear;
> If stone, carbuncle most or chrysolite,
> Ruby or topaz, to the twelve that shone
> In Aaron's breastplate, and a stone besides
> Imagined rather oft than elsewhere seen,
> That stone, or like to that which here below
> Philosophers in vain so long have sought.
>   (3.591–601)

---

[31] *Epitome*, trans. Wallis, pp. 56–7; *Epitome astronomiae*, p. 514: *videri continuare hunc motum, praesidio animae motrieis.*

[32] Stephen M. Fallon, *Milton Among the Philosophers*, pp. 79–110. I find N. K. Sugimura's attempted challenge to the "materialist" reading of Milton – *"Matter of Glorious Trial": Spiritual and Material Substance in Paradise Lost* (New Haven: Yale UP, 2009) – unconvincing.

Apart from its surpassing brilliance and despite the tentativeness of its description, the scene's components are all terrestrial, not ethereal in any sense consistent with the Aristotelian two-storey universe. Moreover, this is true not because of terrestrial influence on the Sun (although, as noted, Milton, along with Kepler, envisages some degree of mutual exchange; see 5.423–5) but vice versa. It is the "Th' arch-chemic sun" that "Produces with terrestrial humor mixed / Here in the dark so many precious things" (3.609–11). The analogy with Earth, of course, is for our benefit, not Satan's; Satan has not yet knowingly seen anything earthly. Nevertheless, Milton underlines the earthly materiality of what Satan beholds: "Here *matter* new to gaze the Devil met / Undazzled" (3.613–14). And typically, Satan is unimpressed by the appearance of so much that is impressive – just as in the following book, he will behold "undelighted all delight" (4.286). A final beautifully imagined feature enjoyed by those standing on the Sun (and those looking on via the poetry) is the absence of shadows:

> For sight no obstacle found here, nor shade,
> But all sun-shine, as when his beams at noon
> Culminate from the equator, as they now
> Shot upward still direct, whence no way round
> Shadow from body opaque can fall.
>
> (3.615–19)

Again, earthly analogy – this time with a critical difference – permits the visualization: Just as sunbeams on the equator (at the equinoxes now but all year round before the fall) are vertical, so on the Sun do they shoot "upward still direct." Therefore, although figuratively Satan is perfectly opaque, he remains a uniquely invisible kind of sunspot. Even the more-than-telescopically penetrating eye of Uriel cannot discern this particular moral filth on the Sun's face.

In his short treatise on the Sun, Ficino points out that light, the first among God's works named in Genesis, precedes the Sun's creation. "Moses says merely that light was created on the first day, and then that on the fourth day it was given its solar, spherical form" (sig. b iv^r). In the sixteenth century, Calvin asserts a similar point in his commentary on Genesis 1:14:

> Moses passeth to the fourth day, wherein the starres were made. Firste he [God] had created the light: but nowe he appointeth a newe order of nature, that the Sunne might be a continuall giver of light, and that the

Mone and Starres might shine by nighte. And hee attributeth this office [*illis officium*] unto them, that we may knowe that all creatures stande at his will, and exequute that which he commaundeth. For Moses reporteth no other thing, but that God had apointed certeine instruments [*organa*], which gave that light by their course and turne which was alreadie created before.[33]

In keeping with the Sun being *shemesh*, merely a created "instrument" or servant of God, and not Shamash, a god or idol, Calvin emphasizes the Sun as filling an "office" and executing divine commands. Milton's invocation to holy light in Book 3 also reflects the chronology of Genesis insofar as the creation of light (1:3) clearly precedes the creation of "lights" (i.e., the Sun and the Moon; 1:14):

> Hail, holy light, offspring of Heav'n first-born,
> Or of th' Eternal coeternal beam
> May I express thee unblamed? Since God is light,
> And never but in unapproachèd light
> Dwelt from eternity, dwelt then in thee,
> Bright effluence of bright essence increate.
> Or hear'st thou rather pure ethereal stream,
> Whose fountain who shall tell? Before the sun,
> Before the heavens thou wert, and at the voice
> Of God, as with a mantle, didst invest
> The rising world of waters dark and deep,
> Won from the void and formless infinite.
>
> (3.1–12)

However, "Before the heavens" – as distinct from "Before the sun" – entirely transcends the chronology of Genesis 1 and places light, at least *holy* light, prior to any of the components mentioned in the first verses of that chapter – be it "the heaven and the earth" of verse 1 or "the earth . . . without form, and void" or the dark-covered "deep" of verse 2. The light that is the addressee of the invocation, even though its influences and traces soon appear in the creation, is precosmological. It is, in a word, theological.

By contrast, the creation story in Book 7 of *Paradise Lost*, narrated by Raphael, dwells within – even as it vastly expands – the sequence outlined in the Genesis account, beginning with the first fiat:

> "'Let there be light,' said God; and forthwith light
> Ethereal, first of things, quintessence pure
> Sprung from the deep, and from her native east

---

[33] Calvin, *A Commentarie . . . upon . . . Genesis*, trans. Tymme, sig. C.i.ᵛ; *Commentarii*, p. 5.

> To journey through the airy gloom began,
> Sphered in a radiant cloud, for yet the sun
> Was not; she in a cloudy tabernacle
> Sojourned the while. God saw the light was good;
> And light from darkness by the hemisphere
> Divided: light the day, and darkness night
> He named. Thus was the first day ev'n and morn."
> (7.243–52)

The synonymous terms "Ethereal" and "quintessence" identify light as part of the new Cosmos and as thus distinct, *qua* creature, from the "bright essence increate" of the earlier invocation to holy light. Created light, like the rest of the emerging pieces of the world, arises by divine fiat from the territory of Chaos – "the deep" – earlier circumscribed by the Creator on the Noughth Day of creation (Gen. 1:1–2 and *PL*, 7.224–34). Moreover, for now, it is literally a nebulous luminescence, tabernacled in a cloud, waiting, sojourning, until it can be transplanted from tabernacle to temple, from shrine to palace.

Through the voice of Raphael, Milton recounts this process of transplantation on Day 4 of the creation and the beginning of the passage follows closely the account of Genesis 1:14–18, which reads:

> [14] And God said, Let there be lights in the firmament of the heaven to divide the day from the night; and let them be for signs, and for seasons, and for days, and years:
> [15] And let them be for lights in the firmament of the heaven to give light upon the earth: and it was so.
> [16] And God made two great lights; the greater light to rule the day, and the lesser light to rule the night: he made the stars also.
> [17] And God set them in the firmament of the heaven to give light upon the earth,
> [18] And to rule over the day and over the night, and to divide the light from the darkness: and God saw that it was good.

Raphael's words are these:

> "Again th' Almighty spake: 'Let there be lights
> High in th' expanse of heaven to divide   340
> The day from night; and let them be for signs,
> For seasons, and for days, and circling years,
> And let them be for lights as I ordain
> Their office in the firmament of heav'n,
> To give light on the Earth'; and it was so.   345
> And God made two great lights, great for their use

> To man, the greater to have rule by day,
> The less by night altern: and made the stars,
> And set them in the firmament of heav'n
> To illuminate the Earth, and rule the day   350
> In their vicissitude, and rule the night,
> And light from darkness to divide. God saw,
> Surveying his great work, that it was good."
>
>   (7.339–53)

In these lines, the only substantive departures from or interpolations into the Genesis text are the identification of the lights' duties as an "office" (line 344, as in Calvin's commentary); the interpretive (and astronomically accurate) gloss telling us that the greatness of the "great lights" is a humanly relative greatness (lines 346–7: "great for their use / To man"); and the theologically important reminder that God's "seeing" of the lights of Heaven, by contrast with our earthly perspective, is actually a *survey* – a viewing from above – of his own work (line 353).

However, these lines of close paraphrase are followed by twice as many that depart almost entirely from the Genesis *Urtext* and offer a tapestry interweaving technical explanation with exuberant celebration of the newly animated cosmic dance:

> "For of celestial bodies first the sun
> A mighty sphere he framed, unlightsome first,   355
> Though of ethereal mold: then formed the moon
> Globose, and every magnitude of stars,
> And sowed with stars the heav'n thick as a field:
> Of light by far the greater part he took,
> Transplanted from her cloudy shrine, and placed   360
> In the sun's orb, made porous to receive
> And drink the liquid light, firm to retain
> Her gathered beams, great palace now of light.
> Hither as to their fountain other stars
> Repairing, in their golden urns draw light,   365
> And hence the morning-planet gilds her horns;
> By tincture or reflection they augment
> Their small peculiar, though from human sight
> So far remote, with diminution seen.
> First in his east the glorious lamp was seen,   370
> Regent of day, and all th' horizon round
> Invested with bright rays, jocund to run
> His longitude through heav'n's high road: the gray
> Dawn, and the Pleiades before him danced
> Shedding sweet influence: less bright the moon,   375

But opposite in leveled west was set,
His mirror, with full face borrowing her light
From him, for other light she needed none
In that aspect, and still that distance keeps
Till night, then in the east her turn she shines,   380
Revolved on heav'n's great axle, and her reign
With thousand lesser lights dividual holds,
With thousand thousand stars, that then appeared
Spangling the hemisphere: then first adorned
With their bright luminaries that set and rose,   385
Glad ev'ning and glad morn crowned the fourth day."
                                                    (7.354–86)

Here, Milton offers a thoughtfully playful glimpse into God's workshop –
into the "how" of astronomical creation not provided by Genesis. Although
beginning with a technical account ("A mighty sphere he framed," made
from "ethereal" matter), the description quickly turns horticultural: The
stars are sown as in a field and the light, already created, is "Transplanted"
into "the sun's orb," which "drink[s] the liquid light." We shall return to the
universal interplay of the "two great sexes [that] animate the world" (8.151).
But in this passage, the interaction is already evident and the scene soon
undergoes a transition from botanical to zoological. The unique consum-
mation of the union of light and Sun is portrayed as an embryonic
transplant of *her* from nebulous container ("shrine") into *him* – into a body
that is receptive, "porous," and yet "firm." The fecundity of the union
establishes the Sun as a place, a palace, that now supplies the other stars of
Heaven (including, as we have seen, Venus) with light. As already indicated, Milton leaves open the question of whether stars have their own
"peculiar" light – but reminds us of their vast distance. And just as the Sun's
and Moon's "greatness" is a humanly relative thing, based on proximity, so
the stars' dimness or "diminution" may be, rather than absolute, simply a
function of their remoteness from us (line 369).

A further significant shift in the tone and substance of the passage then
occurs when the "Regent of day" (etymologically echoing the "rule" of the
Sun in Genesis 1:16) is described as running "jocund" across the heavens
(line 372). Milton thus evokes Psalm 19:5–6, which speaks of the Sun "as a
bridegroom coming out of his chamber, [who] rejoiceth as a strong man to
run a race . . . from the end of the heaven, and his circuit unto the ends of
it." The scene thus suddenly emerges as a marriage celebration complete
with dancing and special lighting – a spectacle that seems to expand
exponentially before our eyes – from the Sun and the Moon to a
"thousand lesser lights" to a "thousand thousand stars" (lines 382–3).

The celebration's gentle sexual *frisson* is reinforced by the interspersing of more than a dozen gendered – male and female – singular pronouns. The Sun's animated joy (as in Ps. 19:5) reappears in the final cadence of the passage, although now attributed to the entire fourth day by way of its termini: "Glad ev'ning and glad morn." By the time it closes, the passage has radiantly emerged as a cosmic epithalamium.

The association of God with light is such a commonplace that it may need little further comment. The invocation to light in *Paradise Lost* posits perhaps as close an identification as (piously) one dare make, although Milton makes the appropriate distinction between light created and "increate" (3.6) and reemphasizes the Sun's secondary, although splendid, nature in the account of Day 4, as we have just seen. Regarding James 1:17 with its reference to God as "Father of lights, with whom is no variableness, neither shadow of turning," Ficino comments in the same vein that the verse is a reminder that "the Sun is not the origin of the Universe."[34] None of these cautions, however, diminish the Sun's potency as a body that symbolizes various divine characteristics. Some commentators have reasonably seen Malachi 4:1–2, with its mention of the coming "Sun of righteousness" – capable of burning and healing – as contextualizing Satan's hostile soliloquy to the Sun,[35] considered earlier in this chapter. But, of course, the most immediate background of Book 4 is Book 3, with its angelic celebration of the Son's announced redemption of humankind. There, the angels' hymn praises the Father as

> "Author of all being,
> Fountain of light, thyself invisible
> Amidst the glorious brightness where thou sitt'st
> Throned inaccessible, but when thou shad'st
> The full blaze of thy beams, and through a cloud
> Drawn round about thee like a radiant shrine,
> Dark with excessive bright thy skirts appear,
> Yet dazzle Heav'n."
>
> (3.374–81)

And next, they sing:

> "Begotten Son, divine similitude,
> In whose conspicuous count'nance, without cloud

---

[34] Ficino, *De sole*, sig. b iv[v]: *admonuit Solem hunc non esse universi principium.*
[35] See, for example, Fowler, *The Poems of John Milton*, p. 610, and *Paradise Lost: The Biblically Annotated Edition*, ed. Matthew Stallard (Macon, GA: Mercer University Press, 2011), pp. 133–4.

Figure 6.1   John Baptist Medina's "engraving" for Book 3 of the 1688 folio
edition of *Paradise Lost*

> Made visible, th' Almighty Father shines,
> Whom else no creature can behold; on thee
> Impressed the effulgence of his glory abides,
> Transfused on thee his ample spirit rests."
>
> (3.384–9)

Given the luminous parallels between Book 3 and Book 4, added to the
well-known Sun/Son pun that the English language affords,[36] it is therefore noteworthy but not surprising that John Baptist Medina, in his

---

[36] One of the most famous meditations on this pun, of course, is George Herbert's sonnet "The
Sonne," published in *The Temple* (1633).

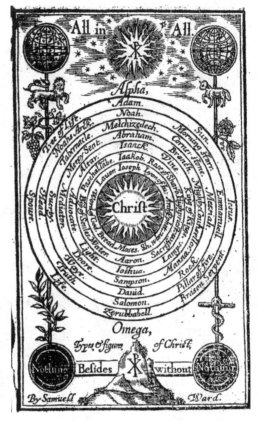

Figure 6.2   Title page of Samuel Ward's *All in All* (1622)

engraving for Book 3 of the 1688 folio edition of *Paradise Lost*, should actually foreground Satan's encounter with the Sun in Book 4. Medina's plate stands accordingly as a visual version of the Sun/Son pun, indicating, by means of his conflation of scenes from the two books, the true object of Satan's hatred (Figure 6.1).

Finally, heliocentrism could hardly avoid strengthening the Christological symbolism of the Sun as universal ruler. With the Copernicans' rediscovery of ancient encomia to the Sun, added to their revised schematic diagram of the Universe – whereby, in Digges's words, "the Sunne ... like a king in the middest of all raigneth and geeveth lawes of motion to the rest, spherically dispearsing his glorious beames of light through al this sacred Caelestiall Temple"[37] – the adaptation of heliocentrism for pious purposes became almost inevitable, as illustrated by the frontispiece of the Puritan preacher Samuel Ward's pamphlet *All in All* (1622; Figure 6.2).

Although the symbolism surrounding the center of Ward's diagram is cluttered and perhaps in the end impenetrable, even a passing glance suggests that some strong hermeneutical challenges and possible theological implications might be created by a new cosmology.

[37] Digges, *A Perfit Description*, sig. M.1ʳ.

CHAPTER 7

Planet Earth

I cannot without great admiration, nay more, denial of my understanding, hear it to be attributed to natural bodies, for a great honour
and perfection that they are impassible, immutable, inalterable, etc.
And on the contrary, to hear it to be esteemed a great imperfection to
be alterable, generable, mutable, etc. It is my opinion that the Earth
is very noble and admirable, by reason of so many and so different
alterations, mutations, generations, etc. which are incessantly made
therein; and if without being subject to any alteration, it had been all
one vast heap of sand, or a masse of Jasper, or that in the time of the
Deluge, the waters freezing which covered it, it had continued an
immense Globe of Christal, wherein nothing had ever grown, altered,
or changed, I should have esteemed it a lump of no benefit to the
World, full of idlenesse, and in a word superfluous, and as if it had
never been in nature; and should make the same difference in it,
as between a living and dead creature.

Sagredo, Galileo's *Dialogo*, 1632[1]

"In my opinion, that [opinion] of Copernicus, for the Earth a heavy
dull grosse body to move and the heaven and Starres who are light to
stand still is as if a Prince should upon a festivall day appoint all the
old and fat men and woemen to dance and all the yonge men and
woemen of sixteen and twenty to sit still."

Edward, Viscount Conway, 1651[2]

". . . consider first, that great
Or bright infers not excellence: the Earth
Though, in comparison of heav'n, so small,
Nor glistering, may of solid good contain
More plenty than the sun that barren shines

---

[1] Salusbury, pp. 44–5.
[2] Edward, Viscount Conway, letter to his daughter-in-law Anne Conway, 22 July 1651, *Conway Letters:
The Correspondence of Anne, Viscountess Conway, Henry More, and Their Friends, 1642–1684*, ed.
Marjorie Hope Nicolson (London: Oxford University Press, 1930).

Whose virtue on itself works no effect,
But in the fruitful Earth ..."
                Raphael to Adam, *Paradise Lost*, 8.90–6

The final two chapters of this study of *Paradise Lost* and the cosmological
revolution can be framed, respectively, around two questions: (1) What
kind of place is Earth and (2) what kind of place is the Universe? The first
of these also raises the question of what was involved in the human process
of reimagining Earth as a planet – something attempted by almost nobody
before Copernicus. That concept, with a few important exceptions, was
entirely foreign to the medieval view of the world.[3] Technically and
classically, as already indicated, "planet" was one of two categories of star:
the "wandering" kind (πλανήτης αστήρ; *stella errans*) and "fixed" stars,
which we now simply call stars in contradistinction to planets. Beyond the
mere technical meaning, however, "star" in the Middle Ages and in
Milton's day evoked many of the same figurative resonances the word still
has when we call an outstanding performer a star or refer to a particular
achievement as stellar. The connotation of specialness or even divinity of a
sort coincides with the classical meaning of planet: Those seven wandering
stars indeed bore the names of gods, echoed in the names of the seven days
of the week – although the Sun, uniquely among them, is now categorized
as a true star.

For most pre-Copernicans, not only was Earth simply Earth and *not* a
planet, but by virtue of its immobility in the center of the Universe, Earth
also occupied the lowest place in creation – axiologically as well as
physically. This means, crucially, that geocentrism did not equate with
anthropocentrism. The former is a geometrical designation: As the heaviest
thing in the Universe, Earth was seen as standing at the center simply
because the center, in Aristotle's physics, draws heavy things to itself.
Anthropocentrism, by contrast – like Eurocentrism, ethnocentrism, and
the like – designates a set of assumptions or attitudes about what is
valuable or what is figuratively and axiologically "central." Put briefly, in
Aristotle's and Ptolemy's cosmology, Earth's position at the center of the
Universe was taken as evidence not of its importance but, literally and
colloquially, of its grossness.[4] Geocentrism thus had *anti*anthropocentric

---

[3] Even prominent historians have occasionally slipped into anachronism regarding this topic, for
example, A. O. Lovejoy, *The Great Chain of Being: A Study of the History of an Idea* (Cambridge,
MA: Harvard University Press, 1936), p. 101: "though the medieval world was ... immense, relatively
to man and *his planet*, it was nevertheless definitely limited and fenced about" (italics added).
[4] Intellectual historian Rémi Brague claims to have found only one medieval writer – a Jewish
theologian from Baghdad named Saadia Gaon (882–942) – who uses geocentrism as an argument

implications. Moses Maimonides (1135–1204), for example, in his *Guide of the Perplexed*, draws various parallels between the Universe as a whole and a human body but goes on to caution that serious differences undermine any simple analogy between macrocosm and microcosm. One of these differences relates to the place and importance of the center:

> Living creatures endowed with a heart have it within the body and in the midst thereof; there it is surrounded by organs which it governs. Thus it derives a benefit from them, for they guard and protect it. . . . The reverse occurs in the case of the Universe. . . . In the universe, the nearer the parts are to the centre, the greater is their turbidness, their solidity, their inertness, their dimness and darkness, because they are further away from the loftiest element, from the source of light and brightness.[5]

This view of our place in the Universe undergirds Maimonides' warning in the same work that we must not "think that the spheres and the angels were created for our sake" (p. 276).

A survey of ancient and medieval Arabic, Jewish, and Christian thought reinforces this axiological dimension of pre-Copernican cosmology. Upward is the direction of improvement and rising importance or value. (For example, within Christianity, Heaven is up; Christ rises from death and into Heaven; the spirits of the devout are exalted – literally, "lifted high" – and so on.) By contrast, downward, toward the center, is the direction of deterioration, corruption, and the grave. In this sense, as Martianus Capella (fl. 410–39) pointed out in his cosmological writings, Earth is "in the middle and at the bottom" position in the universe.[6] Bede declared that Earth "is situated in the world's center or turning point, occupying among creatures the most humble and central place."[7] As the Arab geographer Al-Biruni (973–1048) stated, "in the centre of the sphere of the moon is the earth, and this centre is in reality the lowest part."[8]

---

in support of anthropocentrism. However, comments Brague, this position "is utterly out of tune with the rest of the mediaeval concert." See Brague, "Geocentrism as a Humiliation for Man," *Medieval Encounters* 3 (1997): 187–210 (pp. 193–4).

[5] Maimonides, *The Guide of the Perplexed*, pp. 118–19. A similar evaluation of human cosmic importance was offered earlier by Proclus: "man is . . . a 'being of farness': 'living at the end of the Whole, and farthest from them (i.e. real things), we have a gross and defectuous perception'"; *In Platonis Timeaeum Commentaria*, ed. E. Diehl (Leipzig: Teubner, 1903), pp. 351, 352; translated and quoted in Brague, p. 198.

[6] *Martianus Capella and the Seven Liberal Arts*, trans. W. H. Stahl and R. Johnson with E. L. Burge (New York: Columbia University Press, 1977), 2:318.

[7] *Bedae Venerabilis Opera*, Pars I (Tournai: Typographi Brepols Editores Pontificii, 1975), pp. 227–8: *Terra . . . quae in centro vel cardine mundi sita, humillimum in creaturis ac medium . . . locam tenet.*

[8] Al-Biruni, *The Book of Instruction in the Elements of Astrology*, trans. R. Ramsay Wright (London: Luzac, 1934), p. 45.

Moreover, based on a consistent extrapolation from such views, medieval writers conceived of Hell as being located at the *very* center of the Universe and therefore coincident with Earth's center. Thus, in Dante's *Divine Comedy*, we find the Inferno, Hell itself, in Earth's innermost core. And at its literal midpoint appears Satan: not rolling in a "fiery gulf" – for the element of fire belongs in another place – but immobile, frozen in ice.[9]

While the theology of this picture is Christian, its physics is Aristotelian – from which, again, it is but a short step to the conclusion that Earth itself is gross in more than one sense. Thomas Aquinas (1225–74), in his commentary on Aristotle's cosmology, paid much attention to the passages from *De Caelo* attacking the Pythagorean view that the Sun or "central fire" belongs in the center of the Cosmos because that is the most noble place. Aquinas follows Aristotle in insisting that not Earth but "the sphere of the fixed stars" is "the most honorable" of things; it is this that defines and serves as the essence of the Universe. "In the Universe at large, just as the Earth – contained by all things and dwelling in the very midst – is the most material and the most ignoble of all bodies, so the highest sphere is the most essential and most noble"[10] And if Earth is ignoble, then how logical to extrapolate downward from its surface to its center, where things are conceived to be downright hellish.

The writings of John Buridan reveal how the assumed baseness of our central location colored other cosmological issues, such as that of earthly mobility. Those asserting that Earth moves and that fixed stars are at rest support their claim, says Buridan, by arguing that "the highest sphere [is] the noblest. But it is nobler and more perfect to be at rest than to be moved. Therefore, the highest sphere ought to be at rest."[11] Buridan refutes this conclusion, but he does not challenge the assumption regarding the nobility and ignobility, respectively, of the highest heaven and our lowly Earth.

In fact, "lowly" is one of the milder epithets medieval writers used to describe Earth's central location. Just as often, the center was seen in terms of the bottom of the barrel or of the lower, less noble members of the human body. One neo-Pythagorean writer put it this way: "It is necessary that what is worst should be located in the worst place, which contains the earth, because earth has the rank of a bottom with regard to the universe,

---

[9] Dante, *Inferno*, canto 34.

[10] Aquinas, *Commentary on Aristotle's De Caelo; Opera Omnia*, "Leonina Edition" (Rome, 1886), 3:202.: *Et ideo in toto universo, sicut terra, quae ab omnibus continetur, in medio localiter existens, est maxime materialis et ignobilissima corporum; ita etiam suprema sphaera est maxime formalis et nobilissima.*

[11] Grant, *A Source Book in Medieval Science*, p. 501.

hence, is fit to receive the dregs."[12] And Albertus Magnus, Aquinas's teacher, says that "among the simple bodies, the earth is like an excrement."[13] The Latin noun *faex* (plural: *faeces*), which Albertus uses here, can be translated as either dregs or excrement, but either way, the position that emerges from these major medieval figures is hardly one of Earth occupying a pedestal or enthroned or as enjoying a privileged position in the Universe. Literary and historical scholars of the period have struggled to find new vocabulary to replace the now-popular but fallacious designation of the Aristotelian/Ptolemaic Cosmos as anthropocentric. "The Medieval Model," writes C. S. Lewis, for example, is "anthropoperipheral."[14] A. O. Lovejoy, with Dante's *Inferno* clearly in mind, states that "in the spatial sense the medieval world was literally diabolocentric."[15]

The dominant pre-Copernican cosmology thus pointed not to the preeminence but rather to the sheer grossness of humankind's place in the Cosmos. In this view, Earth appears as a universal pit – figuratively as well as literally the world's low point. This negative view encompasses, finally, not only ancient and medieval Arabic, Jewish, and Christian writers but also many prominent voices more commonly associated with Renaissance humanism – before and after the time of Copernicus. As mentioned in Chapter 6, Giovanni Pico, even within a work that acquired the title *Oration on the Dignity of Man* (1486), referred to our present dwelling place, our Earth, as "the excrementary and filthy parts of the lower world."[16] Later, in 1568, Michel de Montaigne, still assuming a geocentric cosmology, lamented that we inhabit "the worst and deadest part of the universe, ... the lowest story of the house, and most remote from the heavenly arch."[17] Milton will enter this conversation shortly, but for now, it is enough to remember that in his Multiverse, the "dregs" are "downward purged" not *within* our Cosmos but beyond its outer limits – in Chaos. Milton's is emphatically not a Universe with anything ignoble or "tartareous" at its heart (7.237–8).[18]

[12] Anonymus Photii, cod. 249, in *The Pythagorean Texts of the Hellenistic Period*, collected and ed. H. Thesleff (Turku: Abo Akademi, 1965), p. 239, 11–13; quoted in Brague, p. 203.

[13] Albertus Magnus, *De Caelo et mundo*, I, I, 6, pp. 16, 27–9; quoted in Brague, p. 203.

[14] Lewis, *The Discarded Image*, p. 58.

[15] Lovejoy, *The Great Chain of Being*, p. 102. See also Leonard's insightful comments on Lovejoy and geocentrism: *FL*, 2:769–70.

[16] Pico, in *The Renaissance Philosophy of Man*, p. 224.

[17] Montaigne, "An Apology of Raymond Sebond," in *The Essays of Michel de Montaigne*, trans. Charles Cotton (London: Bell, 1892), 2: 134.

[18] See Leonard's agreement with this point – contra C. S. Lewis – in *FL*, 2:806.

This broad, somewhat depressing survey of the implications of geocentrism may, for students of literature, be relatively familiar. Sadly, however, historians of science and in particular science popularizers have endlessly reasserted a quite different picture of the meaning of medieval cosmology and, consequently, also the meaning of its Copernican replacement. Examples of the Great Copernican Cliché – the claim that heliocentrism "dethroned" Earth from its privileged place in an anthropocentric model of the Cosmos – are too many to catalog, although typical is Morris Kline's confident declaration that one of the "prevailing doctrines of Christianity" in the time of Copernicus and Kepler was the "comforting dogma" "that man was at the center of the universe; . . . the chief concern of God" and "chief actor on the central stage."[19] How surprised might Pico and Montaigne be to read, if they could, Kline's confident declaration or countless others of the same ilk, which often proudly (and with unconscious irony) congratulate themselves at having punctured the imagined pretensions of another age or worldview.[20]

By contrast, however, Milton's Copernican contemporaries recognized the prevailing negative value attached to the supposed location of the medieval, nonplanetary Earth and saw themselves, figuratively speaking, as removing and freeing Earth from its incarceration in the universal dead center. But they were not the first to make such a proposal. Two centuries earlier, despite dominant views of Earth as occupying the dark sump of the Universe, Nicolaus Cusanus (1401–1464) seriously proposed that our terrestrial home is indeed a star. In his philosophical treatise *On Learned Ignorance* (1440), whose title hints at the paradoxical and at times mystical nature of its contents, we can discern already a profound shaking of Aristotelian foundations, along with exhilarating hints at new directions for cosmology and for Earth itself.

Perhaps the most startling thing about Cusanus's work is how he arrives at apparently prescient conclusions about the Universe by means that are entirely abstract and speculative. Contrary to still-popular beliefs about the empirical nature of Copernican cosmology, the reevaluation of the Ptolemaic system was in fact grounded on a critical *refusal* to accept

---

[19] Morris Kline, *Mathematics: The Loss of Certainty* (New York: Oxford University Press, 1980), p. 40, and *Mathematics in Western Culture* (George Allen and Unwin, London, 1954), p. 117.

[20] I offer many examples of the cliché, from Cyrano de Bergerac to Carl Sagan, in "The Great Copernican Cliché," *American Journal of Physics* 69.10 (Oct. 2001): 1029–35, and in "Myth 6: That Heliocentrism Demoted Humans From the Center of the Cosmos," *Galileo Goes to Jail and Other Myths About Science and Religion*, ed. Ronald L. Numbers (Cambridge, MA: Harvard University Press, 2009), pp. 50–8.

the evidence of the senses – the apparent diurnal circling of the Sun and stars, the retrograde motions of the planets, and so on. In one sense, it was Aristotle and Ptolemy who were empirical. For thinkers like Cusanus, on the other hand, a true critique of physical reality is possible precisely because there is a higher reality that the physical may imitate but does not comprise. Not unlike Kepler almost two centuries later, Cusanus employs a form of Platonic (or Neoplatonic) deduction to undermine Aristotelian or Ptolemaic tenets concerning the structure of the world. In his discussion of movement, there is even a foreshadowing of the use of imagined extraterrestrial perspectives:

> Clearly, it is actually this Earth that moves, though to us it does not appear to do so; for we apprehend motion only relative to something motionless. Anyone on board ship but not knowing that the water is flowing, nor able to see the riverbanks – how would he, from midstream, apprehend that the ship was moving? This is why to anyone at all, whether he be on Earth, or on the Sun or another planet, it always seems as if he is in the center, immobile as it were, while everything else is in motion. Certainly one always establishes one set of fixed points relative to oneself, whether one inhabits the Sun or the Earth, the Moon or any of the other planets. Thus it is as if the world system had its center everywhere and its circumference nowhere, for God is its circumference and center, and he is everywhere and nowhere.[21]

One of the consequences of this paradoxical deconstruction of location is the qualitative "neutralizing" of place. In contrast to Aristotle or Dante, Cusanus recognizes no "dead center" – no location that marks a body's grossness or baseness. The importance of this contrast with the standard medieval understanding of Earth's place and nature is profound. Among other things, it entails a revision of the doctrine of "influences," according to which the power and quality of stars and planets is communicated downward toward Earth. For if "downward" becomes a merely relative term, then influence may travel a two-way street and Earth itself may be reconceived as a star (a wandering star, of course) shedding its own influence.

> Therefore the Earth is a magnificent star possessing light, heat, and influence different and distinct from all other stars, just as each of these is unique as regards light, nature, and influence. Each star communicates light and influence to the next, though this is not its purpose. For all stars move and shine in order to be most fully what they are, from which their sharing of influence arises as a consequence.

---

[21] All quotations from Cusanus are my translations from *Nicolai Cusani De docta ignorantia libri tres* (Bari: Laterza, 1913) and quoted from *BOTC*, ed. Danielson, pp. 97–8.

As noted in Chapter 4, Galileo arrived at a similar conclusion concerning Earth's stellar nature, although based on observation plus deduction rather than on philosophical speculation.

Thus, although for Cusanus there is nothing unique about Earth's place, like every other star, Earth is unique indeed and has purpose. Moreover, just as mere physical location is no marker of excellence or baseness, so physical *size* for Cusanus becomes a neutral matter. It is instead "intellectual nature" that constitutes excellence. Therefore, even though his speculations lead him to touch on the possible existence of extraterrestrial life, he returns to that intellectual nature here on Earth – and to a suggestion that is actually more anthropocentric than any that raw Aristotelian geocentrism could ever have generated:

> The fact that the Earth is smaller than the Sun and receives influence from it is no reason for calling it more contemptible. . . . It is true, as we see from its shadow in eclipses, that the Earth is smaller than the Sun; yet it is not known by how much the region of the Sun is greater or smaller than that of the Earth. In any case they cannot be precisely equal, for no star can be equal to another. Nor is Earth the smallest star, for, as we know from eclipses, it is greater than the Moon and even, some would say, than Mercury and perhaps also the other planets. From its size, therefore, no argument can be constructed for the Earth's inferiority. . . .
>
> Nor can *place* support such a claim: namely, that this place in the Universe is the home of humans, animals, and plants which are of a less noble rank than those dwelling in the Sun and other planets.

Such are Cusanus's stirring conclusions, with many resonances for a discussion of Milton. Earth is a star. Earth and its inhabitants are not cosmically contemptible. And if Earth is truly a star, shedding influence upon and receiving influences from other stars, then what must become of the notion of the "sublunary sphere" as a unique realm of mutability "quarantined" from the rest of the Universe or of Earth (in the oddly non-Copernican phrase of the Copernican Digges) as "the peculiare Empire of death"? It cannot stand. Proof of change in the heavens would come later with the observation of comets and novas in the last half of the sixteenth century and then with Galileo's astronomical application of earthly geometry and physics. But Cusanus, more than a century earlier, offered a radical view in which the division of the Cosmos into two "zones" of mutability and immutability – the lower storey and the upper storey – simply dissolved. He dared to imagine the *unity* of the physical Universe. In this regard, Milton in his own reading of "the book of God" can be considered among the successors of the visionary Cusanus.

As noted in Chapter 4, for Galileo, the phenomenon of earthshine as described in *Sidereus Nuncius* implied the end of Earth's exclusion "from the dance of the stars" and the death knell of the Aristotelian denigration of Earth as "the sump [*sentina*] where the Universe's filth and ephemera collect." In the *Dialogo*, Galileo returned to this theme and laid the foundation for one of the most profound (if often neglected) shifts in consciousness and values accompanying the cosmological revolution. The mainly Aristotelian conception of the perfection and immutability of the heavens – of the "upper storey" of the two-storey Universe – established the norm against which earthly things were judged and found wanting. But now, in the radically reimagined, physically unified Copernican Universe of Galileo, Earth itself – with all its mutability, contingency, and vitality – was becoming the yardstick for thinking about and measuring the rest of the Universe.

Nonetheless, the persistence of two-storey thinking in the seventeenth century is an intriguing phenomenon in itself. It would be natural simply to assume that such thinking is an entailment of Aristotelian physics and Ptolemaic astronomy, as in part it was. However, quite by itself as a system of values, it had become so ingrained that a reluctance to relinquish it played its own role in creating a reluctance to conceive of Earth as a planet – as nicely illustrated by this chapter's second epigraph, in which Edward, Viscount Conway, at mid-century still displays resistance to Copernicanism based on apparently unshakable preconceptions concerning Earth's grossness and (in several senses) corpulence. It is precisely these preconceptions – expressed by his Aristotelian character Simplicio – that Galileo in the *Dialogo* seeks to undermine.

> SIMP.
>
> ... the Copernican Hypothesis would make great confusion and perturbation in the Systeme of the Universe, and amongst its parts: As for instance, amongst Coe[lestial] bodies that are immutable and incorruptible, according to Aristotle, Tycho, and others; amongst bodies, I say, of such nobility, by the confession of every one, and Copernicus himself, ... bodies, I say once more, so pure, that is to say, amongst Venus, Mars, etc. to place the very sink [*sentina*] of all corruptible matters, to wit, the Earth, Water, Air, and all mixt bodies.
>
> But how much properer a distribution, and more with nature, yea with God himself, the Architect, is it, to sequester the pure from the impure, the mortal from the immortal, as other Schools teach; which tell us that these impure and frail matters are contained within the angust [i.e., straightened] concave of the Lunar Orb, above which with

uninterrupted Series the things Celestial distend themselves. (Salusbury, p. 240–1; *Dialogo*, p. 261)

In this way, twenty-two years after the appearance of the *Sidereus Nuncius*, Galileo continues – as he promised he would – his campaign against Earth's depreciation as a thing enclosed in the "angust" sublunary sphere and so constituting the sump, the *sentina*, that occupies the cosmic center.

In the first day of the *Dialogo*, Galileo resurveys the physical evidence that permits and accelerates the Copernican reimagining of Earth as a planet. There is the Moon's earthlike mountainous roughness, of course, contrary to Simplicio the Aristotelian's persistence in holding the Moon's surface "to be very smooth and even, as a looking-glasse, whereas, we find and feel this of the Earth to be extraordinary montuous and rugged." The similarity and affinity of Earth and the Moon are also reinforced, notes Salviati, by the phenomenon of earthshine, which demonstrates the reciprocity – the open commerce, as it were – between them, one of the two having already long been acknowledged as a wandering star, a planet: "as the Moon for a great part of time, supplies the want of the Suns light, and makes the nights, by the reflection of its own, reasonable clear; so the Earth, in recompence, affordeth it when it stands in most need, by reflecting the Solar rayes" (Salusbury, pp. 54, 52).

Salviati has likewise reminded his conversation partners of other scientific ("philosophical") evidence – including sunspots, comets, and "new stars" (supernovae) – pointing to the breakdown of the sharp division of the Universe into realms respectively of mutability and immutability, of lower and upper storeys:

> in the universal expansion of the Heaven, there have been, and are continually, seen just such accidents as we call generations and corruptions, being that excellent Astronomers have observed many Comets generated and dissolved in parts higher than the Lunar Orb, besides the two new Stars, *Anno* 1572, and *Anno* 1604, without contradiction much higher than all the planets; and in the face of the Sun it self, by help of the Telescope, certain dense and obscure substances, in semblance very like to the foggs about the Earth. (Salusbury, p. 38)

In the *Dialogo*, Salviati also complements this evidence with an "Aristotle vs. Aristotle" ploy, pointing out that even Simplicio's chief philosophical authority affirms "that we ought to prefer that which sense demonstrates, before all Arguments," and therefore that "you shall argue more Aristotelically, saying, the Heavens are alterable, for that so my sense telleth me, than if you should say, the Heavens are unalterable, for that Logick so perswaded Aristotle" (Salusbury, p. 42).

That "the Heavens are alterable": One can hardly overemphasize the philosophical importance of this conclusion. At the physical and cosmo-logical levels, as already noted, celestial mutability shatters the division of the Universe into lower and upper storeys. At the psychological, anthro-pological, aesthetic, and axiological levels, moreover, this unification of the Universe demands a radical redefinition of values as well as perhaps purpose, especially as these pertain to Earth's role, place, and inhabitants. This aspect of the cosmological revolution – not yet fully acknowledged even today – centers on the concept of nobility. In the sunspots debate, as noted, it was a commonplace that the Sun and other heavenly bodies are noble and worthy of high respect. But Galileo, while maintaining the commonplace, pursues its logic earthward. Salviati assures Simplicio: "As to Heaven, your fears are vain for that which you your self hold unalterable and impassible; as for the Earth, we strive to enoble and perfect it, whilst we make it like to the Coelestial Bodies, and as it were place it in Heaven, whence your Philosophers have exiled it" (Salusbury, p. 25). This claim requires a subtle but decisive shift in the meaning of perfection itself. As Donald Friedman brilliantly points out, the cosmology that Galileo opposed "tended to equate perfection with its root meaning of 'completed,' and therefore, with the immutable." However, "the impulse to redefine, to reform, received doctrines of spiritual and formal excellence resonates in Raphael's explanation to Adam (*PL*, 5.524) that God has made him 'perfect, not immutable.'"[22]

The same could be said of nobility. The new understanding that arose from evidence of celestial "alterations, mutations, [and] generations" did not require that the heavens now be considered ignoble. It did, though, imply that Earth's mutability could no longer be taken as evidence of *its* ignobility. We shall return to the lesson of Raphael to which Friedman refers, but the new cosmology's axiological implication can be put this way: The heavens are noble but not immutable; Earth is mutable but not ignoble. Hence Salviati's announced effort to "enoble and perfect" our planet, newly conceived as such. But one can press this logic further: Mutability is not only universal but also, in significant respects, superior to immutability. The factual claim about celestial mutability is

---

[22] Donald Friedman, "Galileo and the Art of Seeing," in *Milton in Italy: Contexts, Images, Contradictions*, ed. Mario a. Di Cesare (Binghamton, NY: Medieval & Renaissance Texts and Studies), pp. 159–74 (pp. 172, 173).

established, again, by sunspots: "if such, so many, and so frequent be made in the very Globe of the Sun, which may with reason be held one of the noblest parts of Heaven, what should make us think that others may not happen in the other Orbs?" (Salusbury, p. 44). But the more radical claim – the case for the positive value of mutability – is enunciated in the *Dialogo* by Sagredo (quoted in the first epigraph to this chapter). What, after all, is so desirable about things that are "impassible, immutable, inalterable"? Indeed, Sagredo's emphatic comment (as rendered by Drake) is that he considers "the earth very noble and admirable precisely because of the diverse alterations, changes, generations, etc. that occur in it incessantly."[23]

In Chapter 4, we pondered ways in which Galileo in the *Sidereus Nuncius* employed geometry – "earth measure" – as a universal yardstick whose application lent support to a vision of a single homogeneous Cosmos. In the *Dialogo*, however, Earth functions as a measure, a criterion, in further profound respects – and now it is the immutable heavens of the Aristotelian/Ptolemaic Cosmos that are found wanting. In fact, in contrast to Earth's "alterations, mutations, [and] generations," the imagined changeless heavens appear a thing uselessly frozen – "an immense Globe of Christal, wherein nothing had ever grown, altered, or changed." In short, in Sagredo's stunning indictment, the difference between Earth and those imagined immutable heavens would be the same "as between a living and dead creature."

Simplicio replies that the heavenly bodies do not *need* to change: "the Sun, Moon, and the other Stars, which are ordained for no other use but to serve the Earth, need no other qualities for attaining of that end, save only those of light and motion." But Sagredo, uncharacteristically passionate, scoffs at such reasoning and counters:

> How? Will you affirm that nature hath produced and designed so many vast perfect and noble Coelestial bodies, impassible, immortal, and divine, to no other use but to serve the passible, frail, and mortal Earth? to serve that which you call the drosse of the World, and sink [*sentina*] of all uncleannesse? ... Take away this subserviency to the Earth, and the innumerable multitude of Coelestial bodies become wholly unuseful, and superfluous, since they neither have nor can have any mutual operation betwixt themselves; because they are all unalterable, immutable, impassible: For if, for Example, the Moon be impassible, what influence can the Sun or any other Star have upon her? ... Moreover, it seemeth to me, that whilst

---

[23] Galileo, *Dialogue Concerning the Two Chief World Systems*, trans. Drake, p. 58.

the Coelestial bodies concurre to the generation and alteration of the Earth, they themselves are also of necessity alterable; for otherwise I cannot understand how the application of the Sun or Moon to the Earth, to effect production, should be any other than to lay a marble Statue by a Womans side, and from that conjunction to expect children. (Salusbury, p. 46; *Dialogo*, p. 52)

Sagredo's brilliantly audacious analogy of the woman and the marble statue echoes vividly his earlier dismissal of the contrast between earthly change and celestial immutability as something amounting to the difference "between a living and dead creature." And it graphically implies a new cosmology in which things of Earth are projected outward into the Universe: change, generation, life, fertility, sex.

For Milton, this aspect of Galileo's new world – resonantly harmonious with various core themes of his own thought – was even more significant than the precise Copernican rearrangement of the heavenly spheres. Friedman has pointed out Galileo's rejection of the Aristotelian "ontological distinctions between the sub- and superlunary worlds" and its consistency with Milton's "mature arguments for the fundamental goodness of matter [and] his adherence to the doctrine of creation from out of divine substance" (p. 164). It likewise resonates with the repeated references in *Paradise Lost* to Earth's status as a star (e.g., 3.722–7; 8.140–2). For Milton, just as matter is divine in origin, so Earth itself is no sublunary aggregation of the Universe's material dross. As Galileo extends earthly fertility and generation out into the Universe, so Milton imagines a Paradise that is no place of stasis or sterility but instead one in which the garden is conspicuously fertile and in which human marriage, still sinless, includes full, joyful coitus. Prelapsarian human prospects include, moreover, migration outward from Earth to "Heav'nly paradises" (5.500), while angels too enjoy love-making, although we are told nothing of their offspring. Finally and most obviously cosmological, the relations among heavenly bodies themselves – those that Sagredo in the *Dialogo* refuses to conceive of as immutable or sterile – Raphael in *Paradise Lost* describes as the intercourse of "male and female light; / Which two great sexes animate the world" (8.150–1).

For Galileo and Milton, the ever more deeply grasped affinities between Earth and the heavens can be read not as a "desacralization of the heavens" (*pace* Friedman, p. 171) but rather as a sacralization of Earth and an extension of its qualities of generation and vitality outward into a newly conceived Universe. At the beginning of the second day of the *Dialogo*, Salviati sums up the previous day's conversation as having set out alternative positions – the first (represented by Simplicio) insisting on the two-storey model, while the second (Copernican) one takes "away such deformity from the parts of the World, [and] holdeth the Earth to enjoy the same perfections as the other integral bodies of the universe" (Salusbury, p. 90). One hears echoes again of Galileo's apt phrase from the *Sidereus Nuncius* regarding Earth's place in "the dance of the stars," an implication not lost on Simplicio, who earlier confesses "a great unwillingnesse [un'estrema repugnanza] to admit this commerce, which you would perswade me to be betwixt the Earth and Moon, placing it ... amongst the number of the Stars" (Salusbury, p. 80; *Dialogo*, p. 90).

Earth's status as a wandering star, a light-reflecting planet – a phenomenon already observed in connection with Satan's and Uriel's glimpses of Earth from the Sun at the end of Book 3 of *Paradise Lost* – initiated a way of imagining Earth that Hans Blumenberg calls "reflexive telescopics." No sooner did Galileo train his telescope upon the Moon than the question arose: How would Earth appear through a telescope? Galileo, of course, deduced that not only does the Moon appear earthlike, but Earth must appear lunar – or, more precisely, planetary, stellar.[24] As Kepler put it so succinctly, Copernicus "gave this Earth the right of citizenship in the heavens."[25] As Uriel says from his station on the Sun: "Look downward on that globe whose hither side / With light from hence, though but reflected, shines" (3.722–3).

The imaginative effort to view Earth from the heavens became one of the most characteristic astronomical thought experiments of the seventeenth century. English instances of its exercise – no doubt influenced by Kepler's *Somnium* as well as by Galileo's works – include Francis Godwin's fiction *The Man in the Moone* (1638), which, among other things, conveys a vision of our own planet as a "new starre" masked "with a kind of brightnesse like another Moone."[26] A second work appearing in 1638, one likewise influenced by Galileo and Kepler, was *The Discovery of a World in the Moon* by John Wilkins, who extrapolated from it the idea of an inhabited Moon. Wilkins, like Godwin (although Wilkins had not yet read Godwin's work), not only vividly described conditions on the Moon but also imagined the shining appearance of our native globe from space, citing Galileo's Copernican associate Paolo Foscarini but also such Aristotelians as Libertus Fromondus and Carlo Malapert (or Malapertius),

---

[24] Blumenberg, *The Genesis of the Copernican World*, p. 675.
[25] Kepler, *De stella nova* (1606); *Joannis Kepleri astronomi Opera omnia*, ed. Christian Frisch (Frankfurt, 1858), 2:683: *Ut Copernicum etiam mittam, qui Telluri ipsi jus civitatis in coelo dedit*.
[26] Godwin, *The Man in the Moone*, ed. William Poole (Peterborough, ON: Broadview, 2009), p. 92.

whom he quotes to the effect that "If wee were placed in the Moone, and from thence beheld this our earth, it would appeare unto us very bright, like one of the nobler Planets."[27]

Nonetheless, as earlier noted, even by mid-century, Earth's status as a planet was no *fait accompli*. The debate over issues contended in Galileo's *Dialogo* raged on in England through the 1640s, most notably in the works of Wilkins and of the reactionary Aristotelian Alexander Ross. Wilkins's *Discovery*, just mentioned, was republished in 1640, together with a new work: *A Discourse Concerning a New Planet, Tending to Prove, That 'Tis Probable Our Earth Is One of the Planets*. Ross's would-be refutation appeared in 1646 under the title *The New Planet No Planet, or, The Earth No Wandring Star, Except in the Wandring Heads of Galileans*. In 1634, Ross's first anti-Copernican work, *Commentum Terrae Motu*, dedicated to the newly appointed Archbishop William Laud, had attacked (in Latin) the Dutch Copernican Phillip Lansbergen as well as the English semi-Tychonic writer Nathanael Carpenter, who accepted Earth's diurnal rotation. In the first half of the twentieth century, Grant McColley, by means of numerous verbal parallels, argued that Wilkins's and Ross's English works engaging this debate served as "the principal immediate sources" for Milton's dialogue on astronomy in Book 8 of *Paradise Lost*[28] – and perhaps they did. In what follows, however, my chief interest is not in reduplicating the hunt for sources but in pursuing answers to the larger question with which this chapter opened: What kind of place is Earth?

One of the most intriguing statements in Wilkins's *Discourse Concerning a New Planet* is the first one that appears, headed Proposition I: "That the seeming Noveltie and Singularitie of this opinion, can be no sufficient reason to prove it erronious"[29] – another reminder that in England almost a century after the publication of Copernicus's *De Revolutionibus* and more than a sixty years after Digges's *A Perfit Description of the Caelestiall Orbes*, an assertion of Earth's planetary status might still, at least to the vernacular reader, appear "singular" and shocking. Wilkins accordingly expends much

---

[27] Wilkins, *Discovery* (1640), p. 150.

[28] McColley, "Milton's Dialogue on Astronomy," *PMLA* 52.3: 728–62. The verbal parallels offered by McColley are helpful, but his interpretations and conclusions are, in my judgment, so thoroughly wrongheaded – for example, that Milton engages in "a vigorous castigation of all astronomical inquiry" (p. 739) – that I have no heart to take them on point by point. Despite Milton's cautions about overreaching and his unwillingness or inability to declare outright for Copernicanism, I hope that his genuine engagement with astronomical and cosmological issues is by now more or less established. See Leonard's extensive and incisive survey of McColley's shifting positions: *FL*, 2:760–81.

[29] *Discourse Concerning a New Planet* (1640), p. 1; cited hereafter in the text.

effort recruiting supporters for his position and anticipating objections based on the authority of Aristotle and of Scripture (exactly the objections Copernicus anticipated in his preface to Pope Paul III in 1543). Indeed, Wilkins recruits rather more enthusiastically than was actually justified. He claims "that since the Science of Astronomy hath bin raised to any perfection, there have been many of the best skill in it, that have assented unto the assertion which is here defended. Amongst whom was Cardinall Cusanus." He goes on to mention genuine Copernicans – Rheticus, Maestlin, Kepler, Galileo – but includes William Gilbert, who accepted only components of the Copernican system, such as diurnal rotation, and Erasmus Reinhold, who used Copernicus's system for drawing up astronomical tables without actually accepting his cosmology. Wilkins also repeats the account of Clavius, who, "when lying upon his Death-bed, he heard the first Newes of those Discoveries which were made by Gallilaeus his Glasse, he brake forth into these words: ... That it did behoove Astronomers, to consider some other Hypothesis, beside that of Ptolemy, whereby they might salve all those new appearances" (pp. 17, 18, 21).

Wilkins identifies among tendencies that oppose the new cosmology a "judging of things by sence, rather than by discourse and reason" (p. 27). This comment echoes an intriguing passage in Galileo's *Dialogo* in which Salviati exclaims: "I cannot find any bounds for my admiration, how that reason was able in Aristarchus and Copernicus, to commit such a rape upon their Sences, as in despight thereof, to make her self mistress of their credulity [far la ragion tanta violenza al senso, che contro a questo ella si sia fatta padrona della loro credulità]" (Salusbury, p. 301; *Dialogo*, p. 325). This dramatic statement of the case accurately specifies the underlying tension between reason – including mathematical calculation – and what the senses actually perceive (the appearances) as well as the Copernican insistence that reason, *rather than* the senses, provides the proper avenue to cosmological discovery. Hence, the identification of reason as "padrona," who, if necessary, will perform "violenza."[30]

Wilkins also tackles other arguments – ones based not on sense but on tradition, including the familiar claim that Earth must be in the center because Hell is in Earth's center and Hell "should be most remotely

---

[30] Michael Hanby, "*Homo faber* and/or *Homo adorans*: On the Place of Human Making in a Sacramental Cosmos," *Communio* 38 (Summer 2011): 198–236 (note 45), refers to Salviati's "metaphor of sense as an 'unwilling mistress' of reason" – thus by means of linguistic gender confusion also failing to see that it is reason ("ragio") who is for Salviati the mistress ("padrona") or, one might even say, "dominatrix."

scituated from the seat of the Blessed," which "is concentricall to the starry Sphaere." Wilkins replies:

This Argument is grounded upon these uncertainties:

> 1   That Hell must needs bee scituated in the centre of our Earth.
>
> 2   That the heaven of the Blessed, must needs bee concentricall to that of the Starres.
>
> 3   That places must bee as farre distant in scituation as in use:

> Which because they are taken for granted, without any proofe, and are in themselves but weake and doubtfull: therefore the conclusion (which alwaies followes the worser part) cannot bee strong, and so will not need any other answer.

> The second sort of Arguments taken from naturall Philosophy, are principally . . . :

> [F]rom the vilenesse of our Earth, because it consists of a more sordid and base matter than any other part of the World; and therefore, must bee scituated in the centre, which is the worst place, and at the greatest distance from those purer incortuptible bodies, the Heavens.

> I answer: This Argument do's suppose such propositions for grounds, which are not yet prooved; and therfore not to be granted. As,

> 1   That bodies must bee as farre distant in place, as in Nobilitie.
>
> 2   That the Earth is a more ignoble substance than any of the other Planets, consisting of a more base and vile matter.
>
> 3   That the centre is the worst place.

> All which, are (if not evidently false) yet very uncertaine. (pp. 107–8)

Here again, we encounter concern with nobility as it relates to the question of Earth's planetary status: in opposition to traditional interpretations of Earth as something essentially vile, ignoble, "sordid and base." Although Wilkins's arguments are directed against the anti-Copernican Fromondus, Ross counterattacks merely by insinuating that Wilkins cares little for the authority of church or Scripture:

> You slight the constant and perpetuall doctrine of the Church from the beginning, concerning the site of hell, which is in the center or bowels of the earth; and you call it an uncertainty; but so you may call any doctrine in Scripture, for where will you have hell to be, but either in heaven or in the earth? These are the two integrall parts of this universe; in heaven I hope you will not place it, except you will have it to be in the moone. But if there

be any hell there, it is for the wicked of that world: as for the wicked of this world, they are not said to ascend to hell in the moone, but to descend to hell in the earth ... Therefore it is called a lake, burning with fire and brimstone; *Abyssus*, a deepe gulfe.[31]

Clearly, the structure of Milton's Multiverse in *Paradise Lost*, with the gulf of Hell being entirely outside and inexpressibly distant from Heaven and our Cosmos, transcends and undermines the simplistic either/or logic with which Ross tries to answer Wilkins.

In *Paradise Lost*, however, what prompts Adam's "doubt" that initiates the dialogue on astronomy is observation ("When I behold") subjected to mathematical calculation ("and compute"):

> "When I behold this goodly frame, this world,
> Of heav'n and Earth consisting, and compute
> Their magnitudes, this Earth a spot, a grain,
> An atom, with the firmament compared
> And all her numbered stars, that seem to roll
> Spaces incomprehensible (for such
> Their distance argues and their swift return
> Diurnal) merely to officiate light
> Round this opacous Earth, this punctual spot,
> One day and night; in all their vast survey
> Useless besides, reasoning I oft admire,
> How nature wise and frugal could commit
> Such disproportions, with superfluous hand
> So many nobler bodies to create,
> Greater so manifold to this one use,
> For aught appears, and on their orbs impose
> Such restless revolution day by day
> Repeated, while the sedentary Earth,
> That better might with far less compass move,
> Served by more noble than herself, attains
> Her end without least motion, and receives,
> As tribute such a sumless journey brought
> Of incorporeal speed, her warmth and light;
> Speed, to describe whose swiftness number fails."
>
> (8.15–38)

That Earth is "as a point" in relation to the magnitude of the sphere of the fixed stars was a commonplace of all mathematical astronomy of whatever stripe. Burton calls Earth "a point insensible in respect of the

---

[31] Ross, *New Planet No Planet*, pp. 58–9.

whole."[32] Wilkins asks: "what is this [Earth] unto the vaste frame of the whole Universe? but *punctulum*, such an insensible point, which do's not beare so great a proportion to the whole, as a small sand do's unto the Earth?" (p. iii; cf. p. 148). And clearly, Adam in Paradise has already taken the observations and made the calculations to establish this firm conclusion.

But the disturbing question for Ptolemaists and Tychonians who held to a stationary Earth – a question eagerly pressed by Copernicans – was: Why should the immeasurably large move while the immeasurably small stands still? Is such a claim, indeed, not literally beyond belief? As Wilkins argued (using some of the same language used by Adam), surely it is unlikely

> that the whole Fabricke of the Heavens ... should bee put to undergoe so great and constant a Worke in the service of our Earth, which might more easily save all that labour by the circumvolution of it's owne Body. ... Or can wee imagine that [Nature] should appoint those numerous and vast Bodies, the Stars, to compasse us with such a swift and restlesse motion ... when all this might as well be done by the revolution of this little Ball of Earth?" (pp. 203–4)

Does a geostatic model not entail, as Adam suggests, stellar movement across "Spaces incomprehensible," a "sumless journey," and swiftness to describe which number appears simply inadequate (lines 20, 36, 38) – in Wilkins's words, an "inconceivable, unnaturall swiftnes," "celeritie ... altogether beyond the fancy of a Poet or a mad man" (pp. 189, 194)? Thirdly, beyond the disproportions in size and motion, there is an apparent skewing in the cosmological logic of values: Is it not disproportionate that nature (God?) should create so many "nobler bodies" "merely" to serve tiny pointlike Earth and its inhabitants (8.28, 22)?[33]

Adam has already partly answered his own question in response to Eve in Book 4, when she asked, as an addendum to her love song to him, about the stars: "But wherefore all night long shine these, for whom / This glorious sight, when sleep hath shut all eyes?" (4.657–8). Adam's

---

[32] Burton, *Anatomy of Melancholy* (1621), p. 327.
[33] Compare Satan's similarly hasty inference concerning the *seeming* uselessness of the heavenly bodies except for their employment in the service of Earth, which Satan designates a

> "Terrestrial Heav'n, danced round by other heav'ns
> That shine, yet bear their bright officious lamps,
> Light above light, for thee alone, as *seems*."
>   (9.103–5; italics added)

reply in effect preempts his own "merely" in Book 8. In keeping with Genesis 1 as well as with Copernicus, there is no denial of the premise that the Cosmos with its stars was made for us, *propter nos*. But that claim does not entail "merely." There are multiple harmonious purposes interwoven in this Universe, of whose fabric we are only one thread. Thus, as Adam replies,

> "... these soft fires
> Not only enlighten [all things], but with kindly heat
> Of various influence foment and warm,
> Temper or nourish, or in part shed down
> Their stellar virtue on all kinds that grow
> On earth, made hereby apter to receive
> Perfection from the sun's more potent ray.
> These then, though unbeheld in deep of night,
> Shine not in vain, nor think, though men were none,
> That heav'n would want spectators, God want praise;
> Millions of spiritual creatures walk the earth
> Unseen, both when we wake, and when we sleep:
> All these with ceaseless praise his works behold
> Both day and night."
>
> (4.667–80)

These interrelations of the stellar and the earthly realms are (even setting aside all things human) no sterile relationship but one in which, to echo Galileo's Sagredo, "diverse alterations, changes, generations, etc. ... occur ... incessantly." The stars' influence is terrestrially fertile and promotes growth.

But that is not all, as suggested eloquently by Wilkins in response to his own Eve-like question about the purpose of stars not seen – in his case, not seen until the advent of the telescope:

> For to what purpose should so many Lights be created for the use of man, since his eyes were not able to discerne them? So that our disabilitie to comprehend all those ends which might be aimed at in the works of nature, can bee no sufficient Argument to proove their superfluitie. Though Scripture doe tell us that these things were made for our use, yet it do's not tell us, that this is their only end. 'Tis not impossible, but that there may be elsewhere some other inhabitants, by whom these lesser Stars may be more plainly discerned. (pp. 130–1)

We shall return to extraterrestrials. But in his response to Eve in Book 4, Adam startlingly proposes that the stars' shining promotes praise among extraterrestrials already invisibly (if not inaudibly) present on

Earth. The stars are there for humans, it is true, but emphatically not "merely" for humans.

Recognizing the potential larger purposes of the heavens thus minimizes the apparent "disproportions" that Adam subsequently worries about in Book 8. At the same time, one should note that his reference to "nobler bodies" (8.28; cf. 8.34) is a comparative; it does not imply that Adam considers Earth ignoble in the standard pre-Copernican manner. Nonetheless, some of Adam's astronomical inferences are presented as illustrative of the kinds of hasty conclusions to which astronomers down the ages may be prone. As Raphael remarks to Adam:

> "Already by thy reasoning this I guess,
> Who art to lead thy offspring, and supposest
> That bodies bright and greater should not serve
> The less not bright, nor heav'n such journeys run,
> Earth sitting still, when she alone receives
> The benefit ..."
>
>   (8.85–90)

Raphael does not affirm that Earth *is* the sole beneficiary of stellar influence; rather, he suggests that "bodies bright and greater" serving the less bright and less large is a possibility not to be discounted. Just as importantly, he denies any automatic equivalence between size or luminosity on the one hand and "excellence" on the other. Our minuscule and non-self-luminous Earth "may of solid good contain / More plenty than the sun" (8.90–5). Raphael thus preempts and undercuts not only Adam's but also other humans' tendency across history to equate size and value. Still today, in popular writings on astronomy, recognition of Earth's smallness is routinely followed, as if by iron logic, by some banal inference concerning Earth's cosmic insignificance.

Raphael indicates furthermore what is at stake in any axiological comparison of the cosmologically large and small. The Sun's beams are to be valued for their capacity to be "active" and to find "vigor" (8.97), life, and, above all, conscious, intelligent life of the sort found on Earth. The Sun and stars thus serve not Earth "but thee Earth's habitant" (8.98–9). And yet, the angelic lesson does not boil down to any facile anthropocentrism. Milton seems aware of that danger, for Raphael carefully articulates the place of humankind within the teleology of creation. *Paradise Lost* affirms a complexity or multiplicity of ends in creation – in effect permitting a *propter nos* but, again, not one that is reductive or exclusive. The challenging issue of cosmic size is not brushed away. Instead, Adam is told:

".. . for the heav'n's wide circuit, let it speak
The Maker's high magnificence, who built
So spacious, and his line stretched out so far;
That man may know he dwells not in his own;
An edifice too large for him to fill,
Lodged in a small partition, and the rest
Ordained for uses to his Lord best known."
(8.100–6)

What emerges from Raphael's lesson is therefore a doctrine of what we might call *multicentrism* or *a manifold teleology*. Yes, the heavenly bodies do shine *propter nos* – but not "merely." There is always a larger *propter Deum*, as there may also be a *propter alios*. More is going on in God's creation than only what concerns us. The situation was (and may still be) beautifully consonant with the new cosmology. As Galileo proved when he discovered the moons of Jupiter, there are in this universe (in the words of Copernicus) "numerous centers."[34] Thus, the cosmic edifice, in all its magnificence and magnitude, reflects that of the Builder. As Wilkins wrote in addressing the issue of the Universe's "bignesse," "God, to shew his owne immensitie, did put a kinde of infinitie in the creature" (p. 131; cf. p. 122). Raphael makes the same point about speed as Wilkins does about size: "The swiftness of those circles attribute, / Though numberless, to his omnipotence" (8.107–8). Thus, our own lodging turns out to be a "small partition." Cosmologically, what we think of as our place – and, in the new cosmology, our *planet* – is, in the proper sense of the word, just a condominium, and yet a place and a location about which Adam and his race might well feel much thankfulness as well as much humility.

Such humility is important, but it was not a requirement unique to any one cosmological party in the seventeenth century. Nor does it automatically signal an antiscience posture. In the astronomical dialogue of Book 8, Raphael draws an analogy between the apparent speed of the starry sphere – the issue with which Adam began the dialogue ("stars, that seem to roll / Spaces incomprehensible"; 8.19–20) – and the actual speed of his own journey from Heaven to Earth:

".. . me thou think'st not slow,
Who since the morning-hour set out from Heav'n
Where God resides, and ere mid-day arrived

[34] Copernicus, *De Revolutionibus*, 1.9 (*Pluribus ergo existentibus centris* ...); *BOTC*, ed. Danielson, p. 115.

> In Eden, distance inexpressible
> By numbers that have name."
>
> (8.110–14)

Milton apparently realized, correctly, that what might be called the "incredible numbers" problem could be urged equally against geostatic and Copernican models, with the *speed* of the starry sphere posing a challenge to the former and the *size* of the starry sphere (and of the stars themselves) to the latter. All parties, moreover, tended to appeal to God's omnipotence.[35] Raphael gently employs the same tactic on both fronts – first, as noted, suggesting that "The swiftness of those circles" be attributed to God's omnipotence (8.107–8) and then, on the brink of sketching a heliocentric model, addressing the question of size and distance:

> "But this I urge,
> Admitting motion in the heav'ns, to show
> Invalid that which thee to doubt it moved;
> Not that I so affirm, though so it seem
> To thee who hast thy dwelling here on Earth.
> God to remove his ways from human sense,
> Placed heav'n from Earth so far, that earthly sight,
> If it presume, might err in things too high,
> And no advantage gain."
>
> (8.114–22)

Again, however, such comments need not be read as any sort of obscurantism because Wilkins – arch-Copernican and among the founders of the Royal Society – likewise, in facing questions of cosmic size and teleology, asserts that "There be many secret ends in these great works of Providence, which humane wisedome cannot reach unto, and as Solomon speaks of those things that are under the Sunne, so may we also of those things that are above it, *That no man can find out the works of God*" (pp. 129–30).

With that caution in place, however, Raphael offers an exquisite sketch of the Copernican-Galilean Universe:

> "What if the sun
> Be center to the world, and other stars,
> By his attractive virtue and their own
> Incited, dance about him various rounds?
> Their wand'ring course now high, now low, then hid,
> Progressive, retrograde, or standing still,

---

[35] See Christopher M. Graney, "Science Rather Than God: Riccioli's Review of the Case for and Against the Copernican Hypothesis," *Journal for the History of Astronomy* 43 (2012): 215–25.

In six thou seest, and what if sev'nth to these
The planet Earth, so stedfast though she seem,
Insensibly three different motions move?
Which else to several spheres thou must ascribe,
Moved contrary with thwart obliquities;
Or save the sun his labor, and that swift
Nocturnal and diurnal rhomb supposed,
Invisible else above all stars, the wheel
Of day and night; which needs not thy belief,
If Earth industrious of herself fetch day
Travelling east, and with her part averse
From the sun's beam meet night, her other part
Still luminous by his ray. What if that light
Sent from her through the wide transpicuous air,
To the terrestrial moon be as a star
Enlight'ning her by day, as she by night
This Earth? Reciprocal . . ."

(8.122–44)

It is true that Raphael does not assert this model definitively; it remains a what-if. McColley is right, moreover, that with its "three different motions," it is technically a somewhat outdated version of Copernicanism; the third motion was dropped by most heliocentric astronomers from Galileo on.[36] However, as we saw in Chapter 5 in the cases of Tycho and Wilkins, who also gestured toward their respective Tychonic and Copernican cosmologies with a what-if, this locution in practice suggests an attitude of open invitation, not necessarily of skepticism. Raphael is gently alerting Adam – who has just displayed his naive if mathematically acute geocentric and geostatic assumptions – to an alternative way of understanding the mechanism of the heavens and Earth. Raphael's account, therefore, not only offers a model with the Sun as "center to the world" but also attends to what Adam actually sees and experiences: the stars with their apparent retrograde motions as well as Earth's seeming steadfastness – a body that in this alternative picture suddenly acquires its now routine appositive "planet" (line 129). Etymologically, the term echoes the "wandering" of four lines earlier, thus implying a strong affinity between Earth and those spheres that dance about the central Sun. So familiar today is the phrase *planet Earth*, however, that it would be easy to overlook the boldness of Raphael's locution. As Wilkins's *A New Planet* has illustrated, the concept was

---

[36] See the earlier discussion at pp. 121–2.

unique and integral to the Copernican model. The central Sun and a planetary Earth are truly two sides of the same cosmological coin.

In what follows, Raphael lists some standard geometrical advantages of heliocentrism (no more "thwart obliquities," etc.) and sketches how diurnal terrestrial rotation replaces the cosmic "wheel / Of day and night," a rearrangement that "save[s] the sun his labor" (8.132–6) – just as Wilkins had said Earth "might more easily save all [the heavens'] labour by the circumvolution of it's owne Body" (p. 203). The climax, however, comes with Raphael's third what-if, which reprises (as noted in Chapter 4, pp. 83–5) the moment in Galileo's *Sidereus Nuncius* when he explains – consonant with Uriel's commentary on the lunar/terrestrial exchange of light (3.722–32) – how earthshine functions and how "the benefit of [the Moon's] light to the Earth is balanced and repaid by the benefit of the light of the Earth to her." This reciprocity – the commerce in sunlight between two wanderers: the Moon and Earth – is what leads directly to Galileo's raptures about Earth's not being excluded "from the dance of the stars." And in *Paradise Lost* it concludes this section of Raphael's speech by recalling the very metaphor with which the angel began his series of Copernican what-ifs: that of the stars and planets – including now the noble planet Earth – brightly dancing together about the central Sun.

CHAPTER 8

Space Flight, ET, and other worlds

For if Tycho Brahe, considering the bare immensity of those globes, believed that it did not exist pointlessly in the world, but was packed with inhabitants, how much more convincing will it be for us, perceiving the variety of the works and intentions of God on the globe of Earth, to adopt a conjecture about the others as well? For He has created species to inhabit the waters . . . ; He has sent into the immensity of the air birds propped up by feathers; He has given to the snowy tracts of the north white bears and white foxes. . . . Has He then used up all His skill on the globe of the Earth so that He could not, or all His goodness, so that He would not wish to adorn with suitable creatures other globes also . . . ? For whose benefit do four moons gird Jupiter, and two Saturn, . . . as this single Moon of ours does our home?

Johannes Kepler, 1619[1]

Very many others, both English and French, all . . . affirmed our Earth to be one of the Planets, and the Sunne to be the Center of all, about which the heavenly bodies did move. And how horrid soever this may seeme at the first, yet is it likely enough to be true, nor is there any maxime or observation in Opticks . . . that can disprove it.

Now if our earth were one of the Planets (as it is according to them) then why may not another of the Planets be an earth?

John Wilkins, 1638[2]

For if the Firmament be of such an incomparable bignesse, as these Copernicall Giants will have it . . . , so vast and full of innumerable starres, [and] If our world be small in respect, why may we not suppose a plurality of worlds, those infinite starres visible in the Firmament to be so many Sunnes . . . ; to have likewise their subordinate planets, as the Sunne hath his dancing full round him? . . .

---

[1] Kepler, *The Harmony of the World*, p. 497; the original Latin appears in *Harmonices Mundi* (Linz, 1619), p. 248.
[2] *The Discovery of a World in the Moon*; quoted from the 1640 edition, pp. 90–1.

179

Though they seeme close to us, they are infinitely distant, and so *per consequens*, there are infinite habitable worlds? what hinders? Why should not an infinite cause (as God is) produce infinite effects ... ?

Robert Burton, 1638[3]

What kind of place does *Paradise Lost* present our Universe to be? Answering this question requires a review of the location and configuration of the Universe and of actual or prospective journeys made to or within it. On the macro scale, it may be helpful to look again at Scheiner's diagram from Chapter 2 (Figure 2.1, p. 39). As earlier suggested, that picture's two inner circles offer a schematic representation congruent with Milton's cosmology, indicating a starry sphere enclosed by "the firm opacous globe / Of this round world" (3.418–19) – a spherical solid boundary that divides Cosmos from Chaos and whose only opening is the "cosmic hatch" that offers passage into as well as out of our world. An important inference from this state of affairs is that in Milton's epic, the synonyms "Universe" and "world" do *not* denote absolutely everything that exists.[4] Indeed, as noted in Chapters 2 and 5, the Universe – comprising Earth, Sun, other planets, and the starry sphere – is vanishingly small compared with the Multiverse that surrounds it, even though it is immeasurably large compared with Earth. The Universe of *Paradise Lost*, accordingly, can seem either immense or minuscule depending on one's perspective or location. Furthermore, it is contingent (2.1052) and created (7.214–42, etc.) – its beginning being clearly subsequent to the creation of the Multiverse. What astronomers in Milton's day called a system of the world – whether the model be Ptolemaic, Tychonic, Copernican, or something else – thus actually describes, according to *Paradise Lost*, a local arrangement *within* the broader canvas of the Multiverse. Such contextualization does not render those cosmological and cosmographical local arrangements trivial. It does, however, suggest that larger philosophical and religious questions about the contingency, createdness, and purpose of the Universe are not answered (at least not fully) by any astronomy or physical cosmology whose domains are merely coextensive with the Universe itself.

As hinted by this chapter's epigraphs, the seventeenth century was an age whose astronomy, even if it could not reach beyond this Universe, certainly raised questions about domains beyond Earth, including

---

[3] Burton, *Anatomy of Melancholy*, expanded edition (London, 1638), pp. 254–5.

[4] Walter Clyde Curry acknowledges this plurality in his observation concerning the cosmic hatch: "the meeting of the three ways at the World's zenith is of tremendous importance in the poet's epic design; here are made 'visible' the roadways to three universes." *Milton's Ontology, Cosmogony, and Physics*, p. 157.

questions concerning possible extraterrestrial life and interplanetary or interstellar travel. As Michael J. Crowe and Matthew F. Dowd remark: "The door that inadvertently let in the aliens was opened in 1543."[5] Even though speculation about ET preceded Copernicus and although such speculation appears to have been no part of his intention, the conclusion that Earth is a planet rendered almost inevitable the analogy that Wilkins put so clearly: "if our earth were one of the Planets ... then why may not another of the Planets be an earth?" As Crowe and Dowd point out, the increased size of the Universe implied by the Copernican model (with no detectable annual stellar parallax, etc.) enhanced the role of the "principle of plenitude" – which coheres with "the claim that God values life and thus would widely populate the universe, not restrict life to the relatively minuscule environment of the Earth" (p. 7). This principle similarly underlies Kepler's profound question, cited in this chapter's first epigraph: "Has [God] then used up all His skill on the globe of the Earth so that He could not, or all His goodness, so that He would not wish to adorn with suitable creatures other globes also?" The same principle is alluded to by Raphael's admission that "such vast room in nature unpossessed / By living soul, desert and desolate, / ... is obvious to dispute" (8.153–8).

"Many worlds" speculation dates from the ancient atomists Leucippus, Democritus, and Epicurus and it was relatively common in early modern England. We have already met with one sixteenth-century example in the *Zodiacus Vitae* of Marcellus Palingenius, who acknowledged: "But some have thought that every Starre a worlde we well may cal."[6] It also made further, apparently unashamed appearances in original poetry written in English. In 1590, in defense of his explorations of Faerieland, Edmund Spenser offered Queen Elizabeth, in the proem to Book 2 of *The Faerie Queene*, the strained analogy of explorers of other lands recently discovered, complemented by a further piece of analogy:

> Yet all these [lands] were, when no man did them know,
> Yet have from wisest ages hidden beene:
> And later times things more unknowne shall show.
> Why then should witlesse man so much misweene
> That nothing is, but that which he hath seene?

[5] Crowe and Dowd, "The Extraterrestrial Life Debate From Antiquity to 1900," in *Astrobiology, History, and Society: Life Beyond Earth and the Impact of Discovery*, ed. Douglas A. Vakoch (Berlin and Heidelberg: Springer, 2013), pp. 3–56 (p. 4).
[6] From Googe's English translation, *The Zodiake of Life*, Book 7, Libra, sig. Y.i.ʳ.

What if within the Moones faire shining spheare?
What if in every other starre unseene
Of other worldes he happily should heare?
He wonder would much more, yet such to some appeare.

Roughly half a century later, Milton's fellow Christ's College alumnus Henry More published *Democritus Platonissans, or, An Essay Upon the Infinity of Worlds Out of Platonick Principles* (1646), whose argument for many worlds appeals directly to a theistically and platonically inflected principle of plenitude:

The Centre of each severall world's a sunne
With shining beams and kindly warming heat,
About whose radiant crown the Planets runne,
Like reeling moths around a candle light.
These all together, one world I conceit.
And that even infinite such worlds there be,
That inexhausted Good that God is hight
A full sufficient reason is to me,
Who simple Goodnesse make the highest Deity.[7]

Although More was a Copernican well informed regarding observational astronomy, his "other worlds" position is more rationalistic than empirical. It may also be remarked, despite his employment of Spenserian stanza, that reading More – witness only his "reeling moths" simile in the stanza just cited – much deepens one's appreciation for the poetic achievements of Spenser and Milton.

Although Galileo himself did not press the issue of ET and other worlds, his luminous account of detailed telescopic observations undoubtedly served as a spur to speculation based on a new grasp of extraterrestrial physical realities. Most influentially, Kepler responded to the *Sidereus Nuncius* with its account of an earthlike Moon, along with still other, "Jovian" moons, by sketching the possibility, even the likelihood, as he saw it, of creatures elsewhere in what we now call the solar system. As Steven J. Dick points out, the positing of physical extraterrestrial environments "capable of sustaining life in the heretofore unchangeable celestial regions was a prerequisite to any discussion of the details of possible inhabitants."[8] Kepler's imaginative comments on lunar geography are remarkable for their tracing of life's adaptation to its environment:

[7] More, *Democritus Platonissans* (Cambridge, 1646), stanza 51; cf. stanzas 19, 26, 57.
[8] Dick, "The Origins of the Extraterrestrial Life Debate and Its Relation to the Scientific Revolution," *Journal of the History of Ideas* 41.1 (Jan.–March 1980): 3–27 (p. 4).

I cannot help wondering about the meaning of that large circular cavity in what I usually call the left corner of the mouth. Is it a work of nature, or of a trained hand? Suppose that there are living beings on the moon. . . . It surely stands to reason that the inhabitants express the character of their dwelling place, which has much bigger mountains and valleys than our earth has. Consequently, being endowed with very massive bodies, they also construct gigantic projects. Their day is as long as 15 of our days, and they feel insufferable heat. Perhaps they lack stone for erecting shelters against the sun. On the other hand, maybe they have a soil as sticky as clay. Their usual building plan, accordingly, is as follows. Digging up huge fields, they carry out the earth and heap it in a circle, perhaps for the purpose of drawing out the moisture down below. In this way they may hide deep in the shade behind their excavated mounds and, in keeping with the sun's motion, shift about inside, clinging to the shadow. They have, as it were, a sort of underground city. They make their homes in numerous caves hewn out of that circular embankment. They place their fields and pastures in the middle, to avoid being forced to go too far away from their farms in their flight from the sun.[9]

Kepler took these speculations about the Moon much further in his posthumous *Somnium* (1634), in which he imagines, as Edward Rosen says, how "the phenomena occurring in the heavens [would] appear to an observer stationed on the moon."[10] Dominant among those celestial phenomena, of course, from a lunar viewpoint, is planet Earth.

Kepler nicely exemplifies a fundamental tension that accompanied the Copernican "expansion" of the Universe – a tension that has not gone away. On the one hand, the discovery of "other worlds" relativizes our planet and its location. In popular accounts today, one still hears that Earth is merely one of innumerable planets, that our Sun is merely one of innumerable stars, that our Milky Way is merely one of innumerable galaxies, and (increasingly) that our Cosmos is merely one among perhaps infinite universes in the Multiverse. On the other hand, the more one learns about the conditions necessary for carbon-based life, the rarer our Earth appears and perhaps the more astonishingly "fine tuned" our Universe itself appears – as one in which, for example, stars may form.[11] Kepler exults in the discovery of Jupiter's moons and he praises Galileo for

---

[9] *Kepler's Conversation*, pp. 27–8.
[10] *Kepler's Somnium: The Dream, or Posthumous Work on Lunar Astronomy*, ed. Edward Rosen (1967; Mineola, NY: Dover, 2003), p. xvii. For much more on Kepler's *Somnium*, see Frédérique Aït-Touati, *Fictions of the Cosmos: Science and Literature in the Seventeenth Century*, trans. Susan Emanuel (Chicago: University of Chicago Press, 2011), pp. 17–44.
[11] Among relatively popular but scientifically informed writings on these topics, see Peter D. Ward and Donald Brownlee, *Rare Earth: Why Complex Life Is Uncommon in the Universe* (New York: Springer,

telescopically discerning that "the countless host of fixed stars exceeds what was known in antiquity." But simultaneously, he strongly resists "[Bruno's] belief in infinite worlds, as numerous as the fixed stars and all similar to our own." Kepler does accept the conclusion that "the fixed stars generate their light from within, whereas the planets, being opaque, are illuminated from without" and accordingly therefore accepts that stars be referred to as "suns." But he is vehemently opposed to seeing our Sun and the stars as essentially equivalent. His cosmology remains truly *helio*centric: "it is quite clear that the body of our sun is brighter beyond measure than all the fixed stars together, and therefore this world of ours does not belong to an undifferentiated swarm of countless others."[12] One cannot but think that Milton attempted a similar, almost impossible balancing act, with Satan sailing past "innumerable stars" that "seemed other worlds" – while yet "above them all / The golden sun in splendor likest Heaven / Allured his eye" (3.565–73).

Kepler complements his heliocentrism with a kind of anthropocentrism: "After the sun, however, there is no globe nobler or more suitable for man than the earth. For, in the first place, it is exactly in the middle of the principal globes. ... Above it are Mars, Jupiter, and Saturn. Within the embrace of its orbit run Venus and Mercury, while at the center the sun rotates, instigator of all the motions" (p. 45). Thus, Kepler redefines earthly centrality itself in a most dynamic manner based on the idea that geometrical comprehension and triangulation require variation of place:

> We on the earth have difficulty in seeing Mercury, the last of the principal planets, on account of the nearby, overpowering brilliance of the sun. From Jupiter or Saturn, how much less distinct will Mercury be? Hence this globe [i.e., Earth] seems assigned to man with the express intent of enabling him to view all the planets. Will anyone then deny that, to make up for the planets concealed from the Jovians but visible to us earth-dwellers, four others are allocated to Jupiter, to match the four inferior planets, Mars, Earth, Venus, and Mercury, which revolve around the sun within Jupiter's orbit?

2000), and Paul Davies, *Cosmic Jackpot: Why Our Universe Is Just Right for Life* (Boston: Houghton Mifflin, 2007). Theoretical physicist Lee Smolin estimates that the probability of a universe existing in which stars can form (stars, with their internal immense temperature and pressure, being a precondition of the synthesis of elements other than hydrogen) is "one chance in 10^{229}." See *BOTC*, ed. Danielson, pp. 473–4.

[12] *Kepler's Conversation*, pp. 34–6. Kepler is quite explicit about the danger that he fears and about the kind of evidence that would confirm the danger: "If you [Galileo] had discovered any planets revolving around one of the fixed stars, there would now be waiting for me chains and a prison amid Bruno's innumerabilities, I should rather say, exile to his infinite space" (pp. 36–7).

Let the Jovian creatures, therefore, have something with which to console themselves. Let them ... have their own planets [i.e., their moons]. We humans who inhabit the earth can with good reason (in my view) feel proud of the pre-eminent lodging place of our bodies, and we should be grateful to God the creator. (p. 46)

Kepler thus posits inhabitants on Jupiter but at once takes pity on them because they are not granted the privileges that we tellurians enjoy, albeit they are divinely supplied with extra moons by way of consolation.

Kepler displays his assumption concerning a common physics across the universe not only by positing planetary and lunar inhabitants but also by imagining interplanetary travel – space voyages on the analogy of terrestrial transatlantic sea voyages:

as soon as somebody demonstrates the art of flying, settlers from our species of man will not be lacking. Who would once have thought that the crossing of the wide ocean was calmer and safer than of the narrow Adriatic Sea, Baltic Sea, or English Channel? Given ships or sails adapted to the breezes of heaven, there will be those who will not shrink from even that vast expanse. (p. 39)

Such imagined voyages illustrate Kepler's views about macrocosmic opportunity and about human microcosmic development:

Let [higher philosophy] ponder the questions whether the almighty and provident Guardian of the human race permits anything useless and why, like an experienced steward, he opens the inner chambers of his building to us at this particular time. ... Or does God the creator ... lead mankind, like some growing youngster gradually approaching maturity, step by step from one stage of knowledge to another? (p. 40)

Without presupposing any direct borrowing on Milton's part, one can accordingly read Kepler as offering a model of how space travel may function as a literal possibility and as a metaphor for or marker of the unfolding of human capacities over history:

Your bodies may at last turn all to spirit,
Improved by tract of time, and winged ascend
Ethereal, as we, or may at choice
Here or in Heav'nly paradises dwell.
(5.497–500)

One Englishman whose ideas of other worlds do descend directly from Kepler – and also from Galileo – is John Wilkins. His first astronomical work – *The Discovery of a World in the Moone: or, A Discourse Tending to Prove, That 'Tis Probable There May Be Another Habitable World in That*

Planet – published when he was twenty-four, openly identifies its sources: "having read Plutarch, Galilaeus, Keplar, with some others, and finding many of my own thoughts confirmed by such strong authority, I then concluded that it was not only possible there might bee, but probable that there was another habitable world in that Planet," the Moon.[13] Wilkins speculates not concerning the nature of the lunar inhabitants but only concerning what their world is like.

Some components of Wilkins's reasoning about the light-sharing aspect of the terrestrial/lunar relationship we have already discerned in Galileo: how the phenomenon of earthshine demonstrates that light from Earth reaches the Moon and in turn how this fact illustrates a reciprocal "trade" in light – along with a shared "stellar" or planetary nature – between Earth and the Moon. Such reciprocity supports the rejection of any qualitative boundary separating these two astronomical bodies and strengthens instead the assumption that they occupy "but one region" (1638; p. 148). Extrapolating still further and referring to his hypothetical lunar inhabitants, Wilkins supports his proposition "that as their world is our Moone, so our world is their Moone" (1638; p. 143). He acknowledges some of the crucial differences between Earth and the Moon – for example, that "there is one [lunar] hemispheare that hath alwaies heate and light, and the other that hath darknesse and cold" and that "the Moone enlightens our earth round about, whereas our earth gives light onely to that Hemisphere of the Moone which is visible unto us" (1638; pp. 144, 158). Nonetheless, despite such concessions and cautions, Wilkins does champion the remarkably bold Keplerian proposal that there may be extraterrestrial environments that support life and that function (in the local sense of this word) as "worlds."

Although Wilkins refrains from describing lunar inhabitants, or Selenites, he devotes a few pages to considering the ancient opinion that "Paradise was in a high elevated place, which some have conceived could bee no where but in the Moone." For, among other reasons, the Moon offers a large territory, "not some small patch of ground, since 'tis likely all men should have lived there, if Adam had not fell." Wilkins mentions in passing the opinions of Tertullian and Augustine, who "affirmed, that the blessed soules were reserved in that place till the day of judgement" (1638; pp. 205, 206). Milton briefly engages a similar speculation concerning the Moon as a possible way station for the righteous:

[13] Wilkins, *Discovery* (London, 1638), pp. 22–3.

Those argent fields more likely habitants,
Translated saints or middle spirits hold
Betwixt th' angelical and human kind.
(3.460–2)

Milton does not pursue this speculation, although its presence in *Paradise Lost* suggests he takes seriously the possibility of the Moon as human environment, in contrast to the parodic environment of the Paradise of Fools described in much greater detail in subsequent lines.

The other Keplerian tactic that Wilkins adopts in his *Discovery* is to defend the novelty of his opinions by declaring a meliorist or progressive view of human knowledge. His peroration, worthy of a future founding member of the Royal Society, deserves to be quoted at length:

> our posterity, perhaps, may invent some means for our better acquaintance with these [lunar] inhabitants. 'Tis the method of providence not presently to shew us all, but to lead us a long from the knowledge of one thing to another. . . . So, perhaps, there may be some other meanes invented for a conveyance to the Moone, and though it may seeme a terrible and impossible thing ever to passe through the vast spaces of the aire, yet no question there would bee some men who durst venture this as well as the other [i.e., sea voyages]. True indeed, I cannot conceive any possible meanes for the like discovery of this conjecture, since there can be no sailing to the Moone. . . . We have not now any Drake or Columbus to undertake this voyage, or any Daedalus to invent a conveyance through the aire. However, I doubt not but that time who is still the father of new truths, and hath revealed unto us many things which our Ancestors were ignorant of, will also manifest to our posterity that which we now desire, but cannot know. . . . Time will come when the indeavours of after-ages shall bring such things to light, as now lie hid in obscurity. Arts are not yet come to their Solstice, but the industry of future times assisted with the labors of their forefathers, may reach unto that height which wee could not attaine to. Keplar doubts not, but that as soone as the art of flying is found out, some of their Nation will make one of the first colonies that shall inhabite that other world. But I leave this and the like conjectures to the fancie of the reader; Desiring now to finish this Discourse, wherein I have in some measure proved what at the first I promised, a world in the Moone. (1638; pp. 207–8)

In the two years following the first appearance of his *Discovery* in 1638, Wilkins gave considerable further thought to "the art of flying." When he revised and reissued the work in 1640, together with his *Discourse Concerning a New Planet*, he added a "Proposition 14": "That tis possible for some of our posteritie, to find out a conveyance to this other world;

and if there be inhabitants there, to have commerce with them." His modest aim in this section is to "answer those doubts that may make [flying] seeme utterly impossible." In the course of considering various challenges, including the sheer distance involved in a journey to the Moon and "how [it were] possible for any to tarry so long without dyet or sleep," Wilkins offers some intriguing suggestions. One is that it is "perhaps not impossible that a man may be able to flye, by the application of wings to his owne body; As Angels are pictured, as Mercury and Daedaelus are fained." Another involves what we would call a spaceship: "I doe seriously, and upon good grounds, affirme it possible to make a flying Chariot." Yet another involves the locomotion of well-trained large birds.[14]

Indeed, right at the end of Proposition 14 and to conclude this volume of his lunar treatise, Wilkins declares that "having thus finished this discourse, I chanced upon a late fancy to this purpose under the fained name of Domingo Gonsales, written by a late reverend and learned Bishop: In which (besides sundry particulars wherein this later Chapter did unwittingly agree with it) there is delivered a very pleasant and well contrived fancy concerning a voyage to this other world."[15] Wilkins's reference is to Francis Godwin's posthumous *The Man in the Moone: Or a Discourse of a Voyage Thither*. Publication of this work, along with that of the first edition of Wilkins's *Discovery* in 1638 – also perhaps the year of Milton's visit to Galileo – supports David Cressy's suggestion concerning the arrival of "England's lunar moment."[16] In retrospect, of course, some elements of Godwin's narrative, such as the tethered flock of geese that conveys the main character to the Moon, appear merely fanciful, along with Wilkins's own suggestion about large trained birds. But Godwin's fictional journey offers a vivid, non-Aristotelian account of physical features, such as gravitation (interpreted under the influence of Gilbert as a kind of magnetism) and Earth's daily rotation ("according to the late opinion of Copernicus"). What Godwin's story perhaps most movingly conveys, however – something repeated more recently by

[14] *Discovery* (1640), pp. 203, 207, 209, 237–8. Wilkins remained fascinated by this topic. His *Mathematicall Magick: or, The Wonders That May Be Performed by Mechanicall Geometry* (London, 1648) included a chapter "Concerning the Art of Flying" (pp. 199–210), in which his favored conveyance remained the flying chariot.
[15] Wilkins, *Discovery* (1640), p. 240.
[16] See Cressy, "Early Modern Space Travel and the English Man in the Moon," *American Historical Review* III (2006): 961–82. The year 1638, writes Cressy, saw "a quickening interest not just in the mechanics and mathematics of planetary motion, but also in what we might call the ethnography or cultural geography of outer space" (p. 967).

NASA's *Apollo* missions – is a vision of our own planet as a "new starre" masked "with a kind of brightnesse like another Moone."[17]

This last comment from the narrator illustrates again the practice of "reflexive telescopics" referred to in Chapter 7. Very often, outward movement into the heavens provides the structure for a visual and philosophical return to Earth. The centrifugal is balanced by the centripetal. The potentially deflating recognition that Earth is somebody else's moon or "just one of the planets" at the same time provides an imaginative platform from which one may look back with affection and admiration on the "brightnesse" of our own world. The elimination of a boundary between the sublunary and the superlunary enhances one's capacity to predicate terrestrial qualities of the extraterrestrial – one of the fundamental assumptions of science fiction. And the principle of plenitude itself can be seen as extrapolating one's awed awareness – as in the epigraph from Kepler – of Earth's own abundance and diversity of climates, landscapes, and species.

The centrifugal/centripetal tension that permeates discussion of other worlds also has a stark theological or christological aspect for the likes of Kepler and Milton. The problem is parallel to one that accompanied the unfolding of Copernicanism. On the one hand, the "placing" of the Sun in the center, together with what I have called Copernicus's "renovation of the basement" – the reconceiving of the cosmic midpoint as one of honor and governmental efficiency – enhanced the Sun's potency as a symbol of deity, even incarnate deity, as in the poetic Sun/Son pun. On the other hand, the mathematics of Copernicanism, especially from Tycho's critique onward, indicated that distant stars were much larger than the Sun. And once one replaced the circumambient sphere of fixed stars with a model of stellar diffusion through possibly infinite space, as suggested by the Copernican frontispieces of Digges and Wilkins, the Sun could hardly any longer be thought of as cosmologically dominant or central.[18]

The same sort of deprivation of universal uniqueness threatened the Sun's symbolic counterpart: the Son. By all appearances in Christian

[17] See William Poole's excellent edition of Godwin's *The Man in the Moone*, pp. 88, 90, 92.

[18] As early as perhaps 1615, John Donne sketched a similar dilemma regarding Earth. He admitted that Copernicus's heliocentrism militated against Earth's gloomy consignment to the dead center but also acknowledged the new cosmology's implications for the remoteness of the stars: "Copernicisme in the Mathematiques hath carried earth farther up, from the stupid Center; and yet not honoured it, nor advantaged it, because for the necessity of appearances, it hath carried heaven so much higher from it." Donne to Henry Goodyear (1615?), *Letters to Severall Persons of Honour* (London, 1651), p. 102.

scriptures and theology, Christ's incarnation and redemption are Earth specific. But if one hypothesizes other suns and with them other earths, what then? Would not the undermining of a truly heliocentric cosmology also encourage abandonment of a Christocentric theology? Although he was no Copernican, Philipp Melanchthon, within a decade of the publication of *De Revolutionibus*, articulated the logic of this predicament:

> The Son of God is one, our Lord Jesus Christ, who came into this world, died but once, and was resurrected. Neither did he show himself elsewhere, nor did he elsewhere die and rise again. We should therefore not imagine there to be plural worlds [*Non igitur imaginandum est, plures esse mundos*], because we should not imagine that Christ is repeatedly dying and rising. Nor should it be thought in any other world without knowledge of the Son of God that people would be restored to eternal life.[19]

Burton mentions the same problem, among others, in his *Anatomy of Melancholy*:

> But who shall dwell in these vast Bodies, Earths, Worlds, *if they be inhabited, rationall* creatures, as Kepler demands? or have they soules to be saved, or doe they inhabit a better part of the World then we doe, or are we or they Lords of the World, and how are all things made for man? . . . These and such like prodigious Paradoxes, inferences must needs follow, if it once be granted, which Rotman, Kepler, Gilbert, Diggeus, Galely, and others maintaine of the Earths motion, that it is a Planet.[20]

Commentators sometimes speak as if Christian theology has no resources for dealing with this apparent dilemma and it is true that the threatened loss of uniqueness of either the Sun or the Son has created anxiety in no lesser a writer than Kepler. Others, however, have not shrunk from seeing Christ's earthly incarnation as having possibly cosmic implications, while others, such as C. S. Lewis, have hypothesized that extraterrestrials, not having sinned, might not stand in need of being "restored to eternal life." In any case, as Leonard has remarked, Milton, despite all his hints about extraterrestrials and other worlds, does not pursue such lines of speculation.[21] And yet, his emphasis on the role of the Son in the creation of the whole Universe – right from the "Noughth Day," as argued

[19] Melanchthon, *Initia doctrinae physicae* (Wittenberg, 1550), fol. 43ᵛ. See Thomas F. O'Meara's admirable discussion "Christian Theology and Extraterrestrial Intelligent Life," *Theological Studies* 60 (1999): 3–30.
[20] Burton, *Anatomy of Melancholy* (1621), pp. 327–8.
[21] See Leonard's detailed discussion, including an engagement of Empson and Lewis on the Christian "dilemma" of ET and other worlds, in *FL*, pp. 760–64. See also the first and best of Grant McColley's articles on Milton and astronomy, "The Theory of a Plurality of Worlds as a Factor

in Chapter 2 – would seem to offer a Christocentric foundation to the world of *Paradise Lost* that precedes questions of soteriology. In any case, Milton took the risks he did with ET without apparently abandoning the central role of the Son in the grand creative and salvific scheme of Providence.

A further engagement with issues concerning other worlds deserves notice before we return again to *Paradise Lost*: Pierre Borel's *Discours Nouveau Prouvant la Pluralité des Mondes* (1657), which soon appeared in English as *A New Treatise Proving a Multiplicity of Worlds*. This useful if somewhat dilettantish survey not only illustrates the currency of many-worlds thinking in the 1650s but also traces it back to the Presocratics, particularly, of course, to the atomists. Borel gives voice to a good number of the Copernican and pluralistic themes already touched upon: the view "That the Earth is a Star situated in Heaven, as well as the other Starres"; a dismissal of those who think "the infinite number of the heavenly bodies are created for the globe of the earth, and for the advantage of its Inhabitants"; and expressions of the theological principle of plenitude – that because "God is infinite, so also ought the Worlds to be infinite." Perhaps most intriguingly, Borel cites and attempts to defang Melanchthon's famous claim that the many-worlds/ET position undermines the unique-ness of Christ: "That if there were divers Worlds, it would be requisite, that Jesus Christ should suffer death several times for to save them all: but what do we know, whether those Men in the Stars are better then those that are in this world[?]"[22]

In *Paradise Lost*, the most visible examples of ET are angels – fallen and unfallen – visitors, of course, not only from beyond Earth but also from beyond this Cosmos. Their visits tell us a great deal – although not as much as we might like to know – about Earth and about the spaces through which they travel to reach Earth. On account of these journeys, especially Satan's, John Tanner has called *Paradise Lost* "perhaps the greatest description of space travel in high-brow fiction."[23]

As Satan nears our Universe in Book 3, Milton describes the Father's vision of that journey:

---

in Milton's Attitude Toward the Copernican Hypothesis," *Modern Language Notes* 47.5 (May 1932): 319–25.
[22] Borel, *A New Treatise Proving a Multiplicity of Worlds* (London, 1658), pp. 28, 31, 125–6, 139.
[23] Tanner, "'And Every Star Perhaps a World of Destined Habitation': Milton and Moonmen," *Extrapolation* 30.3: 267–79 (p. 268).

> ... he then surveyed
> Hell and the gulf between, and Satan there
> Coasting the wall of Heav'n on this side Night
> In the dun air sublime, and ready now
> To stoop with wearied wings and willing feet
> On the bare outside of this world, that seemed
> Firm land embosomed, without firmament,
> Uncertain which, in ocean or in air.
>
> (3.69–76)

At this point in his quest, Satan is still moving through Chaos and the poet's description is consistent with the apparent uncertainty he earlier displays concerning Satan's main means of locomotion – whether it be nautical or aeronautical ("on the calmer wave ... Or in the emptier waste, resembling air"; 2.1041–6). Then, following the scene in Heaven, Satan lands on "the firm opacous globe" and, as noted in Chapter 2, peers through the cosmic hatch, which is said to be "Just o'er the blissful seat of Paradise" (3.527). It is hard to know how much one can infer from this statement cosmologically. It seems to presume a static "opacous globe" and a static Earth. If either sphere were rotating, the hatch would be vertically "Just o'er the blissful seat" for no more than a moment. Perhaps Milton nods at this point or else he is speaking figuratively about the close connection – despite the immense physical distance – between Heaven and the abode of Adam and Eve.[24]

What ought to be clear, however, is that once Satan passes through into our Universe, he encounters no solid nested Ptolemaic globes, which, if they existed, would certainly impede his journey and perhaps make space travel altogether impossible. This was a point well understood by seventeenth-century writers when engaging cosmological matters. As Burton noted:

> With some small qualification, [recent astronomers] have one and the selfe same opinion, about the Essence and matter of Heavens, that it is not hard and impenetrable, as Peripateticks hold, ... but that it is penetrable and soft as the ayre it selfe is, and that the Planets move in it as Birds in the ayre, fishes in the sea. ... If the heavens be penetrable, as these men deliver and no lets, it were not amisse in this aeriall progresse to make wings, and fly up.[25]

---

[24] See in addition Fowler's detailed commentary on Satan's location relative to Paradise, including the suggestion that Satan looks "along the 'length' of the universe, which is lying, as it were, on its side. (The north and south poles are the outer points of *breadth*.)" pp. 593–4.

[25] Burton, *Anatomy of Melancholy* (1621), pp. 324–5.

We may adapt Burton's words to Satan's journey merely by editing "fly up" to "fly down":

> Down right into the world's first region [Satan] throws
> His flight precipitant, and winds with ease
> Through the pure marble air his oblique way
> Amongst innumerable stars, that shone
> Stars distant, but nigh hand seemed other worlds,
> Or other worlds they seemed, or happy isles,
> Like those Hesperian gardens famed of old,
> Fortunate fields, and groves and flow'ry vales,
> Thrice happy isles, but who dwelt happy there
> He stayed not to inquire.
>
> (3.562–71)

The picture is decidedly non-Ptolemaic. For, among other reasons, if the "innumerable stars" – even if not borne by a solid sphere – were whirling about as required by Ptolemaic astronomy, with a "celeritie . . . beyond the fancy of a Poet or a mad man," then Satan, like a pedestrian crossing the M25 in rush hour, would be in danger of being smashed by transverse stellar traffic.[26] The picture Milton presents of Satan winding "with ease / Through the pure marble air his oblique way" is a much more leisurely one than that – suggesting indeed a cosmography closer to the "dispersed stars" model of Digges and Wilkins than to those of Ptolemy or Tycho with their relatively narrow bands of circumambient stars.

From this stage of Satan's space flight, he moves to the Sun – a scene already discussed in Chapters 4 and 6, in which it is evident that the Moon and Earth are considered stars (wandering ones, of course) that in keeping with Galileo's description in the *Sidereus Nuncius* share their reflected sunlight. Once Satan knows where his intended victims are located, however, he takes leave of Uriel

> . . . and toward the coast of Earth beneath,
> Down from th' ecliptic, sped with hoped success,
> Throws his steep flight in many an airy wheel,
> Nor stayed, till on Niphates' top he lights.
>
> (3.739–42)

The modification of Satan's steep flight with "many an airy wheel" again conveys a sense of leisure amid his haste. One recalls once more Burton's use of the commonplace simile (also found in Scheiner and

---

[26] Wilkins, *Discourse*, pp. 194–5; cf. Leonard's discussion, *FL*, pp. 740–1.

others) describing unconstrained movement through the ether: "as Birds in the ayre, fishes in the sea." But here, "airy wheel," interpreted ornithologically, as well it might be, deftly superadds the sense of foreboding one might feel upon observing the gyre of a buzzard or another bird of prey.

The one other major depiction of Satan as a space traveler concerns not his journey to Earth as much as his furtive journey around it just before he returns to Eden to carry out the temptation:

> The space of seven continued nights he rode
> With darkness, thrice the equinoctial line
> He circled, four times crossed the car of night
> From pole to pole, traversing each colure;
> On the eighth returned, and on the coast averse
> From entrance or Cherubic watch, by stealth
> Found unsuspected way.
>
> (9.63–9)

In his notes to this passage, Fowler suggests that the seven days of this journey "travesties the divine week of creation." For three days, Satan circles Earth about the equator – "the equinoctial line" – although this phrase is anachronistic to the extent that before the tilting of Earth's axis (or else the tilting of the Sun's course; 10.668–80), nights and days were equal everywhere on Earth; there was no specific annual pair of equinoxes. Nonetheless, Milton invites us to picture night, in Lewis's words, as "merely the conical shadow cast by our Earth." Moreover (*pace* Lewis), that finger *appears* to revolve "perpetually . . . like the hand of a clock" independently of whether it be caused by the Sun's orbital motion or Earth's diurnal rotation.[27] As for the second phase of Satan's seven-day journey in darkness, Fowler suggests that it "is strictly speaking impossible," for the colures – great circles about the poles that intersect solstitial and equinoctial points – are also anachronistic. If, according to Milton's premise, the prelapsarian Earth were in a state of continuous equinox, then a flight circumnavigating the poles would not take place in full darkness, as Satan intends it should. Fowler concludes that Milton's description is likely proleptic, already anticipating the postlapsarian condition. A more natural, if less complimentary, inference might be that Milton, as he does in Book 10 (see Chapter 5), here atypically loses his technical grasp of astronomical detail.

---

[27] Lewis, *The Discarded Image*, pp. 111–12.

A further episode of angelic space flight involves not Satan but Raphael.[28] By contrast with Satan, Raphael has a clear sense – and a perfectly clear sight – of his earthly destination, even before his departure from Heaven. The scene probably says more about the power of unfallen angelic vision than about any realistic physical detail. Raphael's journey to Earth, however, is cosmographically suggestive and rich. From the gate of Heaven,

> ... no cloud, or, to obstruct his sight,
> Star interposed, however small he sees,
> Not unconform to other shining globes,
> Earth and the gard'n of God, with cedars crowned
> Above all hills. As when by night the glass
> Of Galileo, less assured, observes
> Imagined lands and regions in the moon:
> Or pilot from amidst the Cyclades
> Delos or Samos first appearing kens
> A cloudy spot. Down thither prone in flight
> He speeds, and through the vast ethereal sky
> Sails between worlds and worlds, with steady wing ...
> (5.257–68)

Already in Chapters 4 and 6, we remarked on the contrast of perspicacity between Raphael and Galileo here indicated – not necessarily an insult to the human astronomer, given the nature and status of his opposite number in the comparison. But without gainsaying that contrast, one may also notice the positive analogy between Earth and other heavenly bodies that forms the hinge of this diptych: The unfallen angel observes Earth from afar and perceives that it is "Not unconform to other shining globes"; the Tuscan artist telescopically observes the Moon's surface and finds it to be earthlike. It is almost impossible to imagine that Milton could have made that claim about what Raphael sees had it not been for Galileo's discovery, which in turn undergirded Wilkins's analogy, expressed in this chapter's second epigraph: "if our earth were one of the Planets ... then why may not another of the Planets be an earth?" If Milton here refrains from elaborating on the topic, his framing of it is nonetheless highly significant. For his Cosmos – "the vast ethereal sky" – is truly a *Uni*verse (there is no division between upper and lower storeys); space flight is not impeded by solid spheres; the heavenly bodies are "Not unconform" to each other; the

---

[28] In Book 11 of *Paradise Lost*, Michael makes the journey from Heaven to Earth. Apart from his departure and arrival, however, his "swift descent" (11.127) is only mentioned rather than narrated.

second part of the simile suggests they are like islands one might sail between or among; and, indeed, stars and planets in their multiplicity may properly be thought of as "worlds and worlds."

The two main angelic space travelers of *Paradise Lost*, Satan and Raphael, in keeping with their divergent purposes, likewise offer humans the prospect of cosmic ascent – the former by means of disobedience; the latter by means of obedience. Eve recounts her (satanically inspired) dream, quoting the tempter:

> "'Taste this, and be henceforth among the gods
> Thyself a goddess, not to Earth confined,
> But sometimes in the air, as we, sometimes
> Ascend to Heav'n, by merit thine, and see
> What life the gods live there, and such live thou.'
> So saying, he drew nigh, and to me held,
> Even to my mouth of that same fruit held part
> Which he had plucked; the pleasant savory smell
> So quickened appetite, that I, methought,
> Could not but taste. Forthwith up to the clouds
> With him I flew, and underneath beheld
> The Earth outstretched immense, a prospect wide
> And various: wond'ring at my flight and change
> To this high exaltation."
>
> (5.77–90)

Because this is a dream, one should probably not infer anything too physically precise from it. Nonetheless, in keeping with the rhetoric of his second soliloquy of Book 4, which construed Paradise as a confinement within "narrow limits" (4.384), Satan transfers the same allegation to Earth itself and offers Eve freedom to ascend – to the air, if not yet to the ether. In her dream, Eve accordingly rises to the clouds and takes in a wider prospect of Earth than she thought possible. The focus of her wonder, however, is not creation but her own "flight" and "exaltation."

Superficially, the scenario sketched by Raphael is similar to what Satan offers Eve in her dream. As Empson and Fowler have pointed out, both prospects appear grounded at least partly in what humans eat:[29]

> "... time may come when men
> With Angels may participate, and find
> No inconvenient diet, nor too light fare:
> And from these corporal nutriments perhaps

---

[29] See Fowler's extensive note to 5.496–500, which also cites Empson.

Your bodies may at last turn all to spirit,
Improved by tract of time, and winged ascend
Ethereal, as we, or may at choice
Here or in Heav'nly paradises dwell;
If ye be found obedient, and retain
Unalterably firm his love entire
Whose progeny you are."

(5.493–503)

The exaltations offered, however, are quite different as to their timing: The "Forthwith" of line 86 contrasts with Raphael's "Improved by tract of time" (line 498). In fact, Satan says nothing at all about Eve's being "improved." In his language, Eve's "merit" (line 80) is framed as something innate rather than achieved. Raphael's indicated prospect of moral improvement is crucial to Milton's theodicy, for it destroys any assumption that Adam and Eve were indeed confined to a static state without opportunities for growth and development. Significantly, it also continues to treat earthly existence as a worthy option for humankind's moral destiny – one of the live choices of environment, along with "Heav'nly paradises," for long-term human habitation. There is here no Gnostic shunning of the earthly or the physical.

The cosmological details of these passages, finally, suggest a further contrast. With his repeated "sometimes" (line 79), Satan appears in fact to be offering Eve a kind of tourism – "and see / What life the gods live there" (5.80–1) – or perhaps a "try before you buy" option before she actually takes up residence with the gods. In fact, however, the experience is not even superlunary – it is "in the air"; Eve's exaltation is only "up to the clouds" (5.79, 5.86). Raphael's words, by contrast, imply an ascent that is superlunary – "Ethereal" (line 499) – and perhaps extracosmic depending on whether one reads "Heav'nly" as referring to the sidereal Universe or the empyreal Heaven. The latter reading is certainly possible. But there are enough hints in *Paradise Lost* concerning the possibility of infracosmic extraterrestrial life and habitation that the former reading remains highly plausible.

Among such hints and speculations are those already seen in Milton's description of Satan's descent in Book 3, when he winds among "innumerable stars, that shone / Stars distant, but nigh hand seemed other worlds ... but who dwelt happy there / He stayed not to inquire" (3.565–6, 570–1). We may note here Milton's apparent assumption that the extraterrestrials are happy, so perhaps their dwellings are indeed paradises comparable to the "happy state" (1.29 etc.) of the earthly paradise. Already in Chapter 4 we noticed the openness of Satan's question on his way to Earth – a question whose terms Uriel does not contradict or correct:

> "In which of all these shining orbs hath man
> His fixèd seat, or fixèd seat hath none,
> But all these shining orbs his choice to dwell[?]"
>
> (3.668–70)

That choice, as suggested by the prospect Raphael offers in Book 5, may lie in the future and may include the infracosmic range of options posited by Satan's question to Uriel. This possibility is furthermore supported by the angels' hymn praising God's work in creating this Universe, including "stars / Numerous, and every star perhaps a world / Of destined habitation" (7.620–2). Their use of "perhaps" indicates that the angels of Heaven themselves do not fully know God's intentions and that they too engage in innocent cosmological speculation.

The most decisive cosmological underpinning of "other worlds" speculation in *Paradise Lost*, however, is Raphael's prophecy to Adam – that

> "other suns perhaps
> With their attendant moons thou wilt descry
> Communicating male and female light,
> Which two great sexes animate the world,
> Stored in each orb perhaps with some that live.
> For such vast room in nature unpossesed
> By living soul, desert and desolate,
> Only to shine, yet scarce to contribute
> Each orb a glimpse of light, conveyed so far
> Down to this habitable, which returns
> Light back to them, is obvious to dispute."
>
> (8.148–58)

Leonard is no doubt right that the plural "other suns" is "stupendous" – although not, as we have seen, a rarity in the seventeenth century – and also right that Masson's limp identification of this prospect with the discovery of Jupiter's and Saturn's satellites is misguided and disappointing (*FL*, 2:742). It is much more plausible to take "suns" at face value and to let "moons" be planets – just as Kepler had done in his *Conversation* with the *Sidereus Nuncius*: "the fixed stars generate their light from within, whereas the planets, being opaque, are illuminated from without; that is, to use Bruno's terms, the former are suns, the latter, moons or earths" (p. 34). Moreover, in keeping with Galileo's physics, light is traveling a two-way

street and earthshine is reciprocally repaid to the Moon, whose light we
here enjoy. But the light given off by our Earth and our Moon is female
light. It is starlight and sunlight that are male. The life, the animation, of
our Cosmos depends on the interaction – or, to use an old-fashioned word,
the *intercourse* – of planets and stars, of which our Sun is one.

Something of the operation of this fertile exchange is already suggested
in the lines that precede the "other suns" passage, which encapsulate yet
another of Raphael's cosmological what-ifs:

> "What if that light
> Sent from [Earth] through the wide transpicuous air,
> To the terrestrial moon be as a star
> Enlight'ning her by day, as she by night
> This Earth? Reciprocal, if land be there,
> Fields and inhabitants: her spots thou seest
> As clouds, and clouds may rain, and rain produce
> Fruits in her softened soil, for some to eat
> Allotted there . . ."
>
> (8.140–8)

The sharing of light between Earth and the Moon is again exactly congruent with Galileo's account in *Sidereus Nuncius*. But the engendering
process, Raphael's words suggest, expands beyond the generative exchange
of light to include lunar weather, water, food, and life-forms that eat – a
prospect resonant with the spirit of Kepler's profound question, cited in
this chapter's first epigraph: "Has [God] then used up all His skill on the
globe of the Earth so that He could not, or all His goodness, so that He
would not wish to adorn with suitable creatures other globes also ... ?"
Such divine plenitude, fecundity, and openness to new things are also part
of the lustrous fabric of the world of *Paradise Lost*.

"The meaning, not the name"

In his invocation to the Heavenly Muse in Book 1 of *Paradise Lost*, Milton – seeking instruction, inspiration, and support for his assertion of eternal providence – links his request with actions performed by the Spirit at the creation of the world:

> Instruct me, for thou know'st; thou from the first
> Wast present, and with mighty wings outspread
> Dove-like sat'st brooding on the vast abyss
> And mad'st it pregnant.
>
> (1.19–22)

The *Oxford English Dictionary*'s first given definition of "pregnant" is not "expecting to give birth" but rather "full of meaning." Recently, a student reminded me of the currency of this usage in the seventeenth century and added: "So I think Milton believes the Universe is teleological." Especially after writing the preceding eight chapters, I think so too: The insemination, structure, and story of Milton's Cosmos declare that it is replete with meaning. This may be the most important thing one can say about it.[1]

Such a claim harmonizes well with Milton's invocation at the beginning of Book 7 of *Paradise Lost* to Urania, the goddess of astronomy. Because, typically, Milton worries about correct nomenclature when it comes to divine persons, he adds, in line 5: "The meaning, not the name I call." Here again, I want to say: Yes, he does: Meaning truly is what Milton seeks to call forth. Perhaps this even helps explain why he is frustratingly

---

[1] I am grateful to Eli Zibin for his helpful observation. The contrast with much modern cosmology is perhaps only too obvious. Consider Steven Weinberg's oft-quoted claim from the penultimate paragraph of *The First Three Minutes: A Modern View of the Origin of the Universe* (New York: Basic Books, 1977), p. 154: "The more the universe seems comprehensible, the more it also seems pointless." I might add that to read "pregnant" in the invocation as implying meaningfulness does not preclude the richly sexual possibilities of the word, although it would seem to connect meaningfulness to the divine origin in a way that runs counter to the autonomous, cut-loose picture of Miltonic creation offered by John Rogers, *Matter of Revolution*, pp. 116–17, 123.

noncommittal on matters on which we would like him to take a stronger stand (if *only* Raphael would exchange his what-ifs for a clear affirmation of the Copernican model), yet at the same time, Milton's mind is apparently happily saturated with a Galilean understanding of Earth as participant in the dance of the stars and by extension of the Universe as navigable, fertile, and potentially inhabited beyond Earth. "Copernican" and "heliocentric" – although hugely important for technical astronomy – are merely names. But those fresh glimpses of a generative, unified, "single storey" Universe – and of "male and female light; / Which two great sexes animate the world" (8.150–1) – those are about meaning, teleology, and also earthlings' participation in the Cosmos. At one level, at least for Milton and, I suspect, for many others too, that is above all what the cosmological revolution meant.[2]

Emphasizing the meaning above the name might also helpfully contextualize Milton's apparent hesitations about astronomy itself, particularly as evident in Raphael's disengagement from the rich astronomical dialogue of Book 8, with its concluding imperatives: "be lowly wise" and "Dream not of other worlds" (lines 173, 175).[3] How do these square with the angel's initial affirmation that for Adam "To ask or search" is a blameless activity, "for heav'n / Is as the book of God" (8.66–7)?

Without pretending to crack the riddle entirely, I would suggest that "reading the book" affords a usable analogy. Near the end of *Paradise Lost*, Adam pledges

> "... to walk
> As in [God's] presence, ever to observe
> His providence ..."
>
> (12.562–4)

If, as the Psalmist writes, the heavens declare the glory of God (Ps. 19:1), then there might be a high level of concinnity between observing the heavens and observing providence. In both cases, "observing" will mean *trying* to observe what one cannot always or actually see or fathom. What are impertinent in either case are premature or prideful conclusions about how those things work. To utter that caution, however, is not to forbid

---

[2] For ways in which the rise of Copernicanism specifically made space travel imaginable, see my essay "Ancestors of Apollo," *American Scientist* 99 (2011): 136–43.

[3] Referring to Raphael's concluding comments on astronomy in 8.169–78, Martin Windisch asserts, "Völlig falsch wäre es, dies als eine Absage Miltons an die Leistungen der Astronomie anzusehen" ["It would be completely wrong to regard this as a rejection on Milton's part of astronomy's achievements"]; *Miltons Urania: Poetik im Spiegel der lesbaren Welten* (Berlin: Akademie Verlag, 1997), p. 95.

careful, pious, even eager observation. To trace the Creator's footsteps and to track the paths of Earth, stars, and planets, especially as these concern humans' active appreciation and affirmation of the creation, are, for Milton, parts of our authentic, privileged vocation as sentient creatures made in the image of the great *Opifex*.

In pondering one's observations and in seeking the meaning (not only the name), one undertakes what might be a long, challenging hermeneutical process. Certainly, in astronomy, meaning can be elusive. Two English writers from roughly opposite ends of the cosmological revolution illustrate divergent terrestrial meanings that can be drawn from apparently similar models. In Chapter 3, we noticed how Thomas Digges, vigorous herald and interpreter of Copernicus, nevertheless still considered Earth a "litle darcke starre." However, Thomas Traherne, also having drunk deeply of the new vision of a stellar Earth in a navigable Universe, offered a poetically inflected thought experiment titled "The Celestial Stranger":

> Had a Man been alwayes, in one of the Stars, or confined to the Body of the flaming Sun, or surrounded with nothing but pure Aether, at vast and prodigious Distances from the Earth, acquainted with nothing but the Azure Skie, and face of Heaven, litle could he Dream of any Treasures hidden in that Azure vail afar off. . . . Should he be let down on a suddain, and see the sea, and the effects of those Influences he never Dreamd of; such Strange Kind of Creatures; such Mysteries and Varieties; such distinct Curiosities; such never heard of colors; such a New and Lively Green in the Meadows; such Odoriferous and fragrant Flowers; such Reviving, and Refreshing Winds . . . He would think himself faln into the Paradice of God, a Phoenix nest, a Bed of Spices, a Kingdom of Glory. . . . It would make him cry out How Blessed are thy Holy People, how Divine, how highly Exalted! Heaven it self is under their feet! . . . Verily this star is a nest of Angels![4]

This contrast between Digges and Traherne arises not because one is Ptolemaic and the other is Copernican but because Digges-the-Copernican in 1576 has not yet (it seems) fully absorbed his own model's new implications for space travel, ET, and Earth's radiance within a unified Cosmos, whereas Traherne, although not an astronomer like Digges, has at some point before his death in 1674 imaginatively meditated on the new Universe and grasped its consistency with not a dark but a glorious (if minuscule) planet Earth.

---

[4] *Thomas Traherne: Poetry and Prose*, ed. Denise Inge (London: SPCK, 2002), pp. 112–13. The manuscript of this work lay undiscovered until 1997.

In ways that resonate with the spirit of Traherne's exclamations, Milton, in *Paradise Lost*, offers his readers choice glimpses of things that are beautiful and meaningful, even though very small. In the creation account, for example, he zooms in on insects and worms that

> . . . waved their limber fans
> For wings, and smallest lineaments exact
> In all the liveries decked of summer's pride
> With spots of gold and purple, azure and green:
> These as a line their long dimension drew,
> Streaking the ground with sinuous trace.
>   (7.476–81)

The meaningfulness of such creatures is highlighted by their chirographic activity – drawing, streaking, tracing. And lest we miss that implication, Milton in the next line calls the tiny beings themselves "Minims of nature" – minims being the smallest marks made by pen or printer's type yet integral to the meaning of a text. Bugs and worms too participate in the significance as well as contribute to the beauty of the book of this Universe.

The more we learn about that world and the greater the Cosmos is understood to be, the more likely we *all* are to think of ourselves as minims of nature. It is often popularly assumed that post-Ptolemaic cosmology's "enlargement" of the Universe (which has continued unabated) rendered Earth more puny, more contemptible, more diminished in status than it was under the "Discarded Image." A contrary tendency, however, as evidenced by Traherne's "Celestial Stranger," is to recognize Earth as more of a cosmic exception, more of a peculiarly rich and fertile center of life, and thus an even more rare superconcentration of value than ever previously imagined. Of course, today, a third tendency is to imagine life and perhaps intelligence as more widespread than we yet have any hard evidence for. As already observed in Chapters 7 and 8, the answer to "What kind of place is Earth?" bears directly on any answer to the question "What kind of place is the Universe?" For Earth – our noble, fragile blue-green wandering star – is irrefragably part of the Universe. We may be but minims in that text, but no less an authority than the central character of the Gospels (for example, in Matt. 5:18) might be heard as endorsing the significance of each jot and each tittle to a wider fabric of meaning.

In any case, as remarked in Chapter 2, Milton powerfully imagines the largeness of the Universe amid the immensely greater largeness of the Multiverse – so recognizing the smallness of our own "partition" in the great edifice (8.105) – and yet balancing that with a sense of Earth's glory and of humble thankfulness for the privileges here enjoyed. Among those privileges, for Milton, are ongoing (although since the fall diminished) contacts with persons and voices from the beyond. But as already noted, the extraterrestrials actually "on stage" in *Paradise Lost* are from not only beyond Earth but beyond this Cosmos. The angels (fallen and unfallen) who visit Earth – but most decisively the Son of God himself – bring something into the world from outside the Universe.

Without belittling the efforts of those engaged today in the search for extraterrestrial intelligence, one can say that the contact Milton imagines between humans and extracosmic visitors renders the search for extraterrestrial intelligence (SETI) a relatively parochial and immanent undertaking. Especially for anyone who has renounced the old two-storey Universe, contact that is extraterrestrial but infracosmic can offer no true transcendence. It would indeed be hugely interesting and significant if we could answer the question "Are we alone in the Cosmos?" An even larger question, however, is whether our frail Cosmos itself is alone and solely dependent on itself for meaning – or, alternatively, whether it has a transcendent connection that anchors a deeper teleology. *Paradise Lost* presents the world as not alone, for there is a golden chain connecting our Universe to a higher beyond. And as from the first, the Heavenly Muse remains present, brooding and making pregnant.

The astronomical science of Milton as shown in Paradise Lost

by Maria Mitchell

Maria Mitchell (1818–1889) is known as the first American female astronomer and the first astronomy professor at the first American women's college, Vassar, where there is still a Maria Mitchell chair of astronomy. The following essay, probably composed circa 1857, edited and transcribed by Mitchell's sister, Mrs. Joshua Kendall, was published posthumously, in 1894, in the literary magazine *Poet Lore* (vol. 6). I include it here (only lightly edited) not because I endorse all of Mitchell's opinions but because her stimulating essay is less well known than it deserves to be and because it complements my own words with at least two perspectives that I myself cannot offer: that of a true astronomer and that of a woman.

Milton, like Shakespeare and all truly great poets, becomes greater as we approach him. We have seen objects and individuals through a distorting medium if they dwindle upon a near view. Milton, when read in childhood, fastens his Heaven and Hell upon us; we cannot forget them, we know no other. We see no sunrise without thinking of his lines: "Now morn her rosy steps in th' eastern clime Advancing, sowed the Earth with orient pearl."

Like Shakespeare, Milton has furnished us with many of our daily illustrations. We could not do without the common quotations, "And in the lowest depths a lower still"; "Not to know him argues yourself unknown"; "The world was all before them, where to choose"; "From morn to noon ... from noon to dewy eve."

We should experience the same inconvenience if we dropped these from our language, as that felt by the inhabitants of some of the Pacific Islands, when they drop from their meager dialect the common noun which the King at the time assumes for his proper name.

Read astronomically, Milton may be taken as the poetical historian of the astronomy of his day. The telescope had been known for sixteen years when he was born. Seven planets had been observed. Galileo had made known the existence of the satellites of Jupiter, the belts of Saturn, the inequalities of the moon's surface, and had declared with fear and trembling, which time showed to be well-grounded, the motion of the earth.

Such a crowding together of discoveries was sure to awaken popular interest. To a scholar like Milton, projecting a great epic, it was more than a fleeting interest. Milton became the guest of Galileo while the latter was making his observations; and Galileo, not a mere observer and discoverer, but a philosopher, is reflected again and again from the flowing numbers of *Paradise Lost*.

From his frequent allusions to the novelties revealed by the telescope, it would seem as if the sights were a solace to him in his long blindness. The bright lights of heaven glowed perhaps with more brilliancy to his imagination when, contrasted with his night upon earth, they were set in the gloom of his thoughts as in the deep darkness of the celestial vault.

In his First Book, he alludes to Galileo in these lines:

> The moon whose orb
> Through optic glass the Tuscan artist views
> At evening from the top of Fesole,
> Or, in Val d'Arno, to descry new lands,
> Rivers or mountains in her spotty globe.

And again in Book V, he says:

> As when by night the glass
> Of Galileo, less assur'd, observes
> Imagin'd lands and regions in the moon.

Fesole is a small village in Italy, the capital of Tuscany, situated on a hill overlooking the valley of the Arno. In 1857, I visited the Tower of Galileo, on the hill of Ascetri, the same from which he made his observations when Milton was with him. It is only a short and a most lovely drive from Florence. The tower is in pretty good preservation, and we ascended to the top. It must have been a fine place for sweeping the sky with a little glass; the position is elevated, and nothing for miles around but the lovely scenery, and above, the clear sky of Tuscany.

The absence of water in the moon, now generally admitted, was not then suspected. Galileo had called the prominent points mountains, and had attempted their measurement.

An eclipse furnishes Milton with a fine image in another passage in the First Book:

> As when the sun, new ris'n,
> Looks through the horizontal, misty air,
> Shorn of its beams, or, from behind the moon
> In dim eclipse, disastrous twilight sheds
> On half the nations, and with fear of change
> Perplexes monarchs.

I think that Milton supposes that an eclipse is visible to a whole hemisphere, which it is not in equal degree, but this is a slight liberty to take.[1]

Excellent is the description of the moon, at the close of Book III, as

> that Globe whose hither side
> With light from hence, though but reflected, shines;
> That place is Earth, the seat of man, that light
> His day, which else as th' other hemisphere
> Night would invade, but there the neighbouring moon
> (So call that opposite fair star) her aid
> Timely interposes and her monthly round
> Still ending, still renewing, through mid-heav'n,
> With borrow'd light her countenance triform
> Hence fills and empties to enlighten the Earth,
> And in her pale dominion checks the night.

There is another pleasing idea expressed with regard to the moon's use in creation in Book III. After contending that Chaos is the place where the sinful wander, and "Not in the neighbouring moon, as some have dreamed," he conjectures that

> Those argent fields more likely habitants,
> Translated saints, or middle spirits hold
> Betwixt the angelical and human kind.

This was even in my time a popular superstition. I remember having heard a school-girl speak of it.

In the description of our world, at the close of Book II, as "hanging on a golden chain," pendent, and

> in bigness as a star,
> Of smallest magnitude, close by the moon,

[1] For Mitchell's own beautifully written firsthand description of an eclipse, see *BOTC*, ed. Danielson, pp. 312–16.

there is a confusion of ideas very un-Miltonic about the relative size of the moon and earth. I think he must mean that the earth appeared as small as a small star does when near the moon.

Book IV is so full of human interests that Milton has wisely given us fewer of his learned allusions. We are too much absorbed in our sympathy with his hero and heroine – for I do not call the Devil the hero – to pause for the classical or scientific analogies. Yet in the famous description of the diurnal revolution, given in lines 589–600, he shows us first the glowing hues of a Claude sunset, and then the painting of evening with touches no less graphic of his own.

The beauty of *Paradise Lost* is concentrated in this Book. It has all the charm of the Paradise which it paints, and its effect in a moral point of view is not less excellent. Milton was remarkable for his delicacy of character; and if he has failed to make Eve as intelligent and learned as we require that a woman should be in these days, in all which constitutes loveliness and refinement she is unequalled.

In Book V such improbable suggestions as are made later with regard to the sun's physical nature are applied to the moon. Here Galileo stops, and Milton begins, unsupported by observers or mathematicians; and Milton was pre-eminently a poet. This appears in Raphael's discourse; and with all due deference to Raphael, he is much more unscientific than Milton when speaking for himself. He seems to think that the moon is in process of formation. Doubtless he would have some difficulty in sustaining his theory of grosser elements feeding the purer,

> "the air those fires
> Ethereal, and as lowest first the moon;
> Whence in her round those spots, unpurg'd
> Vapours not yet into her substance turn'd.
> Nor doth the moon no nourishment exhale
> From her moist Continent to higher orbs."

That the moon is a "moist continent" seems especially strange to the science of the present day, when all watery matter is denied to her. An even more striking passage to the same effect, attributing moisture to the moon, is that in Book VII.703–790, where, after Raphael's politic discussion of "whether Heav'n move or Earth," peculiarly interesting in view of Milton's visit to Galileo, he says of the moon: "Her spots thou seest as clouds, and clouds may rain," etc.

It is interesting to notice that mutual admiration societies, though prevalent enough at this day, do not belong to it exclusively. Adam and

Raphael compliment each other much as did the gallant of Elizabeth's age; and we may suppose that the Cavaliers of the time of Milton were equally courteous, even though the Roundheads dispensed with such formalities. In Book VII, Adam goes to the length of telling Raphael that the sun stops in its course to listen to him: "Held by thy voice, thy potent voice he hears," etc. The passage is beautiful.

There is a fine passage, crowded with allusions to the stars, in Book III.543–623, where Milton represents Satan as standing

> high above the circling Canopy
> Of night's extended shade; from Eastern Point
> Of Libra to the fleecy star that bears
> Andromeda far off Atlantic seas
> Beyond th' Horizon; then from Pole to Pole
> He views,

and then, winding his way

> Amongst innumerable stars, that shone
> Stars distant, but nigh hand seemed other worlds,

bent his course

> where the Great Luminary
> Aloof the vulgar Constellations thick
> That from his lordly eye keep distance due,
> Dispenses light from far; they as they move
> Their starry dance in numbers that compute
> Days, months, and years, towards his all-cheering Lamp
> Turn swift their various motions, or are turn'd
> By his Magnetic beam, that gently warms
> The Universe, and to each inward part
> With gentle penetration, though unseen,
> Shoots invisible virtue even to the deep.

The poet here speaks of the probability that the stars are worlds already; and again, in Book VII.620, he speaks of "every star perhaps a world," etc. Before their instruments were delicate enough to detect changes of place, the astronomers were seeking means to discover the distance of these worlds. The sun's magnetic influence was also a conjecture of the time; indeed, Bacon had, a century before, advocated the belief in that of the moon. Galileo had seen the spots on the sun, and with his readiness in turning phenomena to the best advantage, had determined from them the time of the sun's revolution on its axis. Milton, in the above passage, allows himself some liberty in speculating on the sun's physical nature. More recent revelations of the "optic tube" have not made his conjectures probable.

In most cases where Milton confines himself to facts, he is accurate; but his mind was not formed for physical theories, and he fails when he attempts an hypothesis beyond the age.

There is a great difference in the character of men's minds and in the grasp of a subject which they take. I have no doubt that [French astronomer Pierre-Simon] Laplace, sitting in his study, without a glance of his eye at the heavens, and perhaps without power to appreciate the beauty of the universe and the glittering of the myriad suns of heaven, differing only in degrees of glory, had yet a truer idea of the relative position of all these bodies, and in his mind a more correct picture of all their conflicting motions, than the observer who has watched their changes for a lifetime, and can tell you to a second the times of culmination of stars and planets. The mind of Laplace needed not the confirmation of his eyes; he was an architect himself, and could build up a creation with some feeble imitation of the powers of the God whom he denied in his heart.

In a different way, some minds are taught by their eyes, and by a leap, conjecture the cause of phenomena; they cannot prove it, like Laplace, but their eyes see, not only the outward and visible, but as if by intuition they get a glimpse of the hidden and occult. These are the pioneers in discoveries, who give the first start; they detect the game, while stronger minds follow the scent.

The planet Neptune was declared to exist by several persons some half-century before its existence was demonstrated by Lavoisier and Adams.[2]

There are still other minds which neither from reasoning nor observation seem to arrive at a glimpse of the truth, but have a sort of second-sight, a power of prophecy – or if this is not the explanation of it, there is still another, in the conjecture that ages ago our world was as far advanced in literature and science as now, and that there has indeed been a dark age, so dark that its light has not come with sufficient strength to our time to make us sure of its existence. A passage in Ovid, for example, has an allusion to the earth's swinging in space, which seems to show that the power of gravitation was at that time known to exist.

So Milton speaks of meteors as numerous in the autumn, although we, of this age, suppose that this was first known since our recollection.

> Swift as a shooting star,
> In Autumn thwarts the night.

---

[2] "Lavoisier" in this sentence is presumably a transcription error on the part of Maria Mitchell's sister. The two scientists intended here are undoubtedly Urbain Le Verrier and John Couch Adams.

Several comets had appeared in Milton's boyhood, and he is careful not
to forget them:

> Satan stood
> Unterrifi'd, and like a comet burn'd,
> That fires the length of Orphiuchus huge,
> In th' Arctic sky, and from his horrid hair
> Shakes pestilence and war.

The belief in the evil influence of comets cannot be said to be among the
things passed and gone. It may have descended from kings to subjects and
from parlors to kitchens; but it still exists, and must so long as comets are
transiently appearing phenomena, whose physical nature is unknown. To
find out in what way creation began, has always been a favorite speculation
with philosophers. Laplace must have thought that he had discovered it
when he started his beautiful but fallacious theory of star formation from
nebulae, and nebulae from star-dust. The improvements of the telescope
are daily showing the errors of this theory; but many were the minds which
it long held captive, and who hugged their chains, forgetful that though
error may be beautiful, truth is the soul of beauty. Milton makes Light the
original essence, and from that deduces stars, Book III.[708–721]:

> "When at his word the formless mass,
> This World's material mould, came to a heap:
> Confusion heard his voice, and wild uproar
> Stood ruled, stood vast infinitude confin'd;
>
> And this Ethereal quintessence of Heav'n
> Flew upward, spirited with various forms,
> That roll'd orbicular, and turn'd to stars
> Numberless, as thou seest, and how they move;
> Each had his place appointed, each his course,
> The rest in circuit walls this universe."

Again, in Book VII, he describes how

> "Let there be light, said God, and forthwith Light
> Ethereal, first of things, quintessence pure
> Sprung from the Deep and from her native East
> To journey through the airy gloom began,
> Sphered in a radiant cloud, for yet the Sun
> Was not."

I do not know whether Milton here alludes to the supposed existence of
Light beyond the stars, or in spaces where no stars are seen – a conjecture

which I think must have been since his day. It is known that light comes to us from points which seem to be blank space; that there is a diffusion of light. I suppose it to come from suns (worlds) too remote to be seen as such; perhaps brought to us by some light reflecting a light-transmitting medium of which we yet know nothing.

A passing reference in Book II to "concurring signs," which apprised Satan of earth's creation, and another longer allusion in Book X to the "mute signs in nature" which forerun fate show Milton as only on a level with the credulity of the age. Tycho Brahe had been dead only a few years, and Kepler was just in his prime, when Milton was born. Both of these philosophers leaned to the astrological opinions of their time; and Kepler was certainly a believer in them. He calculated nativities when pressed for money, and published astrological almanacs, though he admitted that such procedures were little better than begging. Walter Scott has allowed Guy Mannering, though a scholar and a gentleman, to be a believer in these fallacies, and to cast a horoscope of the young Laird of Ellangowan – though he places the period of the story after the death of Milton.

We meet in Book V with another proof that if Milton was vastly beyond his age in most respects, he yielded at times to the superstition of the period; or perhaps he did not do so seriously, but only employed it as poetic imagery. If we see so strange an illusion as that by which spirits are supposed to hold converse with us through the vulgar means of raps upon furniture, and ungraceful antics performed by inert material, it should not surprise us that at an earlier day the more elegant belief prevailed that the heavenly bodies, as they moved, sang to the praise of their Creator. Addison has said, "Forever singing as they shine." Kepler, who was thirty-seven years old when Milton was born, studied seriously the music of the spheres, from which study resulted laws, not only as harmonious as the notes which he fancied he heard, but more lasting, for their vibrations have reached to the present day, and made themselves heard in the reasoning by which Neptune was made known. The passage alluded to begins:

> "Moon that now meetst the Orient sun, now fli'st
> With the fixed stars, fixt in their orb that flies,
> And ye five other wandring fires, that move
> In mystic dance, not without song."

A beautiful passage poetically, though not scientifically, is that in Book VII beginning, "Again the Almighty spake: Let there be lights"; and describing how first the sun, "unlightsome first, though of ethereal mould," "a mighty sphere, was framed," and then the moon, "globose, and every magnitude of stars," he says, "of light, by far the greater part," was placed "in the sun's orb." Here Milton departs from his usual prudence, and advances a theory. And so on for some time, he describes the sun's physical nature, and its ability to receive light, "made porous to receive and drink the liquid light." Where Milton confines himself to phenomena, he is very accurate; but when he attempts to reason, he reasons as a poet, but not as an astronomer. The whole passage is very fine, but, like most of Raphael's speeches, far from sustaining the received theories. He uses the term "longitude" for east and west, without regard to the sun's orbital motion.

As a woman, I do not like Book VII. I felt, even when a child, indignant that Milton should represent Eve as so careless of the angel's discourse that she must tend her flowers just at that juncture. The poet thus shows an ignorant and a manoeuvring woman. It seems to me that the childlike Eve should have remained and listened, asked questions, and kept up the dramatic interest. The educationists of to-day would scarcely be willing to say to an inquiring child, "Solicit not thy thoughts with matters hid." But everywhere Milton's Adam and Eve are the man and woman of Milton. Adam's speech, "When I behold this goodly frame," etc. (VII.650), and the answer of the angel, are not very scientific. I think the angel "dodges" the questions, but the whole is very interesting. The angel is very non-committal; he is plainly ignorant, but does not like to have Adam know that he is so; there's a sort of shuffle which is not manly, though it may be angelic. Adam expresses himself as fully satisfied, which I own is more than I am, and I suspect more than Eve would have been.

The new cosmogony, made necessary by the Fall and expulsion from the eternal spring of Paradise is curiously and at length described in Book X.649–691, in the course of which occur allusions to the moons of Jupiter and the inclination of the ecliptic:

> The sun
> Had first his precept, so to move, so shine,
> As might affect the Earth with cold and heat
> Scarce tolerable, and from the North to call
> Decrepit Winter, from the South to bring
> Solstitial Summer's heat. To the blanc moon
> Her office they prescrib'd, to the other five
> Their planetary motions and aspects
> In Sextile, Square, and Trine, and Opposite.

Some say He bid his angels turn askance
The poles of Earth twice ten degrees and more
From the sun's axle; they with labour push'd
Oblique the Centric Globe; some say the sun
Was bid turn reins from the Equinoctial road
Like distant breadth to Taurus with the seven
Atlantic Sisters and the Spartan Twins
Up to the tropic Crab; thence down amain
By Leo and the Virgin and the Scales,
As deep as Capricorn, to bring in change
Of seasons to each clime; else had the spring
Perpetual smil'd on earth with vernant flowers,
Equal in days and nights, except to those
Beyond the Polar Circles. . . .
                                        . . . At that tasted fruit
The sun, as from Thyestean banquet, turn'd
His course intended; else how had the
World Inhabited, though sinless more than now,
Avoided pinching cold and scorching heat?

This last of the passages astronomical in *Paradise Lost* may well close the evidence that Milton's epic reflects through a poet's lens, but with considerable learning, the state of astronomical knowledge in his time.

Bibliographical note

Rather than provide a bibliography of such heterogeneous materials as have fed into this study, I would direct interested readers in the first instance to my footnotes, which provide full citations of texts quoted or referred to. Many authors appearing there may be searched in the Index. Primary works are also increasingly searchable and accessible electronically. I particularly recommend the following access points:

EEBO (Early English Books Online, based on the *Short Title Catalogue*) Accessible via major research libraries.

www.worldcat.org
WorldCat offers enhanced access via major research libraries and provides direct links to many digitized rare books.

www.e-rara.ch
Digitized rare books published from the fifteenth to the nineteenth centuries and held in Swiss libraries.

www.bsb-muenchen.de
Bavarian State Library (offering access to many digitized rare books).

www.hab.de
Herzog August Bibliothek, Wolfenbüttel (offering access to many digitized rare books).

If one wishes to explore the history of astronomy and cosmology further, one cannot do better than to sample the writings of the great astronomers themselves: Copernicus, Tycho Brahe, Kepler, Galileo. Wilkins's *Discovery* and *Discourse* are likewise highly worthwhile, as is Burton in his function as a gatherer of miscellaneous opinions (in the "Digression of Air" in *The Anatomy of Melancholy*). Michael J. Crowe's *Theories of the World From Antiquity to the Copernican Revolution* provides an accessible introduction to the problems of astronomy. Albert Van Helden's *Measuring the Universe: Cosmic Dimensions From Aristarchus to Halley* is also informative and historically interesting. My own anthology *The Book of the Cosmos: Imagining the Universe From Heraclitus to Hawking* offers stimulating, historically organized excerpts from more than eighty prominent cosmological writers across more than two millennia. Another useful and intriguing anthology is Crowe's *The Extraterrestrial Life Debate, Antiquity to 1915: A Source Book* (South Bend, IN: University of Notre Dame Press, 2008). Two large, ambitious studies of Copernicanism are Blumenberg's *The Genesis of the Copernican World* and, more recently, Robert Westman's *The Copernican Question: Prognostication, Skepticism, and Celestial Order* (Berkeley: University of California Press, 2011). Also indispensible in this category, of course, is Thomas Kuhn's *The Copernican Revolution: Planetary Astronomy in the Development of Western Thought.* Finally, few studies are as informative and stimulating as John D. Barrow and Frank J. Tipler's *The Anthropic Cosmological Principle* (Oxford: Oxford University Press, 1986).

Most articles on Milton are searchable and accessible electronically via the Modern Language Association (MLA) bibliography and via the JSTOR collection. Many of the books relevant to Miltonic themes pursued in this volume are given astute critical attention in John Leonard's magisterial final chapter of *Faithful Labourers*, "The Universe" (pp. 705–819), in addition to appearing in his extensive bibliography.

Index

Adams, John Couch, 210
Adams, Robert M., 44
Addison, Joseph, 212
Airy, George Biddell, 116
Aït-Touati, Frédérique, 183
Albertus Magnus, 158
Al-Biruni, 156
Albrecht, Duke of Prussia, 75
Allegri, Alessandro, 141
Ambrose, St., 135
American Dialect Society, 132
angular motion, 17, 19–20, 24
anthropocentrism, xviii, 155–6, 159, 174, 184
Apelles. *See* Scheiner, Christoph
Apian, Peter, 7, 9, 11, 53, 57, 62, 69
Aquinas, Thomas, 25, 157–8
Aristarchus of Samos, 25
Aristotelianism, xviii, xix, 5, 9, 11–12, 14, 16, 20, 23, 25–6, 31, 47, 58, 68–71, 74, 76, 81–2, 89–90, 131, 145, 157–63, 165–6, 168, 188
Aristotle, xxi, 5–9, 11–12, 14, 16, 20, 22, 25–6, 55, 57, 65, 88, 155, 157, 160, 162, 169
atomists, 31, 87, 96, 181, 191
Augustine, St., 29–30, 32, 34, 90–1, 93, 186

Babb, Lawrence, 120
Bacon, Francis, xix, xviii, 94–7, 99, 101, 209
Barbour, Ian G., 4
Barker, Peter, 55
Barrow, John D., 216
Becker, Barbara, 126
Bede, 156
Bellarmine, Robert, 101
Blagrave, John, 76
Blake, William, 38
Blumenberg, Hans, xiii, 167, 216
Blundeville, Thomas, 65
Boesky, Amy, 143
Bonaventure, St., 2

Book of Nature, book of the heavens, 1, 3–4, 92–4, 103, 161, 201, 203
Borel, Pierre, 191
Brague, Rémi, 155
Brownlee, Donald, 183
Bruno, Giordano, xx, xxi, xxii, xx, 87, 89, 114, 184, 198
Buridan, John, 25–6, 157
Burton, Robert, 21, 51, 66, 97, 114, 122, 171–2, 180, 190, 192–3, 215
Butler, George F., 78

Calvin, John, 2, 91–3, 133, 145–6, 148
Capella, Martianus, 108, 156
Carpenter, Nathanael, 76, 168
Casaubon, Meric, 30–1, 38
Castelli, Benedetto, 109
Chambers, A. B., 33
Charleton, Walter, 31–2, 34
Clavius, Christoph, 2, 100–1, 112–14, 141–2, 169
Coleridge, S. T., xiii, xiv, xv
Conklin, G. N., 35
Conway, Edward, Viscount, 154, 162
Copernican model, xiii, xvi, xx, 2, 14, 23, 26, 38, 40, 50, 56, 61–3, 65, 68–72, 74–6, 83, 85, 88–9, 91, 94, 97, 100–2, 104, 107–10, 113–16, 118, 120–2, 126, 128, 131, 137, 139, 156, 159, 161–3, 166–70, 174, 176–8, 180–1, 183, 189–91, 201–2, 215–16
Copernicanism, xv, xvi, xviii, xix, xx, 54, 56, 61–3, 65–6, 69, 72, 74, 76, 80, 84, 91, 94, 98, 101–2, 104, 106, 109, 111–14, 116–18, 162, 168, 177, 189, 201, 216
Copernicus, Nicolaus, xv, xviii, xx, 2–5, 9, 11, 14, 19, 21, 24, 26, 38, 46, 52, 54–6, 58, 60–2, 64–6, 68–72, 74–5, 77, 82, 88–92, 94–6, 98–100, 102, 107, 109, 112, 114, 116, 121–3, 126, 129–32, 154, 158–9, 167–9, 173, 175, 181, 188–9, 202, 215
Coriolis force (or effect), 118

217